SILENT WARRIOR
THE MARINE SNIPER'S VIETNAM STORY CONTINUES

Charles Henderson is a veteran of more than twenty-three years in the United States Marine Corps, with a distinguished career spanning from Vietnam to the Gulf War, after which he retired as a Chief Warrant Officer. In addition to writing his own books and for various publications, he also runs his family's cattle enterprise in Peyton, Colorado. His first book was the critically acclaimed military classic *Marine Sniper*, which first chronicled the exploits of U.S.M.C. sniper Carlos Hathcock. He is also the author of *Marshalling the Faithful*.

Marine Sniper
93 Confirmed Kills

"Highly readable."
—*Publishers Weekly*

SILENT WARRIOR

THE MARINE SNIPER'S VIETNAM STORY CONTINUES

CHARLES HENDERSON

BERKLEY BOOKS, NEW YORK

SILENT WARRIOR

A Berkley Book / published by arrangement with
the author

PRINTING HISTORY
Berkley hardcover edition / October 2000
Berkley trade paperback edition / October 2001
Berkley mass-market edition / January 2003

Copyright © 2000 by Charles Henderson
Cover design by Oyster Pond

All rights reserved. This book, or parts thereof, may not be reproduced
in any form without permission. For information address:
The Berkley Publishing Group,
a division of Penguin Putnam Inc.,
375 Hudson Street, New York, New York 10014.

Visit our website at
www.penguinputnam.com

ISBN: 0-425-18864-7

BERKLEY®
Berkley Books are published by The Berkley Publishing Group,
a division of Penguin Putnam Inc.,
375 Hudson Street, New York, New York 10014.
BERKLEY and the "B" design
are trademarks belonging to Penguin Putnam Inc.

PRINTED IN THE UNITED STATES OF AMERICA

10 9 8 7 6 5 4 3 2 1

FOR
ELLY LAND,
A CARING MOTHER TO
ALL MARINE CORPS MARKSMEN
AND MARINE CORPS MARKSMANSHIP
COMPETITORS . . .
SHE KEEPS US IN TOUCH.

Whoever is first in the field and awaits the coming of the enemy, will be fresh for the fight; whoever is second in the field and has to hasten to the battle will arrive exhausted.

Therefore, the clever combatant imposes his will on the enemy, but does not allow the enemy's will to be imposed on him.

Hence, that general is skillful in attack whose opponent does not know what to defend; and he is skillful in defense whose opponent does not know what to attack.

O divine art of subtlety and secrecy! Through you we learn to be invisible, through you inaudible; and hence we can hold the enemy's fate in our hands.

—SUN TZU WU, *THE ART OF WAR*

(written 512, B.C.–496, B.C.)

Contents

Preface

CERTAINLY, NO ONE CAN KNOW WHAT IS IN THE MIND of a dying man who is unable to communicate with or even recognize the people around his bed. For this reason, I extend my apology to Carlos Hathcock's family, friends, and my readers for the liberty I have taken in that regard. I believe that I knew Carlos well enough to realize what he might have been thinking as he passed his final hours. I honestly believe his wife, Jo, and his son, Carlos III, his family and his love for them, was what dominated his final thoughts. I seriously doubt that his Vietnam experience was something he wanted to spend his last night reliving.

With his family, I believe that he recalled the good days he spent competing with his rifle. The good days he spent shark fishing with his friend Steve McCarver. I also believe that he thought about his many friends in law enforcement, and how much he loved his Marine Corps family and being a Marine.

I used Carlos's dream state as a tool to tell his story in this book. My dilemma was how to cover events that occurred during the same period as my book *Marine Sniper*. How could I write *Silent Warrior* as a companion book to *Marine Sniper*, yet have it stand alone on its own merit? Thus, I imagined it is possible that he could have recalled these events, though unlikely, simply as a means of tying additional stories about Carlos's Vietnam experience with events that transpired after the publication of *Marine Sniper*.

I drew the events that occurred prior to 1985—told in *Silent Warrior*—from my research documents, notes, and tape recordings of interviews that I used to write *Marine Sniper*. More than 300 pages were cut by the publisher simply to reduce *Marine Sniper*'s length for marketing purposes. Obviously, they had no idea that *Marine Sniper* would become a classic among books of military themes. However, what was disturbing for me then has become a blessing now. *Silent Warrior* has not only provided the opportunity to tell these stories cut from *Marine Sniper*, but also to follow the rest of Carlos Hathcock's life. Much of what occurred after the publication of *Marine Sniper* I collected from my own personal experiences with Carlos, and from newspaper articles and other documents. Jim and Elly Land are greatly responsible for providing this documentation, and to them goes a great deal of credit.

Additionally, I was able to add in greater dimension the Viet Cong and North Vietnamese viewpoint from interviews I conducted in Vietnam in 1994. During my travels there, I spent many hours hearing former Viet Cong and North Vietnamese veterans describe their combat experiences. Most significantly, I had the good fortune on two occasions to sit down privately with General Tran Van Tra, Commander in Chief of the Viet Cong, and hear his perspectives of the war.

I believe that it is important that we tell more of Carlos Hathcock's story because he was one of the greatest Americans to ever wear a military uniform. I consider him great because he sets an ideal for everyone, especially for those young people who enter military service today and in the future. Carlos did get in trouble, broke the rules, as did most of us Marines. That makes him human. But the important lessons he demonstrates are his priorities, putting others ahead of himself, his honor and his devotion to his country, and his friends and his family. His family also includes everyone who wears or has worn the Marine Corps uniform.

Together with *Marine Sniper*, this second volume in the saga of Gunnery Sergeant Carlos N. Hathcock II provides not only exciting reading but good lessons in values, courage, and integrity. If you have not read *Marine Sniper*, I urge you to read it, too. If it inspires you, then in your prayers ask God to thank Carlos Hathcock. We Marines truly love him.

—Charles Henderson

Acknowledgments

My thanks go to Jim and Elly Land for their support, friendship, and assistance. Also thanks to my many friends and fellow Marines who encouraged my efforts. Special thanks go to the handful of these friends who took time to read this manuscript and gave me their honest feedback.

Tom Colgan, Executive Editor of The Putnam Berkley Group at Penguin Putnam, deserves great praise for his courage to roll the dice with me. He put a lot on the line in his enthusiasm for this book. He took the heat and kept it off me. A Max Perkins kind of editor. I will not forget it.

I would have no career as a writer without the friendship and ceaseless encouragement of my agent, Bob Markel. He has stood fast with me for the past fifteen years, and remains my friend and confidant. I look forward to the future with optimism because he has been and will remain in my corner, whether good times or bad.

Lastly and most important, my heart, eternal love and thanks go to a special lady whose name I need not mention. A perfect angel. I would have been lost without her—she saw what I needed to be doing, pointed me in that direction, and then helped me to get with it. She put me back on track. Her love keeps me smiling. *123!*

1

Semper Fidelis

METAL TASTE. COPPER. IT FELT LIKE A MIX OF ACID and adrenaline in Carlos Hathcock's mouth as he knelt just inside the cover that the trees and ground foliage provided him. Slowly he raised the Model 70 Winchester to his shoulder and looked through the 10-power Unertl scope mounted above the rifle's receiver.

He turned the focusing ring on the long slender tube, bringing the white plaster house and the sandbagged compound that surrounded it into focus. Even with the powerful telescopic sight the structures and the few men he saw around them still looked tiny. Nearly a mile and a half away, Carlos considered that he still had a lot of ground to cover before he could make the shot.

"I gotta go worm-style," he said in his mind. "Grass is shorter than I thought, too."

He considered his odds and didn't like them at all. The metal taste grew stronger, and he pulled out his canteen and took a long, slow drink of water.

"Make myself look like a bush. Like a hump of grass," Carlos told himself as he slowly and methodically plucked handfuls of grass at the jungle's edge. He stuffed as much as he could carry inside his shirt and crept to deeper cover where he could work.

Carefully, he cut little slits along the backs of his shirt and trousers. Taking a small bunch of grass in his fingers, Carlos stuffed their ends through one of the incisions he had cut in his clothing and brought the short ends through another opening next to the primary slit, thus securing the camouflage tightly. The grass laid at a slight angle, so he gently spread the blades so that each clump would stand and look natural.

Carlos had taken light green and dark green camouflage paint and covered every speck of skin on his face, ears, neck, hands, arms, even his eyelids.

With his Winchester cradled beneath him, Carlos knelt slowly and deliberately, and then spread himself, stomach down, on the ground.

Now, well into the night, Carlos inched himself forward. Oozing like a worm. His motion so purposeful and slow, one could hardly detect any movement at all.

Carlos reminded himself of what Captain Jim Land had taught him.

"A sniper's best defenses are cover and concealment, and long-range accuracy. Most important," Land had taught, "one shot, one kill."

CARLOS HATHCOCK GASPED FOR AIR. IT SEEMED AS though he had the weight of a car sitting on his chest. He blinked.

"Where am I?" he thought. He felt the dampness of the sheet and mattress cover beneath his back. It was not 1967. This was not Vietnam.

None of the faces in the room seemed familiar, so the tired and aging Marine sniper simply closed his eyes. His memories kept him company now.

The multiple sclerosis that he had fought for nearly thirty years had finally worn him out. Although he persisted in trying to walk, for the past few years, the wheelchair had become more and more a constant in his life. His balance was bad. He could manage to totter just a few steps. Although only three months shy of his fifty-seventh birthday, his body had spent its course.

Outside, cold wind moaned through the trees as Carlos lay in bed, dying. His body was numbed by drugs and the illness that now raged through him, blocking most conscious recognition.

He had developed a urinary infection. Infections of all sorts were an increasing hazard to him as his immune system weakened with the rest of his body. While trying to recover, pneumonia had invaded his lungs. His body just could not take any more.

Now, well after midnight, February 23, 1999, Carlos Hathcock slept as the last measure of sand drained through the hourglass of his life. His vision had turned inward, and played back scenes of an incredible life. Still, he could never quite understand why so many people made all the fuss about him. "I just did my job," he had always said.

Although there are snipers who reported more confirmed kills than Carlos Hathcock's ninety-three, it was the nature of those missions and the impact that his service had on the Marine Corps that made him the legend. The Marine Corps drew from his vast experience to develop its sniper doctrine, its sniper programs, and the training of snipers that followed him. For Carlos, that meant much more than any score.

He had more than 300 probable kills in addition to his ninety-three confirmed. That is the way with most snipers. However, Carlos always rejected the thinking of people who measured a sniper's success by the numbers. He considered the sniper's role as a support element to be more important than any other. Many times, his job was simply to observe, or to shoot an antenna.

"You would have to be crazy to enjoy killing," Carlos always said. "I never enjoyed it. It was my job. It was important that I did it well. If there was a meaningful thing about numbers, it would have been the number of lives I saved. Not the number I took."

Until the book *Marine Sniper* had made him famous, and confirmed him as a legend among United States Marines, Carlos Hathcock was just another retired Marine living a quiet existence in Virginia Beach, Virginia. His gentle, soft-spoken nature, his slight build, and his kind spirit, hid from most people the courageous, silent warrior. Yet, it was that loving, sensitive part of him that had enabled Carlos to be such a hero and great Marine.

Once a person came to know Carlos Hathcock well, his contradictory nature—the gentle man combined with steely killer—made perfect sense. He was that valiant Marine because he cared so greatly for others.

Carlos had always regarded himself last, and placed his family, his brother and sister Marines, and his country first. His selflessness and devotion, his deep sense of honesty and honor had, in every case, guided his decisions. Always at the root of the decision was this question: His life or the good of his brethren? Himself or his family? Himself or the mission? He equated the good of the mission to that which was best both for his family and his fellow Marines. The mission always came first.

Certainly he, like any other person, feared death and injury. Carlos was just an average man, after all. But, unlike so many others, he held a clear set of values. The values were perfectly logical to him, and the importance of his own well-being meant much less.

His love of others. His gentle caring. His simple, uncluttered rationale that focused itself on the good of others, his community and nation, remained constant with Carlos Hathcock until he could no longer acknowledge the presence of anyone.

Now, he could only remember. Lying quietly, he watched film reel after film reel play the best parts of his life through the windows of his mind.

*   *   *

SEATED IN HIS WHEELCHAIR, CARLOS'S HANDS SHOOK so violently that he could hardly maintain his grip on the black metal gunnery sergeant insignias that he was about to pin on his son's collar. This was his favorite memory. He had told his friends that it was one of the most important moments of his life.

The next day's newspapers had written, "Is the world ready for two Gunnery Sergeant Carlos Hathcocks?" That made Carlos beam. The world would just have to deal with it, he thought.

Most newspapers seemed to always get Sonny's name correct: Carlos Norman Hathcock III. But Carlos could never understand why so many newspapers insisted on referring to him as Carlos Norman Hathcock, Jr. He had always made it a point to impress on every reporter that he was not Junior. He did not even care for the name Junior. His parents had named him Carlos Norman Hathcock II. And it was very important to him that everyone respect this aspect of his name. Some people thought, What is the difference, the second or junior? However, it made a big difference to Carlos. He had guided his life, had succeeded on the battlefield as one of the greatest snipers the Marine Corps, or America, had ever known, by this simple aspect of his nature. He paid attention to detail. Detail was important. And his name, Carlos Norman Hathcock II, not *Junior*, was a very important detail.

Today, as he always had, Carlos made a special effort to ensure that the reporters covering his son's promotion knew better.

For Sonny Hathcock, making gunnery sergeant stood as one of his life's great accomplishments. He had dreamed of this day from the time he was a schoolboy and had first put on a Naval Junior ROTC uniform. He had known then that he wanted to be like his dad. He had joined the Marines, had competed in the marksmanship programs, led the Cherry Point shooting team. Now, at last, he had achieved this dream. Who else other than his father should pin on his stripes?

Fumbling with the rank pin, Carlos took hold of the left collar of Sonny's Marine Corps camouflage utility uniform. The younger Hathcock, while maintaining a presence of attention, leaned over his father's wheelchair to enable Carlos to pin the stripes. First the collar slipped from his grip. Then he fumbled again with the pin. Sonny remained at a leaned-over position of attention, patient.

Even for healthy fingers, the tight, tough weave of this uniform is difficult to pierce. For Carlos, with his weakened, crooked, and burn-scarred fingers, the cloth seemed impenetrable.

A well-meaning lieutenant, standing in the ceremony stepped to Carlos's side, and asked, "May I help you with that, sir?"

Those who knew Carlos well, including his own son, felt lumps gather in their throats. They knew this was trouble. When Carlos meant to do something, he would not accept help.

Carlos Hathcock narrowed his eyes, and through pursed lips he sharply whispered to the lieutenant, "Sir. I don't need no help!"

Hushed and reddened, the lieutenant snapped back to attention and retreated to his post. Carlos, now heated by his solitary determination pressed the insignia's two sharp posts right through Sonny's collar. Then, in true Marine Corps fashion, he slapped the insignia down hard against the younger Hathcock's collarbone and smiled joyfully.

CARLOS STIRRED FROM HIS SLUMBER. HE FELT CHILLED and breathless. His chest rattled with each shallow and labored breath he took. A small lamp near his bed gave a soft halo of light about him. The light quickly fell to darkness beyond his bed, where loved ones stood vigil. Light from the hallway spilled into the doorway, illuminating a path to the foot of Carlos's bed. He was at peace, and dreaming. The film reels of his life flickered onward in his mind.

THE TAN, SMILING FACE OF A TALL, DARK-HAIRED LANCE corporal, who stood leaning in the doorway of the sniper hooch in Chu Lai, Vietnam, began growing bright in Carlos's mind. The lad held a warm can of Orange Crush in his left hand, and leaned his right shoulder against the doorjamb while resting his right foot on his boot toe, crossed in front of his left. He wore a green sateen Marine Corps utility cover tilted back on his head, the band wet with sweat, and the dampness creeping up the sides of the hat's starched and ironed crown.

Carlos always liked to remember his friend and partner, John Roland Burke, like that. Smiling.

Both Hathcock and Burke shot the same zero, so when they switched duty on the sniper rifle, neither Marine had to make any adjustments. Ron McAbee was the only other Marine in Hathcock's entire life who also shot the same rifle sight settings as he did.

However, remembering John Burke also caused Hathcock's heart to ache. Of the more than 600 men that Carlos trained into qualified snipers, Burke was the only one of them that he knew of who had not come home from the war. Anyone would point out to the Marine sniper that 599 out of 600 represented quite a record. It told of the superior training that Carlos provided these men. But for Carlos that made no difference. Each of them had a face and family, people who loved them. They had an entire life ahead of them. To have one of them die in combat remained unacceptable to Hathcock.

Carlos tried to move his mind from the sadness that came with remembering John Burke. He focused more on that smiling face. That hot day in Chu Lai. Jim Land had just begun to organize the sniper unit and school, and everyone there was new.

Those days seemed carefree now. Although in reality they had been anything but carefree. Once they moved to Hill 55 life in the field became very serious.

How many times had he and Burke confronted impossibility and made reality of it? The three days in Elephant Valley had been one of those seeming impossibilities.

It had actually been fun, in a dark way. He and John had encountered an entire company of North Vietnamese Army replacement troops hiking along a faint roadway that bordered a rice field in the middle of Elephant Valley.

Neither sniper had dreamed that they could do much more against that many enemy soldiers than pick off a few of them and then run. However, Carlos's strategy of taking out the men who wore pistol belts first proved sound. Without leadership the frightened company dove for cover behind a long rice paddy dike.

It might seem the best move to the unschooled, but Carlos knew that diving behind that dike was the worst thing a patrol could do. It was almost suicidal. They should have turned into the fire, returned their own fire, and attacked the ambush. For many, this immediate action tactic was a hard lesson to learn, but hundreds of dead soldiers who had sought cover in the killing zone stood as testament to its folly.

The NVA had lain behind that paddy dike for three days with no water while Burke and Hathcock lost count of the kills they made during those days and nights. The two snipers had taken turns catnapping while the other kept illumination rounds called into the valley through the dark hours.

Running low on ammunition, the two Marines called in artillery salvos to finish their work that third day while they retreated up the slopes and around the mountain called Dong Den.

One thing about having Burke as a partner, neither man ever let impossibility cloud his thinking. Perhaps that is what finally used up Burke's life—facing impossible odds because the lives of his fellow Marines depended on his courage, his will to fight against bad odds.

But, then, they never considered enemy strength, because they always planned to hit and escape. Much the same tactic that the Viet Cong had used for decades. As long as they could hit, then disappear, it didn't matter how many of the enemy they faced. The sniper controlled where, when, and how to fight. With that he controlled the battle. He never gave the enemy the opportunity to launch an attack on him. His elusiveness left the enemy with no idea of where, when, or how to find him.

This chess match of deception had played itself to the extreme as he and Burke had faced and methodically taken out the majority of an enemy sniper platoon, trained in the north expressly to eliminate Carlos Hathcock. It was a private, very personal war that they waged in the midst of the greater conflict.

How many missions had he made with Burke? Most of them, he thought. He had several with Jim Land, a few with Charlie Roberts, but most were with John Burke.

Next to Carlos, the young lance corporal was the best sniper in the division. Together, the two snipers made a team capable of accomplishing the seemingly impossible. Thus, it was no wonder to Carlos that he and Burke more often than most faced the unusual and even the bizarre.

Over time, a special bond grows between men facing the extreme together. The two snipers had lived at life's edge, side by side, for eight months. They survived on peanut butter and John Wayne crackers. Placed their trust in each other and their faith in God. Burke had become more of a brother to Carlos than simply a partner or fellow Marine. Although the last time Carlos had seen John Burke was in the spring of 1967, the memory of him that day remained clear in every detail.

He could see himself joking with Burke and the other

snipers while standing behind the diesel "six-by" truck, waiting to climb in the back of the canvas-covered cargo bed and make the rough trip to Chu Lai. Carlos had dreaded how his kidneys would ache after the long ride in the hard-bouncing truck. Burke and the other snipers had kidded about drinking plenty of beer so that the kidneys would flush good after the jolting.

Carlos nearly cried when he said good-bye to Burke that day. He remembered looking out of the dark canvas cavern as the diesel droned down Hill 55, and seeing John Burke waving farewell in the billows of red dust. His smile. Wide and happy. Showing the purity of his soul.

He thought of Burke and how he, too, loved shooting. John had excellent talent and would certainly have found himself competing in Quantico on the Big Team. Carlos would have enjoyed shooting with his friend. After the work of war, the pleasure of competition would have made up much for both of them. Shooting. Competition. Nothing in his life had ever seemed more satisfying.

"LICK 'EM AND STICK 'EM PRIVATES," A SCRATCHY VOICE droned over the public-address system. A hundred Marine Corps recruits wearing yellow sweatshirts and green herringbone utility trousers frantically raced to patch the bullet holes in the fifty targets. They slapped black adhesive paper patches over the black centers of the targets, and white adhesive patches over the white areas. The recruits used many more white patches than black.

A sergeant seated inside a shack at the center of the line of targets lowered in the butts at Camp Pendleton's shooting range began to shout over the loudspeakers, "Hurry up! Hurry up, Privates. Another relay of shooters is ready on the firing line."

"Stand by!" the sergeant cried out, and paused, waiting for the secondhand on the wall clock in the target shack to cross the twelve o'clock position. "Targets!" he continued.

Fifty targets rose together from the butts, and in that same instant forty-nine bullets ripped through the paper pasted on cheesecloth.

Recruit Private Carlos Hathcock adjusted his knee slightly and closed his eyes for a second and then opened them. The black center of the target remained in the center of his sight. He let out half a breath, allowing the front sight blade of the M-1 rifle to stop in the center of the black bull's-eye. As it settled, he began increasing pressure on his right index finger, drawing back the trigger. He was in his bubble.

When the rifle cracked, sending his shot 200 yards downrange and into the target, he placed a pencil mark on the center of the small target picture in his shooter's data book.

"I think I got a pretty good one off that time," he thought to himself.

In a few seconds, the target rose with a white marker in the center of the black bull's-eye. A recruit in the butts beneath the target pushed a white painted metal disk on the end of a pole in the air. With it he covered the center of the target, indicating Hathcock's score: a five.[1]

---

[1]*Marine Corps Marksmanship Training Manual Testing and Scoring Information*: In 1959 the Marine Corps used the A-Course of fire at rifle ranges to teach and test marksmanship skills. It is very similar to the Known Distance Course, used today, but employed a different set of target faces at some of the firing lines. Today, 200- and 300-yard rapid-fire uses "Dog" targets, which are head-and-shoulders silhouettes, rather than the "Able" and "Baker" targets, containing round bull's-eyes, which were used on the A-Course. Scoring awards five points for any shot that breaks the paper in the black bull's-eye. The next ring outside the bull's-eye awards four points, and progress farther out to a three-point ring. Shots outside the rings but on paper net a two-point score. A miss nets nothing. Firing is from 200, 300, and 500 yards. With a total of 250 points possible. The V-ring is at the center of the bull's eye, but does not provide additional points in Marine Corps rifle qualification tests. The V-ring is used in marksmanship competition as a tiebreaker. In today's

A voice came from behind Carlos. "Where is your point of aim, Private?"

"Sir, at six o'clock bull, sir," Carlos said to the primary marksmanship instructor, reciting what the *Guidebook for Marines* taught.

"You made an excellent shot, but why is your call at center mast?"

"Sir, that is where the private last saw the front sight blade when the bullet broke, sir," Carlos answered respectfully in the third person, as was the custom for recruits speaking to any Marine.

"But you know to hold at six o'clock bull?" the instructor asked in a way that was more a reminder than a question.

"Sir, yes, sir," Carlos answered.

Carlos took a second .30-06-caliber round from the loading block and slid it into the rifle's chamber, sliding the butt back into his right shoulder. He laid his cheek back to the exact same spot on the stock where it had been when he had shot the first bull's-eye. Taking a breath, relaxing, closing his eyes, and reopening them, the target again rested center mast on his sight blade.

A guilty feeling swept him, and he eased his elbow forward on his knee, allowing the sight to move downward to the six o'clock position.

"It just don't make any sense. Where you aim ought to be where the bullet hits," he thought to himself as he added one click of elevation to his rear sight aper-

---

marksmanship competition, the center of the bull's-eye contains an X-ring rather than a V. Scoring is from a ten-point center and progresses outward with one less point per ring. Firing is from 200, 300, and 600 yards, and all targets use round bull's-eyes. In all marksmanship, the target is divided into areas corresponding to a clock face. Marines are generally taught to hold their front sight blade at the six o'clock or bottom center position of the bull's-eye. However, many competitive marksmen, such as Gunnery Sergeant Carlos Hathcock, hold "point of aim, point of impact," meaning that they hold the front sight blade at the point on the target that they expect their bullet to strike. Thus, Hathcock would hold his sight at the center of the bull's-eye.

ture. "Not six inches below it. Here I am on qualification day, and he's asking me questions."

Carlos closed his eyes, then opened them. Satisfied that his position was solid and aligned with the target, he squeezed the trigger.

When the target was raised back up, a white spotter rested in the six o'clock position of the bull's-eye. Carlos cleared a lump from his throat and wrote the score in his data book. Behind him, a recruit with Carlos's scorecard noted the second bull's-eye. Another five. Two in a row.

While the target was in the butts, Carlos looked downrange, careful not to watch his hand as he adjusted his elevation back to its former setting. "What they don't know won't hurt 'em," he told himself.

The next shot struck center, in the V-ring.

Carlos marked his call at six o'clock in his data book, and made a little check by the score. "Me and God will know it's center mast," he told himself.

He had placed all of his shots sitting and kneeling at the 200 yard line in the black. As he rose to his feet, adjusting his sling tight to a "parade" position, the recruit keeping his score whispered, "Bet you drop one out here."

Carlos narrowed his eyes and glanced back over his shoulder at the fellow private. The young man smiled, and Hathcock went back inside his bubble. He focused his concentration on the target, placed his left elbow against his ribs, and rested the rifle on his palm.

The day had begun gray. A cool breeze ruffled the red range flag on the left side of the berm bordering the range. The air was wet and heavy, and now a fine mist began to soak the cotton shooting jacket that Carlos wore. Even though it was July 1959, and usually warm in Southern California, the cold Pacific Ocean turned Hathcock's breath into a white cloud. "Lights down, sights down," he told himself.

Fog drifted across the 200 yards of clear area between the shooting line and the targets as Carlos's first shot broke paper on the left side of the bull's-eye.

"Nine o'clock," he told himself as he marked the call on the page of his data book and picked up his second round in the standing or offhand position.

He always tried not to think about the last shot or the next. Only this shot. As calm settled over him, the front sight blade of his M-1 rifle became so clear he could see the mill marks on its back.

A second offhand bull's-eye. It felt good.

After his third bull's-eye, Carlos glanced back at the private keeping his score. Hathcock avoided smiling at the fellow, but only looked him in the eye. The recruit smiled and gave Carlos an encouraging nod.

His fourth and fifth shots also struck black. A clean score, sitting, kneeling, and offhand.

Carlos loved the 200-yard rapid-fire, and the 300-yard rapid-fire almost as much. But four of his rounds drifted out of the black on the 300, and nearly wrecked his concentration. His shots had all struck in a tight cluster, but at the three o'clock position on the target, leaving the four rounds in the white.

He felt like kicking himself. He had nothing but black through the entire 200-yard string of fire, and cleaned the 300 slow fire, too.

"Damned wind," he told himself as he walked back to the 500 yard line.

"Pay attention to the range flags. This is where it is all made or lost," he said aloud as he sat on his ready box and adjusted his sling around his left bicep. He slid the thick shooting glove on his left hand tight against the front sling swivel and pulled hard, tightening the loop around his arm so that his fingers felt as though they would burst.

"Tight sling, solid position, adjust with your toes," he said as he dropped to his knees when the targets rose. Although he knew the range officer in the booth at the center of the firing line had called out to commence firing, Carlos never really heard it. He only saw the targets and heard the noise on the loudspeakers.

He never shot first. Never rushed. He looked one last time at the dial on the side of the rifle sight, making sure he had truly adjusted in his 500-yard dope.

"Out on the right," Carlos mumbled. He felt his heart pound seeing the red face of the disk come up in the center of the target. It was the fifth red face he had seen this day. Another four.

The wind became unyielding and unpredictable, gusting and shifting. Visibility also worsened. Anyone would be lucky to strike black now.

Carlos studied the range flags. The ones nearest him fluttered rapidly. Those at the 300 yard line lay limp. The flags at the 200 rose and fell.

A TELEPHONE RINGING PULLED CARLOS'S AWARENESS from that rainy day at Camp Pendleton back to his bed. The room remained quiet and he could hear a voice somewhere, talking to whomever had called. The voice was familiar, but he could not place it.

He felt himself smiling, remembering how he had won the high shooter award for his series in boot camp. That day he finished his qualification with a score of 241 out of a possible 250. He was only one shot away from tying the Marine Corps qualification record. That was his first trophy for shooting well.

Lying silently, Carlos's mind drifted into his early past. He thought of his mother and his father. Their lives had been difficult. His father drank excessively when Carlos was little. It prompted several separations between his parents. On those occasions his mother always took him to live at his grandmother's home, at the end of Butler Road in Geyer Springs, Arkansas.

She had a gray, rural route mailbox mounted on a post by the dusty gravel-covered road. Someone long ago had painted FRANCIS SWANNER on its side, in black block letters. Whenever his grandmother had an outgoing letter, Carlos always asked to take it out to the box. It wasn't so much putting the letter inside that he enjoyed, but raising the small red metal flag. Carlos loved to snap it up from its resting position, signaling the postman to stop and pick up his grandmother's letter.

How could such a simple thing, he thought, mean so much to a kid?

More than anything, however, Carlos, from the time he could first remember, loved shooting. He and his dog, Sassy, along with an old Mauser rifle his father had brought back from the war, passed many days alone in the woods, enjoying the best part of his life. His spirit thrived in the outdoors, in the country, and pushed against the walls of city life that constrained his need for freedom.

As a lad in Kansas City, Kansas, while his mom and dad were together, Carlos had gotten a Daisy pump BB gun for his birthday. Of course, his parents thought that he would only shoot around the house, up in the trees or at cans.

However, Carlos had an adventurer's spirit. Day by day he expanded his hunting range until it reached the grounds of a nearby Catholic church.

"Pigeons," Carlos said as he raised the air rifle to his cheek and took aim.

Several of the gray-and-white birds crowded on the edge of the church's roof. *Plink*—a pigeon jumped just as the BB struck the gutter beneath him. Carlos moved closer.

This time Carlos worked the pump on the rifle so much that he could barely snap it back in place. Carefully, he lined his sights on a pigeon.

"Stop! Stop right now!" a voice shouted to him.

Carlos dropped the BB gun from his cheek and turned to see four nuns running at him. He wanted to run. Flee the scene of the crime. But he knew better. In his disciplined home life, he had learned to stand and take responsibility for his actions.

"Young man," a nun whose face was pale and wrinkled said in a stern tone. "Thou shalt not kill! This church and its grounds are sanctuary for all of God's creatures."

Carlos said, "Yes, ma'am." He thought to himself, "I wonder if that applies to the mice in the basement?" He had always considered pigeons and starlings pests, too. They nest in rafters and leave a nasty mess.

The nun reached to take the BB gun. When she pulled it, Carlos's finger snagged on the trigger. *Splat*—the BB struck a sheet of water, puddled over with mud, in a flower bed only a foot away from Carlos and the nun. Speckles of mud splattered on both of their chests and faces. It left brown spots on her glasses, her white starched collar, and the white starched headpiece over which she had her black veil draped. Brown spots also speckled her pale face and tightly pursed lips.

"I am sorry," Carlos said sincerely, and let go of his gun.

"I will keep this," she said, "until your mother or father comes to retrieve it."

Young Hathcock walked home and confessed his sins to both of his parents, who forgave his transgression. However, no one went to the church to retrieve the BB gun.

CARLOS WAS LIVING AT HIS GRANDMOTHER'S HOUSE when he joined the Marine Corps. His mother worked in Little Rock and his father was somewhere else, welding for the railroad. His seventeenth birthday. What a day! His mother and grandmother had taken him into town where Mom signed the waiver allowing him to join the Marines. May 20, 1959, that same day he took his first plane ride to bootcamp in San Diego and began the first day of service in an organization that to him became more a family than a career.

Memphis, Tennessee, he recalled as his mind drifted back into his dreams. How could he ever forget the day he decided to be a Marine? Only eight years old, and he knew then what he wanted in his lifetime.

During those days, Carlos's father welded train parts for Tennessee Fabricating Company in Memphis. His mother worked in a department store. The Hathcock family resided in an upstairs apartment. Downstairs a Marine Corps recruiter lived with his wife.

The Marine stood straight and tall beneath a white barracks cap with its bright gold eagle, globe, and anchor emblem. He dressed in blue trousers with red stripes sewn down the side of each leg. The trousers never showed a wrinkle, and always hung straight with their sharp creases breaking just above the Marine's spit-shined shoes. His fine wool shirt had two sharp creases down the front and three sharp creases down the back. The recruiter had three stripes and a rocker sewn on his sleeve, and several rows of colorful ribbons. Beneath the ribbons, Carlos was awestruck by the two silver badges that dangled crossed rifles and crossed pistols.

Carlos knew the first time he saw the man in uniform that he, too, would be a Marine and wear that awesome uniform. He had never seen anything so grand, and never saw another uniform nearly as handsome. It spoke to Carlos of toughness, of courage, of discipline. Carlos could not imagine being anything better than a Marine.

At fifteen years old, Carlos had dropped out of school and gone to work shoveling cement for the H. W. Tucker Company of North Little Rock. He was as hard as the hundreds of pounds of concrete that he lifted each day. From the time he could first speak, his life was structured and disciplined. He always said, "Yes, sir." So bootcamp, for Carlos, presented few challenges to his body or his mind. He felt at home in the rigid structure that surrounded him.

He was proud the day he graduated recruit training and was then allowed to finally call himself a Marine. Carlos strutted in his tan tropical wool uniform, wearing a matching barracks cap, and the crossed rifles of a sterling silver expert shooting badge hanging from his sharp-creased shirt.

CARLOS OPENED HIS EYES FOR A MOMENT, HEARING THE voice of the person still talking on the telephone. Every few minutes he saw the figure of someone walking to the side of his bed, leaning over him, adjusting things and saying something he could not understand. He closed his eyes to the confusion and drifted back into his past.

WIND RATTLED THE TIN ON THE ROOF OF THE HOOCH where Carlos Hathcock sat at the foot of a cot writing a letter to his wife and son, who waited for him to return from Vietnam. New Bern, North Carolina, seemed so far away.

Sweat left brown trails through the dirt that covered his face, and he felt his legs trembling again. His hands shook, too, and his head felt light, off balance.

"Had to be that helicopter ride from Duc Pho," he said to himself. "This heat, too. I just need a good drink of water and some rest."

Carlos set the tablet and pencil on his footlocker and took his canteen cup to a large green vacuum can filled with water. He filled the cup once, drank it all, and filled it again. Walking back to his cot, he recalled the chopper flight back to the sniper platoon headquarters on Hill 55 earlier that afternoon. The aircraft had skimmed the treetops to avoid enemy fire, and the wind from the open doors felt cool as the helicopter beat its way through the air with its big twin rotors, racing northward.

Carlos had looked out the door of the CH-46 Sea Knight helicopter, watching as the green jungle carpet skimmed beneath his feet, and thought of home.

November 10, 1967, would mark his fifth wedding

anniversary. These five years of marriage had passed quickly for Carlos.

Although Jo was a few years older than he, their marriage had been very happy so far.

Jo did not like being a "shooting team widow." But when she married Carlos, she knew what lay ahead: He would be gone from home quite often, competing in regional, state, and national shooting matches, both military and National Rifle Association events, which took place in many cities throughout the United States.

Carlos would leave on Thursday and come home on Sunday night. Monday, Tuesday, and Wednesday he worked from five A.M. until six P.M. at the rifle range. In the evenings, he lay on the floor, in front of the television, and practiced "getting into position"—the tightly contorted stances (standing, sitting, kneeling, and prone) from which he fired in the matches.

It seemed to Jo that from March through April he did nothing but shoot. And he did.

However, she had resigned herself to that lifestyle— at least for a while—when she decided that she wanted to spend the rest of her life with him as Mrs. Hathcock.

Had anyone asked her if she would ever make that decision when she first met him, she would have laughed in their faces. Carlos, on the other hand, thought Jo was swell—nice looking and a great personality.

Carlos formed that opinion the day that he walked into the bank in New Bern where she worked as a teller. That was in January 1962. Carlos had just reported to the Marine Corps Air Station at Cherry Point from the 1st Marine Brigade in Hawaii.

That had been a dramatic change for Carlos—departing that tropical paradise, with its brown-skinned girls and wonderful liberty nights, for coastal North Carolina, with its tobacco-lined country roads and gas station entertainment.

Gas station entertainment was nothing new to him, rural Arkansas had offered little more during his youth.

And he had enjoyed those teenage years, too. But after graduating from recruit training, during Infantry Training Regiment at Camp Pendleton, California, Carlos discovered the world of entertainment that surrounds military bases and large cities.

Southern California offered its own special brand of "liberty" for the new Marine.

Following the rigors of infantry training, and like many of the Marines there, Carlos and his buddy Private David C. Holden joined the staging battalion at Camp Pendleton, a unit where overseas-bound Marines awaited their port calls to arrive.

During bootcamp, while on what had seemed an endless tour of mess duty, he had become fast friends with David Holden. Holden was a happy-go-lucky kid from Chicago who graduated Infantry Training Regiment with Carlos and later accompanied him to Hawaii.

While at ITR Carlos and David spent their first liberty weekend following along with the usual stream of Marines to Disneyland—looking for girls.

After a fruitless weekend at the land that Mickey Mouse built, Carlos and David met a couple of California Marines who took them along on liberty to the Norwalk and La Mirada area of Los Angeles. There, Carlos and David met girls.

Disneyland could not compare with what the two Marines encountered in Norwalk, and there they returned weekend after weekend for liberty.

But this weekend liberty—their last weekend in Southern California before they shipped out for Hawaii—was going to be different. They were going to do this weekend up right. It was going to be a weekend at a motel—girls and good times, and no platoon sergeants to barge in and stop their fun.

The summer of 1959 lingered hot on that September Friday afternoon when Carlos and David picked up their liberty cards and headed for the bus station where they caught a ride into Oceanside, California. There

Carlos had arranged to rent a 1953 Chevy coupe with a reworked engine.

As the two Marines cruised up the coastal highway to La Mirada, the old car purred as the sounds of Bobby Vee singing "Rubber Ball" drifted from the radio. David and Carlos felt excited about what the weekend promised.

The breeze from the Pacific Ocean whipped in the car's windows, ruffling the sleeves on their khaki-colored uniforms. But Carlos kept hearing a *bump, bump, bump*—something was wrong.

Carlos wheeled the old car to the highway's shoulder. "What's wrong?" David asked.

"Don't know. I keep hearing this bump or something. I want to look under the hood. It sounds like something's loose."

Carlos raised the hood and then slammed it down. He walked back and sat down behind the steering wheel and looked at David. "No tie-down on the battery."

"Any problem with that?" David asked.

"Don't think so. It looks like it's riding all right. Just bangs against the fender now and again. That's the noise I heard. Let's get on to the motel."

"You bet!" David exclaimed. "I can't wait to get there and get started."

The neon light flashed VACANCY in the fading orange of the late-summer afternoon as Carlos and David wheeled the old Chevy into the motel driveway where they would unwind for the weekend. Their liberty would expire at noon Sunday, so for the next forty hours they planned to have the time of their lives.

They checked into their room and then headed for the local drive-in hamburger haven to see who they could interest in unwinding with them.

It didn't take long before Carlos and David were hosting one of the more active parties La Mirada or Norwalk teen life had seen during the summer of 1959. There were girls and light rum, music and laughter.

Just before midnight, a loud banging on the motel

door brought the revelry to morgue silence, except for the giggling of a girl who sat on the corner of the bed, sipping on a rum and Coke, oblivious to the sudden intrusion.

Someone said, "Who is it?"

"Police. Open up."

David dove across the bed, grabbed the rum bottle from the nightstand and rolled off onto the floor, shoving the bottle up into the box springs—hiding it from the law.

Even though Carlos and David were both old enough to join the Marines, they were still teenage boys—too young to legally buy or consume alcoholic drinks. And certainly their guests were not legal-aged drinkers either.

One blonde girl, whose hair hung in stiff tangles, which a few hours earlier had sat neatly atop her head, peeked between the louvers of the blinds and screamed, "My mom's out there."

Carlos calmly opened the door, barefooted and wearing only his uniform trousers and T-shirt. When he opened the door, he saw the angry faces of the mothers of the La Mirada and Norwalk girls they had lured to the motel room for drinks and dancing.

"Yes, sir, could I help you?" he quietly asked the police officer who stood between Carlos and the group of irate mothers.

"Julie! You get out here now!" one woman commanded her daughter with a shrill cry that made Carlos cringe.

The blonde struggled to pull a brush through her ratty nest of hair. The embarrassed girl slung her long-strapped, saddle-style purse over her shoulder and walked toward the door, hanging her head and still pulling the brush, now less hastily, through her hair.

A stream of troubled girls followed, accompanied away from the motel room by their angry mothers who cautioned them about "boys such as these."

One woman looked Carlos squarely in the eye. "You

soldiers ought to stay where you belong—away from proper people. Don't you ever come back here, corrupting our daughters! There ought to be a law to keep you people away!"

The words stung. Carlos had never considered himself anything but upstanding, although not always proper. And Marines were beyond reproach in his book. He thought most Americans believed that, too. With that sudden scorn, however, he learned that not everyone shared his opinion of Marines or servicemen. Carlos learned that being in the service of his country also carried a stigma for which he, like most servicemen, would suffer discrimination. Carlos wondered if the hatred would have been the same if he and David had been La Mirada teens themselves. If anyone had checked ID cards, they would have discovered that Carlos, at seventeen, was the youngest of the group.

And it had been the rat-haired blonde who had gotten the bottle of light rum, bought by her older sister.

The policeman looked at Carlos and David and said, "I got out of the Corps last year so I'm not going to check your room, but you two better be more careful. Word about this bash spread pretty fast."

"Thanks a lot, sir," Carlos told the policeman. "We won't be any more trouble. I promise."

He closed the door and fell into a plastic-covered chair.

David looked at Carlos, reached under the bed and pulled out the half-full quart of rum. "Buddy. You need a drink!"

Two girls suddenly burst out of the bathroom, laughing and shrieking. Both Carlos and David laughed, too. They had nearly thirty-six hours of liberty left.

The Friday night party carried over into Saturday night, La Mirada and Norwalk teens coming and going, and Carlos and David enjoyed the bawdy weekend for which they had hoped.

Late Saturday night, the two Marines, accompanied by two girls, drove their rented Chevy through the backstreets of the La Mirada neighborhoods. They made drinks from a fresh quart of rum.

Del Shannon whined loudly over the radio about his "Runaway, run run run run Runaway." The four care-free youngsters sang along in high-pitched voices as the old Chevy cruised from curb to curb on the backstreets.

The joyous singing stopped with an abrupt thud as the car crashed through a wax-leaf hedge and skidded to a halt on the front lawn of a white, hacienda-style home with red curved tiles on its roof. Lights flashed on behind the decorated ironwork that covered the windows.

"Damn! Carlos, let's get out of here!" David yelled from the backseat.

"Something's wrong. Engine won't start. Something messed up under the hood."

Carlos leaped out of the car and popped up the hood.

"Damn! Dave! Get out here. The battery's gone through the radiator!"

David shoved the front seat forward and bounded out the door. "What can we do, Carlos? People will be coming out any second."

"Help me get the battery back up on the platform," Carlos commanded. "Look at that. This thing won't go far leaking water like that."

David reached beneath the battery while Carlos pulled near the corner that was embedded in the radiator.

"*Pulllll,*" Carlos grunted.

"Shit!" Carlos yelled, yanking his hand out and sling-ing it rapidly at the wrist. He shoved his knuckles into his mouth and sucked hard. "Christ Almighty, Dave! I raked all the skin off my knuckles."

"Come on, Carlos," David pleaded, "you can suck your knuckles when we get outa here. Let's pull on that battery again."

Both Marines reached under the battery and again pulled hard. This time it came free with a thud, dump-ing acid as it tipped upside down.

"Damn! That shit burns," Carlos cried out as acid ran into the fresh wounds on his hand. He dropped to his knees and wiped his skinned knuckles on the wet grass. David set the battery again on its rectangular platform.

"Can we get out of here? Now?" David begged.

"Let's see if she'll turn over," Carlos said calmly.

Carlos sat behind the wheel and turned the starter. It groaned and groaned. David squirmed anxiously, watching from the backseat now.

"Carlos! The guy's coming out."

At the same moment that a man wearing a bathrobe and slippers, and carrying a flashlight started across his front yard to see what damage the runaway car had caused to his lawn, flower bed, and hedge, the Chevy's engine fired to life. Carlos popped the clutch, sending turf spraying from under the wheels. Through a cloud of blue engine smoke, the man ran behind the fishtailing car, yelling and waving his flashlight over his head.

The man only saw one head showing above the car's windows as it squealed around the corner, white smoke pouring from the rear tires.

Inside the car, David and the two girls lay low in the seats, hiding until they felt safely out of sight.

Carlos took backstreets and alleys as the quartet of fast-sobering youths returned to the motel, hoping to avoid any police cars that might be searching for them now.

The angry home owner had reported the incident to police, but he could not give them a good description of the car, and he only saw one youth, who he mistook for an Hispanic.

The next morning, Carlos and David both awoke late. Their heads ached and Carlos's hand throbbed from the skinned knuckles.

At ten o'clock, he and David raced through Garden Grove, heading back to Camp Pendleton on a Los Angeles expressway. Carlos watched the temperature gauge needle go from the C to the H in a matter of minutes as they sped southward.

The one-hour drive turned into more than two as the Marines stopped at each exit and refilled the leaking radiator. They knew they would be late back from liberty. They both dreaded their inevitable meeting with the first sergeant.

At 12:30 P.M. Carlos pulled the car off the expressway and coasted down the Oceanside exit. Blue smoke belched from the tailpipe and a white cloud of steam boiled from behind the grill.

"That's it, Dave, we walk from here. She won't make it another ten feet without that engine seizing up."

As David stepped out of the car, he shook his head. "We're dead. We were supposed to have our liberty cards checked in thirty minutes ago. What are we going to tell the first sergeant?"

"The truth," Carlos replied. "We had car trouble."

Carlos locked the car and the two Marines walked, ditty bags in hand, back to the rental company to explain their problem.

As Carlos and David walked up the rental agency's driveway, the manager, an old man who wore a silvery crew cut and smoked foul-smelling cigars, looked at the thin gold watch stretched around his fat wrist.

"You boys are about two hours late."

"Yes, sir," Carlos acknowledged. "We had car trouble. Your battery wasn't tied down, and when we were headed down a ramp in L.A., we hit a pothole and it fell through the radiator.

"Rather than burn up the engine by driving back here on time, we stopped at every exit and refilled the radiator. Now Dave and I are late back to base because of your car. I'm sorry, but your car didn't make it all the way back. It's parked just off the expressway. The engine was smoking. I'm real sorry."

"You're sorry?" the man asked. "I'm sorry! I thought we had tied that battery down. You boys being late back from liberty, I know what that means. I was a sergeant major, you know, and I remember what I had to do with my Marines who showed up late.

"Don't you worry about the car. I'll send the truck up to get it. But first, I gotta call your first sergeant and square all this for you.

"I'll have one of my boys take you back to base."

As soon as Carlos and David arrived back at their Camp Pendleton barracks, they immediately changed into freshly starched and ironed utilities and spit-shined boots. At two o'clock they marched into their first sergeant's office.

At rigid attention, holding their starched and ironed utility hats in their right hands, Privates Hathcock and Holden stepped to the front and center of the first sergeant's desk.

"Sir, Private Holden reporting as ordered, sir," David said first. Carlos immediately followed suit.

"Okay, you two," the first sergeant said, "stand at ease and let's hear it."

"First Sergeant, sir, we sure are sorry we are late getting back," Carlos pled. "But we did have car trouble, and the man did call."

"Right," the first sergeant said. "You two are still late. The way I see it, car trouble or anything else is no excuse. Late is late. U-A is U-A. Your cock-and-bull story may have worked on that old man in Oceanside but you don't fool me any. Just take a look in the mirror. Those pretty red eyes and baggy faces say one thing. You two liberty hounds decided that these California split-tails and the good times are more important than your duty, otherwise you would have made it, car trouble or not.

"Hathcock, you and Holden will remember to plan a little bit better from here on out. I will see to that.

"To make it sink in, I have a small chore for you men over in the headquarters building."

The three Marines walked to the staging battalion headquarters where the first sergeant issued them a bucket of soap and water, and two stiff brushes.

From 2:30 P.M. until nine o'clock that night Carlos and David scrubbed boot marks from the stairs in the building. Both men smiling—recounting the weekend—the entire time.

THREE DAYS LATER, CARLOS AND DAVID LEFT CAMP Pendleton for Treasure Island, where they caught a troop ship from the San Francisco Bay to Hawaii. There they joined the same squad as machine gunners in the weapons platoon of Company E, 2nd Battalion, 4th Marines.

And like the battalion's nickname—"The Magnificent Bastards"—the two did their best to maintain that image throughout their tour in Hawaii.

TO YOUNG MARINES IN HAWAII, FIRST LIEUTENANT JIM Land looked hard. Intimidating. He had a crew cut and a square jaw. He rigorously kept his body lean and muscular. A platoon commander in the 4th Marine Regiment his first year in Hawaii, Land then became the officer in charge of the Hawaii Marines shooting team because of his experience as a competitive marksman.

Together with Marine Gunner Arthur Terry, a mentor of competitive shooters, he devised a way not only to justify competitive marksmanship there, but also to increase the Brigade infantry units' effectiveness by training selected Marines to be scouts and snipers. In 1960, Land and Terry commenced their first two-week scout/sniper course.

That same year, Carlos Hathcock won the intramural individual shooting championship. Besides engraving his name on the big trophy, 1st Brigade sent him as one of their representatives on the Hawaii Marine Shooting Team.

"Sir, Private Carlos Hathcock reporting for duty, sir," Carlos barked as he stood at attention six inches

in front of Lieutenant Jim Land's desk, his eyes fixed
straight ahead.

"At ease, Private," Land said in a friendly voice.

Carlos snapped his feet apart and clasped his hands
behind his back, but remained rigid, his eyes still fixed
on the wall behind Land's head.

"Would you please relax," Land said. "I want to talk
to you, not inspect you."

Carlos let his eyes drop to Land's face, and breathed
a little easier, yet he still maintained a certain amount
of rigidity out of respect for the Marine Corps officer's
rank.

"When I saw you win the intramural title, weren't
you a private first class?" Land asked.

"Yes, sir," Carlos answered, offering nothing more.

"Do I have to pry it out of you, or will you just tell
me what happened," Land said while thumbing
through Carlos's Service Record Book to find its "Page
12," where an administrative clerk would have recorded the young Marine's violations and punishments.

"Says here your company commander found you
guilty of Article 134, conduct unbecoming a Marine,"
Land said. "That's the catchall. So what kind of conduct are we looking at?"

"I hit a lieutenant," Carlos said.

A MONTH EARLIER, CARLOS HAD CELEBRATED HIS
twenty-first birthday, and typical of many Marines who
crossed the threshold that allowed him to legally walk
into any bar, he and several of his Echo Company buddies went out to Hotel Street in Honolulu to celebrate.
Famous for its prostitutes and steamy nightclubs, Hotel
Street is that lighted strip of establishments focused on
cleaning out military paychecks from their recipients
twice monthly. Nearly every city that hosts a military
base, also hosts its version of Hotel Street.

Since Carlos would have nothing to do with the
women of easy virtue who trolled the nightclubs, at

midnight he found himself alone, sitting at a bar beneath a thatched awning, sipping Jim Beam whiskey, waiting for his buddies to return so that they could go back to the base.

Carlos straddled a bar stool wearing a sharply creased, tan tropical wool uniform with a long-sleeved shirt, matching tie, and one stripe on his sleeve. His expert shooting badge with a third-award bar added to it dangled from his shirt. Although drunk, he had kept his collar buttoned and tie snugged up. He had tucked his garrison cap neatly under his belt when he had sat down next to a young man with short-cropped hair, wearing a blue and red flower-covered Hawaiian print shirt, khaki Bermuda shorts, and shin-high white socks with sandals.

Filled with whiskey-born bravado, Carlos chuckled to himself as he noticed the man's white socks and sandals. He would never be caught dead looking like that, he had thought to himself.

The man took immediate offense at the look Carlos had given him and the chuckle that followed. He had drank well beyond a reasonable quota of beer, and like Carlos sat in a booze-tilted haze. He glanced at Carlos's shooting badge and said, "You really earn that third award, Private? Or did you just buy that at the PX and decide to wear that instead of a toilet seat?"

"What did you say?" Carlos responded, and felt his stomach tighten as his face filled with blood. "These crossed rifles was awarded to me in bootcamp when I was series high shooter. It's pure silver. I just got through winning the intramural championship for the second year in a row, my third expert award. Next month, I am reporting TAD to the Hawaii Marine Rifle Team."

Carlos's breath had shortened and his hand trembled as he picked up his glass and brought it to his lips.

"Another shooter," the man said scowling at Carlos. "You have any idea what a waste of space you guys are?"

Carlos did not want to acknowledge the comment. He kept his line of sight fixed on the several rows of bottles at the back of the bar, and out of the corner of his eye he glanced at the mirror to see what this drunk would do next.

"I'm talking to you, Private," the man said, taking Carlos by the shoulder and turning him. "You better look at me when I say something."

With the help of Jim Beam, Carlos unloaded. He slid off the bar stool, and in the same move swung a round-house right fist into the man's nose and cheek.

"That is PFC, you asshole," Carlos said as the man fell off his bar stool and cupped his hands over his now bleeding nose.

"It's lieutenant to you, Private," the man told Carlos as he looked up through tear-filled eyes.

CARLOS LOOKED AT JIM LAND AFTER DESCRIBING THE incident. Then he quickly snapped his gaze back to the wall.

"That lieutenant wanted to run me up and disk me at battalion office hours," Carlos explained, "but I was lucky. My captain at Echo Company found out from witnesses there that the lieutenant was drunk. He convinced the colonel to keep it at company. So I lost a stripe and a month's pay."

"You're damned lucky you're not doing a year in the brig," Land said. "They could have given you a special court-martial, and booted you out with a dishonorable discharge."

CARLOS BEGAN HIS STINT ON THE HAWAII MARINE RIfle Team by graduating Land's sniper school and then winning the Marine Corps' Pacific Division Rifle Championship. A few months later, in the fall of 1961, he received orders to report to the commanding general,

2nd Marine Aircraft Wing, Cherry Point, North Carolina.

With a newly sewn PFC stripe on his arm, Carlos
wondered what rationale had possessed the person who
decided to send him, a machine gunner and rifleman,
to an air station.

"What are they gonna do, strap me on a wing with
a machine gun?" Carlos said to himself as he stepped
briskly down the sidewalk in front of the 2nd Marine
Aircraft Wing, Headquarters Squadron administrative
offices. He wore custom-tailored khaki trousers and a
starched crisp shirt. His spit-shined low-quarter shoes
clicked noticeably from the horseshoe cleats nailed to
the heels. This was a standard look for Brigade Marines
who often spent many months at sea visiting exotic
ports and wanted to look sharp.

Carlos believed in always being sharp—squared
away, he called it. But as he made his way to the first
stop of his check-in route he felt let down. As though
someone had tossed him off a pedestal and into a scrap
heap. These Marines wore their hair long. For Carlos,
long was seeing any length of hair above one's ears and
below one's cover. High and tight was Carlos Hathcock's standard.

Worse yet, these air wing Marines looked disheveled
instead of squared away. Their uniforms fit loosely. Instead of starched utilities and khakis, they were fluff-
dried and wrinkled. Their boots were dull and scuffed,
and many sported rolls of fat above their belts.

Back at Brigade in Hawaii, the company gunny had
told him as he checked out that he wouldn't like it at
the wing. "The officers are not Marines," he had said,
"they are naval aviators. They have no idea what it is
to hump, or be a grunt."

Recalling what the gunny had said, Carlos concluded
he had been correct. These air wing fellows at one time
knew how to look and act like Marines, but without
the same brand of disciplined leadership they experienced in basic and infantry training, they fell slack.

They ate too much fat, did not exercise, and lost pride in their appearance.

When Carlos checked in at Headquarters Squadron, the personnel chief, a round-bellied gunnery sergeant with a ruddy face, suggested that they could put him to use at the gymnasium with special services. But after a brief conversation about Hathcock's marksmanship skills, Carlos found himself seated on a bus, bound for the rifle range.

After Jim Land had learned of Hathcock's orders, he gave Gunnery Sergeant Paul Yeager a heads-up telephone call. He told the Cherry Point shooting team captain that the Pacific Division rifle champion was on his way. So by the time Carlos knocked on the duty hut door and reported to Yeager, the gunny was expecting him.

IN THE NEXT THREE YEARS EVERYTHING ABOUT CARLOS'S life changed. On November 10, 1962, he got married. He lost his PFC stripe for a second time, too. He had been hospitalized and failed to properly check back into the squadron, so he was listed as an unauthorized absence. Even though he was at work, where he belonged, the squadron commander still took his stripe.

A year later, 1963, he won so many titles that the Marine Corps invited him to Quantico to join the "Big Team." Feeling it was just too quick a move up, Carlos declined the offer. In 1964 he was glad that he had. He had a tough time that year, and did not finish in the medals. However, because of his standing at Cherry Point, Carlos was able to compete in the National Championship at Camp Perry, Ohio, where he won a silver medal.

The points that medal carried put him so close to the top that in his first competition in 1965 he achieved every competitive marksman's goal. He became Distinguished, and received the gold Distinguished Marksman shooting badge.

During 1965, his team regularly beat the Marine Corps team. Cherry Point had the Marine Corps' best shooters, and Carlos was among the best of those men.

His greatest prize, however, came at Camp Perry, Ohio, concluding that year's shooting season in the National Championship matches. There, Carlos won the Wimbledon Cup. With that achievement, the shooting world hailed him as America's best shot at 1000 yards. It was his best year at Cherry Point, and concluded his competition there. His next team, as Carlos liked to put it, was "in that big shooting match across the pond."

SWEAT STUNG CARLOS'S EYES, BUT HE COULD NOT MOVE. He dared not breathe. Frozen in place, all he could do was look into the ruby eyes of a deadly bamboo viper that lay coiled in front of him. The bright green serpent waited, poised with its head raised. It flicked its black tongue from its yellow-rimmed mouth, only inches from the Marine sniper's face.

"What's going on?" Carlos asked in his mind. He could not recognize this person, or another who now walked at the foot of his bed. Blurs in a white light.

He shut his eyes.

Carlos thought about the snake. The thought of it still frightened him. He hated snakes, and especially that one. A two-stepper, he called it. It bites a person and all he gets is two steps. Yet Carlos had to lie there and allow this deadly viper to taste the air next to his face, and satisfy himself that this thing in his way presented no threat. In a matter of seconds, the creature whisked silently away, disappearing in the grass.

The snake represented one of the exclamation marks that punctuated this most demanding and dangerous mission. Carlos had oozed four days and three nights across more than 1,500 yards of open ground, covered only by grass, to take out an enemy commander. A general at his own headquarters, far away from any of Carlos Hathcock's friendly forces.

Pure suicide. He took the assignment, voluntarily, because he knew he was the best available. He had the best chance, if there was any chance at all. Carlos certainly did not want to die. Yet, he could not accept a less skilled sniper dying in his place.

That was in the spring of 1967. His last mission of that first tour.

Vietnam.

There were good memories. Memories of men that he considered brothers. Men like Corporal Burke, Captain Land, Gunny Wilson, and Top Reinke. Buddies like David Sommers and Ron McAbee.

But with them came the other memories. The unforgettable. Impressions burned so deeply in his mind that even the details of that deadly green snake he had watched for less than a minute remained vivid after more than thirty-two years.

2

Newbee in Chu Lai

I T HAD BEEN A YEAR SINCE HIS PROMOTION TO COR-
poral, and Carlos Hathcock sat in front of a television,
touching up his metal utility uniform chevrons with
EmNew. He dabbed the black paint with the tiny brush
inside the bottle cap, covering spots where the brass
shone through the original paint. On the TV's black-
and-white screen, a Navy journalist read the latest news
from the Far East Network, transmitted from Kadena
Air Base, Okinawa.

There only one day and Carlos had written two letters home already. While other Marines in transit to
Vietnam took advantage of liberty opportunities in Kin
Village, just outside the gates at Camp Hansen, Carlos
remained close to the barracks. He saw a movie at the
base theater and bought a box of stationery at the PX.
He had dumped a dollar's worth of quarters into a slot
machine at the NCO club, but became bored with that
and returned to the barracks.

Since he would never think of being unfaithful to his
wife, he saw no use in going into the "ville," paying

higher prices for watered-down whiskey, and wasting money on Okinawan *naisans* who would probably give a guy the clap anyway.

Carlos laughed at his buddies mimicking the girls they had entertained. "I love you, GI, no bullshit. You take me Stateside? You buy me Honda? You take me big PX?" they would say.

Ironically, many of these same Marines who spouted such sarcasm about the bar girls' intentions, were completely broke when the plane lifted off from Kadena, bound for Chu Lai.

On the plane, one Marine commented, "So I pulled out my wallet and told the girl, 'Here take all my money. Let's just get this over with fast, so I can go back to the barracks.' "

The Marines knew the absurdity of spending their money on these cold-hearted girls, who the very next night would be with another Vietnam-bound GI, taking all his money, too. But, what the hell. Their prospects for the future did not appear all that bright. Death loomed for any number of the men, just outside the gates at Chu Lai.

THE PLANE TAXIED PAST ROW AFTER ROW OF STALLS constructed of sand-filled, fifty-five gallon barrels, stacked six and seven high. These provided cover for the fighter and attack planes quartered there. Suddenly Carlos's gaze was caught by the red archway sign at the tarmac's edge that displayed WELCOME TO CHU LAI, 1ST MARINE DIVISION HEADQUARTERS, painted in yellow block letters.

Carlos followed the line of Marines, seabags on their shoulders, as they walked across the hot concrete apron and fell into formation. Humidity and temperature hovered at about the same number—100—beneath the broiling April afternoon sun. Carlos felt his sweat soak through his green utility uniform, leaving the starch feeling sticky against his skin.

"First I was a machine gunner," Carlos mumbled to himself as he laid his seabag next to his right foot. "Then they send me to an air wing. I wonder what they have in store now?"

A gunnery sergeant read names off a long roll call list. As each man answered, "Here," he announced the unit's name to which he should report.

"Corporal Hathcock, Carlos N.," he said.

"Here," Carlos responded.

"1st Military Police Battalion."

"That's about right," Carlos mumbled as he picked up his seabag and joined a group of three other Marines also assigned MP duty. None of them had a clue about his new job.

"CORPORAL HATHCOCK," MAJOR GEORGE E. BART-lett, the military police commander, said as Carlos stood before his desk. "Good to see you again."

Carlos recognized his new commanding officer from the firing lines at Quantico. He had competed against the senior Marine on several occasions. Marines called Bartlett hard. He shot a good group.

As the officer glanced through Hathcock's Service Record Book, Carlos felt an immediate sense of belonging.

"I see you are due for sergeant," the major said.

"Yes, sir," Carlos responded.

"We'll have to take care of that on the next quota," Bartlett said. "You are well into the cutting score, and we need sergeants here."

If reporting to a fellow marksman wasn't good enough, making sergeant right off the bat went beyond Carlos's expectations. He had thought that he would have to go through promotion boards, and those Marines who had more time in the unit would get the stripe. With such a positive welcome, Carlos thought that life could not get much better.

*   *   *

MILITARY POLICE DUTY AROUND THE CHU LAI AIRFIELD and 1st Division headquarters compound became a monotonous chore for Sergeant Carlos Hathcock. As watch commander and desk sergeant, he toured all MP posts and ensured that his subordinates followed orders. Glorified guard duty. But, instead of four weeks or six weeks of a detail, he had an entire year.

Whenever he could, Carlos would duck out of desk sergeant duty to honcho security on the truck convoys that moved from the supply warehouses in Chu Lai to the various outposts and fire support bases that lay to the north, west, and south.

The young sergeant would position himself in one of the middle trucks, usually behind an M-2 .50-caliber machine gun. At that station he could see the front and the rear of the column well, and direct his men's fire, if they came under attack.

During the entire month of May, Carlos had not fired a shot in anger. The motorized patrols had gone with few incidents. Most of the action came from either the lead truck or the rear truck, when a lone VC gunman or sometimes a pair took potshots and then fled. The Marines riding shotgun on those trucks lit up the brush with machine-gun and rifle fire, but had yet to claim a Victor Charlie life.

CARLOS HATHCOCK HAD JUST PULLED OFF HIS BOOTS and lay back on his cot when the shooting at the flight line started. The sun had dropped behind the mountains, leaving the grayness before dark. Under its cover, the saboteur had sneaked through the coils of German tape and barbed wire that covered the airfield perimeter. Beyond that, he had carefully stepped through the crisscrossed barbed wire that the Marines had stretched six inches above the ground and extended out fifty feet. Along the coiled wire fence, claymore mines guarded the low avenues where a VC sapper might try to hide.

Inside the wire, Marines watched from fighting holes. They held rifles, .30-caliber and .50-caliber machine guns. They had radios and the trigger controls to the claymores. From each hole the Marines held fields of fire that crossed into the field of fire of the next hole. To Carlos, it seemed virtually impossible for a human being to negotiate the tangle-foot wire, work through the several layers of concertina wire, and avoid being shot by a Marine sentry or dusted by a claymore mine.

Sergeant Hathcock ran from his hooch, shirtless, his untied boots flopping on his feet.

"What's all the shooting?" he called to a staff sergeant named Cooper who jogged just ahead.

"Charlie slipped through the wire and emptied a magazine into a Huey," the staff sergeant said.

"They get him?" Carlos asked.

"Don't think so," Cooper answered, stopping for a moment so that Carlos could catch up.

"You mean he got in, shot a helicopter, and got out with nobody seeing him?" Carlos said in a tone that was more an exclamation than a question.

"That's about the size of it," Cooper responded.

Ahead of them the flashing red lights of crash trucks and police vehicles flickered in the evening. The crews pointed floodlights at the damaged helicopter, and Carlos could see Major Bartlett tracing his hand along the pattern of bullet holes.

Flight line crewmen and other curious Marines gathered in a growing crowd at the side of a hangar less than 100 yards from the shot helicopter.

Carlos stopped short and said, "Looks to me like they got her under control. I'm heading back."

"Go ahead, but I am going to take a look where this hotdog might have come through," Cooper said as he walked on.

*   *   *

AT THREE O'CLOCK THE NEXT AFTERNOON, CARLOS SAT at his desk, finishing his daily report. His shift relief had already arrived, and he sat in a chair reading *Mad Magazine*. On the wall over their heads an oscillating fan did its best to stir the hot, damp air.

"We located that gunman," Staff Sergeant Cooper called inside the police hut to Carlos. "One of our ARVN translators found a woman who saw the guy running from the base. We located his village and have spotters there now, looking for him. You got anybody willing to pop this guy?"

Carlos looked up.

"None of our guys wants to do it," Cooper said.

"You ready?" Carlos said to his relief sergeant as he stood.

"Sure, go ahead," the relief answered.

"I suppose I could do it," Carlos said as he walked at Cooper's side. "I had two weeks of sniper training at 1st Brigade, and I shot on the Cherry Point team for the past three years. I imagine it would be me or Major Bartlett who would be best to do the job."

The jeep wound its way westward, crossing Highway 1 and following a narrow trace that led to a knoll overlooking a hamlet of thatched huts. Surrounding the small village were rice fields and farther back a line of trees. Staff Sergeant Cooper parked his vehicle on the road behind two other jeeps, where two Marines with rifles stood watch.

As the two sergeants climbed the knoll, Carlos could see four other armed Marines lying on their bellies, looking toward the hamlet with binoculars.

"This our sharpshooter?" a lieutenant said, looking over his shoulder at Hathcock and Cooper, who low-crawled next to the officer.

"Good evening, sir," Carlos said, offering an appropriate greeting, and avoiding an exchange of salutes.

"Sergeant Hathcock is an MP desk sergeant," Cooper said. "He also had sniper training, and he won the 1000-yard shooting championship last year."

"Then this should be no trouble, Sergeant," the lieutenant said. "I guess that old boy's neighborhood isn't much more than 500 yards."

Carlos Hathcock moved ahead of the other Marines and found a flat spot where he could take a solid, prone position. He put his M-14 rifle to his shoulder and sighted at a hut.

"Breeze coming in off the ocean gives me a little left to right wind," Carlos said as he began turning clicks on a knob at the side of his rear sight. "Shooting downhill increases the challenge."

While the four other enlisted Marines lay on the backside of the knoll, smoking cigarettes, swigging water, and discussing the latest news from rumor control, Carlos and the lieutenant studied the village.

During the hours that they waited, several villagers had walked along the trails that followed the tops of the rice paddy dikes. Each time a villager appeared, Carlos whispered, "That him?"

"Nope," the lieutenant would respond.

By seven o'clock the grayness of evening had begun to darken the countryside. The air felt cool now, and the sweat that had beaded and dripped from their faces dried.

"Don't suppose we're gonna see him," Cooper whispered to Carlos as he moved back to his side.

For a moment Carlos did not answer as he studied some movement with his binoculars.

"You give up too easy," he answered. "Take a look at that tree line that comes from behind those hooches and out yonder past those rice paddies."

"What is it?" the lieutenant asked.

"Keep watching along the bottoms of the trees," Carlos said.

"I see it now," the lieutenant said as he picked up the flash between trees of a man hurrying toward the village.

"That him?" Carlos asked.

"Can't tell," the lieutenant said.

Hathcock laid his front sight post at the midsection of the man as he moved from tree to tree, stopping behind cover for a moment and then hurrying to the next tree.

"He sure acts guilty," Carlos commented as he kept his sights on the man.

Just as he stepped from the tree line and hurried toward the hut nearest to the trees, Carlos said, "He's got a rifle."

"That's him," the lieutenant said.

Carlos shot.

The man fell backward, the impact of the bullet lifting him off his feet. He never moved again.

Carlos lay quietly, looking at the dead man through his binoculars. The finality of the shot left Hathcock fighting a knot that drew tight in his stomach. His heart beat rapidly and he felt his legs and arms begin to shake with nervousness. It was the first time he had ever shot at another human being. It was the first time Carlos Hathcock had ever killed a man.

By ten o'clock, Carlos lay on his cot wearing a T-shirt and boxer shorts. In the darkness he could hear the snoring of the other sergeants and corporals who shared his hooch. He felt extremely tired, but could not sleep. The vision of the man falling backward, almost as if he had jumped, kept replaying in Hathcock's mind.

He reminded himself of what Jim Land had told his class in Hawaii five years ago: "When a sniper shoots the enemy it is an intimate thing. A good sniper values life, and does not take one casually. But he cannot allow it to eat at him. It is important to remember that when you kill the enemy, you have prevented him from killing your fellow Marines."

Carlos turned the philosophy over and over in his mind. All he knew about this man was that he had shot a few holes in a helicopter. However, he did have a rifle. Tonight it might have been a Marine.

* * *

No rain had fallen around Chu Lai in six weeks. June had ended hot and dry, and the first half of July offered nothing better. On this July 14th, as French expatriates across Vietnam celebrated Bastille Day, Carlos Hathcock started another watch as desk sergeant.

"If the wind would just come in off the ocean, I think it would be cooler," he said as he set the black briefcase next to his desk. The Marine Carlos had relieved finished tucking paperwork into his own black briefcase and now walked toward the duty hut's open door.

"Yup," the Marine responded to Carlos. "That wind coming out of the southwest is hot as an oven, and dryer than a popcorn fart."

Carlos chuckled at the analogy. "Keep your head down and your powder dry," he said to the departing sergeant.

The Marine turned and smiled at Carlos. "Not hard to keep anything dry with this weather, but I will keep my head down."

Ten minutes had not passed when Carlos heard the sound of a grenade exploding, and then the chop of several automatic rifles. He kicked back his chair, threw on his flak jacket, and was about to run outside when the duty phone rang.

"Military police desk sergeant," Carlos said quickly, "Sergeant Hathcock speaking, sir."

"You need to get your react squad and get over to the Highway 1 intersection," an anxious voice commanded.

"Who am I speaking to, sir?" Carlos asked, turning his logbook and jotting down the time in a left column and beginning to identify the phone call in the wider right-hand column.

"Captain Smith, division officer of the day," the voice responded.

"Aye, aye, sir," Carlos answered. "Can you give me some information about what has happened? I heard an explosion and automatic weapons fire a minute ago."

"Five females with BAR's [Browning Automatic Rifles] ambushed the afternoon logistics- and mail-run to Da Nang," Captain Smith said. "We are mustering a rifle platoon from 7th Marines to pursue these ladies, but your squad needs to get a jump on them to see if you can find a trail."

Carlos hastily wrote the information in his logbook, and then sat down at a two-way radio where he ordered his corporal of the guard to report to the duty hut with the reaction team. He again noted the time and entered that information in his duty log.

The phone rang again. Carlos rattled off the prescribed greeting, and then responded, "Oh, yes sir, Major Bartlett. I just got through talking to the officer of the day, and ordered Corporal Henry and the react squad to report here."

"I am on my way out there now," Bartlett said. "Put a duty at that desk and meet me with the react squad ASAP."

"Where?" Carlos asked, scrawling information in the logbook.

"Catch up with me at the front gate," Bartlett said, and hung up before Carlos could answer.

Carlos stood behind the M-2 .50-caliber machine gun mounted on a ring above the canvas-covered cab of the six-by truck that also carried the eighteen-man reaction squad. As they sped out of Chu Lai's main gate, he could see a jeep and driver with Major Bartlett riding in the right seat and a third Marine seated backward, resting an M-60 .30-caliber machine gun over the jeep's spare tire.

Peasants along the roadside scurried away from the truck as it sped westward toward Highway 1. Carlos fastened the chin strap on his helmet and pulled down the goggles that he had strapped around the steel hat. Gripping the handles of the machine gun he swung it to the right as the truck bounded around the corner where the Chu Lai road intersected with Highway 1. Less than a half mile ahead, he could see Major Bartlett's jeep and three trucks parked at the roadside.

Dust still filled the air from the jeep skidding to a stop when the truck pulled in behind it. Before the driver could shut off the engine, the reaction squad began bailing over the tailgate. Carlos grabbed a lance corporal by his canteen belt and pulled him back.

"You know how to operate this gun?" Carlos asked.

"Sure," the lance corporal said.

"Stand watch here while I go report to the major."

Jogging alongside the three mail-run trucks, Carlos could see metal parts and oil scattered beneath the lead truck.

"These women tossed a grenade under that truck," Bartlett told Carlos, pointing to the mess. "It took out the transfer case and drive shafts, and sent shrapnel up through the floorboard, wounding the driver."

"Anybody else hurt, sir?" Carlos said, now looking at the rows of bullet holes sprayed along the sides of all three trucks.

"Two other Marines," the major said, "hit by flying metal from the bullets. Nobody really serious except the driver. He got some pretty good blast wounds and shrapnel in his legs.

"They ambushed the trucks from the right side," Bartlett continued, "and then fell back into the brush, trying to draw out the Marines riding shotgun. Then they circled around and crossed the road at that little bend up ahead. Looks like they headed back west."

"My guess is that they live out yonder," Carlos said, pointing across the road where rice fields lay checkered between hedgerows at the foot of jungle-covered mountains. "Where do you want me to deploy this squad?"

"Sergeant," Bartlett said, looking across the green fields and the thickly grown trees and brush that spread across the overlooking hills, "I need your Marines to fan out around these trucks so we can have some kind of defense while we get this mail-run reorganized and headed to Da Nang."

Just inside the tree line, Carlos found dozens of empty

shell casings scattered in circular bunches. Farther back
he found more empty cartridges, but instead of lying in
bunches, they lay randomly scattered in threes and
fours.

"BAR's all right, every one of them," Carlos told a
corporal from his squad who had joined him. "They
were all on the ground up there when they opened up
on the convoy. All their empties were pretty close together and in five bunches. Five women. They were
shooting on the run back here, because the casings went
every which way."

In the next three weeks the same five women firing
Browning Automatic Rifles hit four other convoys.
They killed one Marine and wounded ten others. Ma-
rines at Chu Lai had begun calling them the BAR Team.

DURING AUGUST, CARLOS HAD BEGUN RIDING ALONG
with every motorized patrol that he could. Many days,
he took a morning patrol and assumed his duties at the
Military Police desk the same afternoon, working until
after midnight. After four or five hours of sleep, he was
up again, reporting as a machine gunner for another
morning patrol.

Sitting in a duty hut, getting out only to check sentries bored him. Carlos wanted action. Most of all, he
wanted a shot at the BAR Team.

Rather than riding atop a truck at the center of the
convoy, Carlos took a position behind the machine gun
on the lead vehicle. Goggles strapped on his helmet and
binoculars around his neck, some of the Marines on his
patrol began calling him Field Marshall. But Carlos
laughed it off. In his years of competitive marksmanship, he had learned to value eye protection. He had
seen more than one receiver blow up in a shooter's face.
Although they had cuts and metal embedded in their
cheeks and foreheads, shooting glasses had kept the
shrapnel out of their eyes. Carlos knew that good eye-
sight was critical for a marksman. He knew that losing

his would cost him his dream of one day competing in the Olympics.

The trucks had just turned west off Highway 1 and had began a dusty journey toward a firebase when Carlos noticed a flash of movement behind the brush on the left side of the narrow dirt road.

"Whoa!" he shouted, slapping his hand on the canvas above the driver. "Stop! Stop!"

The driver hit the brakes, sending two Marines lounging on boxes tumbling toward the front of the truck bed.

Carlos snapped the goggles off his face and onto his helmet, and began searching the brush with his binoculars. Suddenly he dropped them and opened fire with the machine gun.

"Ambush!" he screamed as he poured a stream of 700 grain bullets into the foliage.

The two Marines who had tumbled, now stood in the front corners of the truck bed and fired their M-14 rifles at a dozen Viet Cong who fled toward a group of huts. Carlos had dropped one man with his machine gun, but followed several other smaller figures who carried large weapons in their hands and ammunition bandoliers strung across their shoulders.

"The BAR Team!" Carlos shouted to the two Marines who fired their rifles beside him. He walked a stream of tracers up a rice paddy dike to the trail where the five women fled. Suddenly the machine gun stopped.

Carlos pulled the charging handle and let it go. The bolt slid halfway and stopped. He released the receiver cover and used an empty shell casing to clear the jam. He laid the ammo belt back in the gun and slammed the lid shut. He drew the bolt back and let go. As he pressed his thumbs on the butterfly trigger, positioned between the gun's handles, he realized that the BAR Team had disappeared from sight.

Hathcock took a green package of cigarettes from a pocket on the front of his flak jacket, shook one out, and lit it. Leaning over the big gun, he stared at the tree line to where the BAR Team had escaped. A knot of frustration grew in his stomach and he slapped his hand on top of the machine gun. "So close," he thought, "only to slip through my fingers. Damned gun jam, anyway."

He saw the women only once more while still serving as an MP at Chu Lai. It occurred a week later while Carlos was again on motorized patrol. The BAR Team apparently decided that the heavily armed caravan presented too much risk. So they fled, again to the west.

Carlos released several bursts of fire while other Marines potshot with their M-14s. But the BAR Team held too much distance and cover for anyone to have a realistic chance at hitting them.

BY THE LAST WEEK OF AUGUST, JIM LAND HAD ALREADY arrived in Vietnam, receiving his marching orders from Major General Herman Nickerson, who had just assumed command of 1st Marine Division.

Nickerson knew that Land had been one of the marksmanship officers at Quantico who selected rifles and equipment, established doctrine and tactics, and developed a viable table of equipment and organization for the first sniper organization in Vietnam. Major Robert A. Russell led the unit within 3rd Marine Division, under the command of Major General Lewis W. Walt.

Captain Land had already spent half of his one-year overseas tour at Camp Butler commanding the base ordnance company when General Nickerson saw him there. Nickerson told Land that he was no ordnance officer, and that he had only thirty days to go to Vietnam, organize a 1st Marine Division sniper school and tactical unit, and have it operational.

When Jim Land arrived at Chu Lai, he immediately began scouring the division's personnel rosters, looking for the best sniper candidates to man his unit. On the rolls, he found Master Sergeant Donald L. Reinke, Gunnery Sergeant James D. Wilson, Staff Sergeant Charles

A. Roberts, Sergeant Carlos N. Hathcock, and Lance Corporal John R. Burke. The captain requested that General Nickerson reassign the Marines to Temporary Additional Duty with him.

He selected each of the five Marines because of their superior marksmanship skills, their adaptability and confidence in the field, and their mental stability. In addition, each of the men had a history of dedication to their missions and to the Marine Corps. The most important and common attribute to each, however, was his great respect for human life.

CARLOS HATHCOCK PUSHED OPEN THE DOOR TO HIS new hooch with his boot toe. He carried a seabag on his shoulder and dragged a footlocker. The place was empty except for a Marine wrestling the end of a cot.

The lance corporal sat on the floor, pulling with both hands and pushing with both feet, trying to maneuver the end stick in place on his cot. Still straining, he glanced at Sergeant Hathcock and then grunted as the device finally popped into place.

"There's an easier way of doing that," Carlos said as he took a folded cot from a pile at the far end of the hooch and brought it where he had lain his footlocker and seabag.

In a minute he had the canvas bed unfolded and one end stick in place. He walked back to the pile of cots and pulled out another end stick. Using it as a lever, he popped his cot's other end stick in place in a matter of seconds.

"After you put enough of these together, you figure out an easier way of doing business," Carlos said with a smile.

"I'm Lance Corporal Burke. John R.," the Marine told Carlos. "Pretty much everybody just calls me Burke though."

Burke extended his hand and Carlos took it, giving it one shake and letting go.

"Sergeant Hathcock, Carlos N.," Carlos said, mimicking Burke's introduction. "Pretty much everybody just calls me Sergeant Hathcock."

Both Marines walked to a pile of bedrolls next to the cots, and began searching for the cleanest and most serviceable of the bunch.

"Be nice to have a pillow," Carlos said as he pulled the knots out of the tie strings on his bedroll and let it unfurl on top of his cot.

Burke looked at Hathcock and smiled. "Hold on just a minute, I got an idea." Then he trotted outside.

In a few minutes the youthful Marine from Alabama jogged back to the hooch and handed Carlos one of two empty sandbags he had gotten.

"Wad up some old skivvies or utilities in 'em, and I think they'd make pretty good pillows," Burke said.

Carlos immediately liked John Burke. He stood nearly a head taller than Hathcock, with dark hair and a deeply tanned face that made his bright, wide smile stand out. Burke always seemed happy.

THE SNIPERS SPENT SEPTEMBER GOING ON SHORT PAtrols as a six-man team north and west of Chu Lai. Jim Land used a sniper tactics book written during World War I. Unbelievably it was the newest version available; however, the tactics proved to be sound. Land merely adapted them to the conditions, terrain, and enemy tactics of Vietnam. Rather than working the fringes of large units, Land adapted the methods to guerrilla warfare. The basics remained identical: Engage the enemy at great distance with one shot. Rely on cover and concealment as the primary defense.

From the field training at Chu Lai and the guidelines that the World War I sniper manual provided, Land and his men developed a basic doctrine for Vietnam. Chief among these rules: One shot, one kill. Never fire a second shot from the same position. Never return to the same hide. Always remain alert: smelling, tasting, seeing, hearing, and feeling. Always be part of the environment: smelling, looking, and acting in unity with it. Always keep a good logbook. Never take a life casually.

3

Welcome to Da Nang

SWEAT POURED FROM THE LIEUTENANT'S FACE WHILE he sucked water from his canteen. It seemed to flow out of his skin as fast as he could drink it.

With his right hand, he lifted the steel helmet covered with green camouflage fabric off his head, and with the same forearm he wiped the sweat from his eyes. They burned from the salty perspiration.

Hungry and tired, he gazed across the valley below him. In another hour the unit he accompanied could be across and at a landing zone where helicopters would carry them home. Food, a cot, and getting the boots off his aching feet seemed a great reward to him now.

Before daylight, he had eaten creamed chipped beef on toast, two eggs, bacon, and a grapefruit. On his way out of the chow hall he had emptied a container of salt packages into the cargo pocket on the right leg of his trousers.

Now, waiting on the trail, he reached into that pocket and took out two of the brown paper packets. He tore the ends off, and dumped the salt they contained onto his tongue. The young Marine swigged more water, quickly washing the salt down his throat.

"Pew," he said, frowning at the bad taste. A Vietnamese soldier, who squatted two feet from him, smiled.

"Bad taste, huh," he said.

"That's right Nguyen," the lieutenant said. "Bad taste, but keeps heat cramps away."

The young officer had learned about taking the salt packets from the chow hall when he had prepared for this duty in Okinawa. The Marine had learned about heat the hard way.

During the rappel phase of the combat preparation program, the sergeants instructing the lieutenant's class took the men to the top of a cliff face. There, they spent the morning roping down, and then running up a trail to the top.

There were three lieutenants in this group: himself and two classmates from his platoon at The Basic School.[1] The rest of the men were junior enlisted Marines and Navy Hospital Corpsmen destined for reconnaissance or similar units.

After two hours of the hard exercise in the Okinawan heat, several of the men became sick to their stomachs. Some threw up. Others simply sat in the shade, their faces pasty and wet.

"Virus going around," a crusty sergeant said to the three green officers as he walked by them, helping a lance corporal to a seat in the shade.

---

[1] Known among Marines as TBS and located in the western training area of the Marine base at Quantico, Virginia, The Basic School provides newly commissioned Marine Corps officers and warrant officers with basic combat, leadership, and administrative skills. Today, whether aviation or ground, all Marine officers are required to successfully complete TBS. During the Vietnam War, Marine Corps Naval Aviators were not required to attend TBS. During the late 1970s and early 1980s the Marine Corps rescinded this exemption for aviators, citing the Corps' requirement that all Marine officers, regardless of primary specialty, be qualified to lead an infantry platoon in combat.

The lieutenants rested beneath the shadow of the cliff, stomachs hurting, feeling dizzy, and sporting complexions like cold cans of beer. Pale and sweaty.

The lieutenant's two fellow officers headed down the trail to get aid from a Corpsman on duty at the cliff base. He and a Marine assistant sat by a green, jeep-style, tactical ambulance with a large red cross painted on the canvas that covered the vehicle's cargo area.

"Got anything to make me feel better?" the lieutenant, who had remained on the cliff top, asked the gruff instructor.

The sergeant smiled.

"Oh, now the officers want to listen?" he said. "I got the impression that you three gentlemen already knew everything you needed."

"Okay, Sergeant," the lieutenant said, "I am humbled, and get the point. You have my attention."

The sergeant gave the lieutenant four salt packages, and said, "Pour these in your canteen cup, swish it around, and sit over there in the shade and sip it. Loosening your clothing will help, too. Heat cramps, sir. That's all."

"Don't want to get heat cramps, Nguyen," the lieutenant said, and tossed two packets to the Vietnamese soldier.

The American officer wore the tiger-stripe uniform typical of advisors assigned to work with South Vietnamese units. He was a trainer and observer.

Two canteens and an ass pack dangled from the back of his cartridge belt. A K-Bar knife and several pouches of ammunition hung at his side. He had unhooked the buckle, and let his suspender straps transfer the load to his shoulders instead of his hips. A model M-1911A1 .45-caliber Colt pistol tucked in a black shoulder holster rode beneath his arm at his left side, over his metal-plated flak vest. In his hands he carried Colt's latest rifle, the AR-15.

Only a few years earlier, Americans serving as advisors in Vietnam could not carry firearms on patrol. The lieutenant was glad that rule had changed. This would be a bad place to go unarmed.

The patrol had stopped at the side of a trail that led along a hogback mountain that 3rd Division Marines had named Charlie Ridge. Victor Charlie controlled this countryside. It was his ridge and valley, a prime spot for ambushes.

The Marine looked down at the green, peaceful valley landscape, checkered with fields along the valley floor and dotted with random clusters of small huts. But the fields stood fallow and the huts empty. The South Vietnamese government, as part of their "Strategic Hamlet Program," had relocated the valley's resident farmers to "safer territory."

The lieutenant considered this, and blew a breath of air in disgust.

"Farmers, right," he said to himself. "Most likely Viet Cong."

These days, when patrols encountered anyone on this ridge or Dodge City and Happy Valley, below it, they treated those people as hostile. Almost anything that moved got shot. The ARVN took few prisoners here.

In regard to this land, the lieutenant had long ago decided that those who weren't VC before the relocation certainly had the motivation to join the VC afterward. Being forced from one's ancestral land and homes did not sit well with him either. While he may have had a jaded attitude about the fidelity of the farmers, he nevertheless felt compassion for their plight.

He had grown up working on his father's farm in the south-central region of Kentucky, a short ride from the Tennessee line, near the town of Franklin. His family raised tobacco, corn, and beans, and ran a small herd of crossbred Angus/Hereford cattle.

An honor roll student in high school, the young man received an ROTC scholarship. After graduating from the University of Kentucky in Lexington, he began his active duty payback in the Marines.

Walking at the head of the second platoon, the lieutenant took small steps to maintain the wide interval both between him and the platoon ahead and the men who followed single file behind him.

THE COMPANY-SIZED PATROL FROM LIEN KET 70 DIVISION, Army of the Republic of Viet Nam [ARVN], had begun their trek at daybreak. The sun had now turned deep orange as it began to drift behind the mountains to the west.

As the patrol wound its way off the ridge and turned eastward, a gunshot cracked the air.

Soldiers dropped to cover, and fired blindly into the trees and undergrowth. When nothing responded to their barrage, they stopped shooting. The soldiers crouched nervously behind what cover they could find at the trail side, and waited for orders.

Sprawled facedown in the dust, a pool of blood spreading beneath him, the Marine lieutenant lay motionless. The gap in the front of his flak jacket, which he had unzipped for better ventilation, had offered the enemy sniper an unprotected avenue to the American advisor's heart.

The .30-caliber bullet had shattered his breastbone and pulverized the vital organ and vessels beneath. He died in seconds.

Shaken by the sudden death of the American, the Vietnamese major who led the patrol crouched next to his radio operator and reported the casualty.

"Only one shot. Enemy not sighted," he had advised his battalion headquarters. He told them that the gunman had hidden somewhere ahead and below them.

Anxiety now rode heavy in the major's heart. Darkness loomed. His patrol had fallen badly behind, and they faced at least another hour's hike to reach their pickup point.

Little things had slowed their progress all day long. Missed checkpoints, poor land navigation, more frequent rest stops than he had anticipated, unexpected investigations of suspected enemy positions.

Pushed to the brink of panic, the major urged his men to step more quickly. He was anxious to reach the landing zone that lay just beyond this quickly darkening valley. From there, helicopters could whisk them out of this place.

Watching the patrol from below, the Viet Cong sniper slid quietly from her firing point. Her face revealed French ancestry, yet her heart beat steadfastly for the Vietnamese that predominated her heritage. Dirty yet still hauntingly attractive, the woman crept silently back to the hiding places where her Viet Cong platoon waited.

American intelligence officers had begun calling her the Apache. Her reputation exceeded the most gruesome tales told about Apache warriors in the American West. Burying a man in an anthill, burning him alive, bleeding him slowly to death with a thousand cuts paled in comparison to the tortures she had devised for her prisoners.

Quietly, she informed her guerrillas that she had killed the American, and that the enemy company now advanced hastily toward the killing zone. Moving stealthily to their ambush positions, the Viet Cong platoon then lay silently as the sound of many footsteps approached them.

The Apache waited until the first platoon had begun to pass the apex of her patrol's ambush and the second platoon had strung itself dead center. Then she opened fire, signaling for the slaughter to commence. Her platoon's rifles, machine guns, and command-detonated mines chewed the South Vietnamese patrol in half. Panic-stricken, the company's remnants fled in two directions, retreating as fast as they could run.

Half of the first platoon, half of the third platoon, and nearly all of the second platoon lay dead or wounded. The Apache had scored a great victory.

Saving celebration for later, she maneuvered her platoon quickly away from the site. She anticipated the possibility that the South Vietnamese unit could manage to regroup and launch a counterattack. Her men would likely prove ineffective at attempting to hold a defense, even against what was left of the ARVN company.

Quiet as cats, the Apache and her platoon spread along a line through the forest. The black-clad guerrillas then stalked eastward, hoping to sweep in a straggler or two from the disarrayed unit.

Two soldiers wearing tiger-stripe camouflage uniforms ran eastward. Both men had lost their helmets and rifles when they escaped the ambush. Now they hoped that they could quickly reach the landing zone, where their unit would regroup and where the helicopters would rescue them.

Sweat soaked the men's hair and faces. Their eyes opened wide in the darkness, trying to see what might lay ahead of them. The two unarmed soldiers ran, overcome with fear. They never thought to look down.

As though struck by a lightning bolt, both men tumbled to the ground when their shins struck three parachute cords stretched among the trees. Just as the two soldiers fell, six Viet Cong swarmed them. The guerrillas tied their ARVN captives' hands behind their backs, and gagged and blindfolded them.

"Didi, didi mao," the woman growled at the two men, telling them to move out quickly. She had more business tonight.

Her soldiers tied cords around the prisoners' necks, and led them like dogs as they rushed eastward.

JUST AFTER MIDNIGHT, SCREAMS ECHOED FROM THE distant tree line below Hill 55. As 3rd Division Marines spent their last night on this dirty knob, southwest of Da Nang, the sickening despair of the two tortured men deprived them of sleep once again.

Most of these Marines had lost count of how many nights the Apache had serenaded them with her bloody music, sung by slowly dying victims. Each night that she performed her gruesome act, the tortured lullaby did its work on the minds of the men who sat helplessly listening. It had become a well-worn tune, but remained effective.

Psychological warfare, the Intel and Ops guys called it. For the grunts, just more bad dreams. Leaving the Apache behind made going north into Quang Tri, As-hau, and other equally delightful shit holes seem almost attractive.

At daylight, a patrol cautiously crossed the wide fields below Hill 55 and entered the forest. Even the hardest grunt had difficulty handling the sight when they finally located the two men.

Neither of the prisoners showed any signs of bullet or stab wounds. The Marines concluded that the Apache had spent the night peeling and cutting the derma away from the men's flesh while they cried out from the pain. She had sliced numerous gashes across their faces, and from the neck down, had skinned them.

No doubt the Apache had taken her time. Perhaps she skinned one man while the other watched, making sure the screams lasted through most of the night. She was an artist at her work, sculpting nightmares.

The patrol cut the men from the trees where the Apache had left them tied, and zipped the bloody corpses inside body bags. Now, well into the morning, the Marines dragged the two dead soldiers up Hill 55 where the South Vietnamese liaison could then take them home.

MEANWHILE AT CHU LAI, 1ST DIVISION MARINES fin-ished packing and began their movement north.

"That's about it," Carlos Hathcock said as he pushed up the tailgate on the six-by truck. He and the other snipers had loaded their heaviest equipment onto the bed of the big vehicle bound for Hill 55, the snipers' new home.

"Worst is over," Jim Land said in a sarcastic tone as

he wiped sweat off his arms and face with his utility jacket. "All we have to do now is carry this other mountain of gear to the flight line, and get on the chopper."

"Hope it's a darn site cooler up on that hill than down in this hole," Carlos said as he slipped his uniform top back on.

"Don't count on it," Master Sergeant Reinke said, picking up his seabag and two rifle cases. "We gotta go a lot more north and a whole lot higher up to find anything cool."

"Wait a second, Top, don't go knocking our new place prematurely. I found a nice hooch for us, set out on Finger 4, with two good sandbagged emplacements. It's an excellent vantage point that covers two sides of the hill and a lot of country," Land said as he lifted his seabag and rifles onto the back of a truck that would take the six men to a row of helicopters waiting at the flight line. "And sitting out on that finger, we ought to catch plenty of breezes."

"Yes, sir, breezes off incoming fire, I'll bet," Top Reinke said with a smile as he piled his gear aboard, too.

Marines from the 25th and 26th regiments, deployed to Vietnam from the recently reactivated 5th Division at Camp Pendleton, had already begun movement this October morning. Their infantry battalions traveled both by helicopter and ground transport to the Hill 55 compound where Land's snipers would join them.

That same day in October 1966, Marine Corps numbers had swelled to 60,000 now serving in Vietnam. Their areas of responsibility since March 1965 had grown from eight square miles around Da Nang to more than 1,800 square miles and one million people. Current plans estimated that this area of responsibility would expand to covering 2,700 square miles and two million people.

During that eighteen-month period, Marines in Vietnam carried out 150 regimental- and battalion-sized operations, killing 7,300 enemy, and fought more than

200,000 small unit actions, accounting for an additional 4,000 enemy dead.

In those same months, more than 9,000 Marines suffered wounds in combat, eighty percent of whom returned to duty. Sadly, however, nearly 1,700 Marines died in action.

Lieutenant General Lewis W. Walt, nominated for his third star by President Johnson in February, held overall leadership of the eighteen infantry battalions and supporting Marine air and ground units in Vietnam as Commanding General, III Marine Amphibious Force. Until March, General Walt had also directly commanded 3rd Marine Division. However, with the escalation of Marine numbers in Vietnam, Major General Wood B. Kyle assumed Walt's command of 3rd Division. Major General Herman Nickerson commanded 1st Marine Division.

With the expansion of Marine forces, 3rd Division now moved from Da Nang into the northern reaches of I Corps. As many as seven battalions of Marines and three ARVN battalions, since early August, had fought the North Vietnamese Army's 324-Bravo Division and their reinforcing elements. Daily, the Communist enemy to the north sent scores of fresh troops southward, continually replacing the NVA soldiers they had lost in the battles.

During July alone, in northern Quang Tri Province, Marines killed 824 of the enemy. From early August through the end of January, Marines in this fight, called Operation Prairie, would kill an additional 1,397 enemy soldiers, most of whom were NVA regulars.

This 3rd Division hunting ground began at the 1954 Demarcation Line, the 17th parallel, better known as the Demilitarized Zone, and stretched east to west along the Ben Ha River, just above Highway 9. From that northern border, the Division's territories reached southward to the Hai Van Pass outside Da Nang.

Their new Tactical Area of Responsibility included such garden spots as Khe Sanh, Con Tien, The Rock

Pile, Camp Carroll, the Ashau Valley, Dong Ha, Quang Tri, Hue, and Phu Bai.

1st Marine Division's new TAOR stretched from the Hai Van Pass westward to Cambodia, and southward to Phu Cat. It included its own variety of unpleasant attractions such as Charlie Ridge, Happy Valley, Dodge City, Elephant Valley, Antenna Valley, Que Son Hills, and the Riviera. Marines and soldiers alike called it Oklahoma Territory, westward from Da Nang, and Arizona Territory southward. Both famous as "Indian Country."

While 1st Division headquarters joined III MAF at the top of Freedom Hill, identified on the maps as Hill 327, Captain Land and his sniper unit boarded an H-34D helicopter bound for Hill 55. Each man carried a seabag filled with his most important personal possessions, and packed in cases slung over their shoulders, their rifles.

The snipers' weaponry included several M-14s, as well as a number of Model 700 Remington .30-06 Springfield rifles with Redfield 3 × 9 power scopes, and Model 70 Winchester .30-06 Springfield rifles with 10-power Unertl scopes. They fired full-copper-jacketed, 173-grain, Sierra boat-tail bullets set in match cartridges, manufactured to exact specifications by the Lake City Arsenal.

With the top-grade ammunition, all of the rifles held groups in a less than one-inch wad. Describing it, Carlos would hold his index finger and thumb together in front of his face, and say with a grin, "Tighter than a gnat's ass."

Although heavily laden on the helicopter, Land believed that the overland route up Highway 1 from Chu Lai to Da Nang presented too great a risk for their most important equipment, riding aboard the cargo trucks.

Between these two major compounds lay miles of potential ambush sites. Hot spots such as the Que Son Hills and the several hamlets of Cam Ne, places always

certain to offer American caravans ample helpings of
VC fire.

"I heard that your trucks got held up at that big iron
bridge, a few miles south of the turnoff that heads up
here from Highway 1," a captain from 3rd Division
Operations said to Jim Land, and extended his hand to
greet the new Hill 55 tenants.

"No, Skipper," Land said, dropping from the tailgate
of a truck that had carried him and his snipers and their
most valued gear from the compound's landing zone.
"I hadn't heard that."

After a quick handshake, Land walked to his team's
new hooch, and lifted its screen door, which lay side-
ways, twisted on its bottom hinge and torn away from
the door at the top. Debris, discarded during the previous inhabitants' departure, littered the floor and the
area in front and behind the hardbacked shelter. Most
of the screens that wrapped the hooch as a continuous
series of windows from shoulder height to the metal
rooftop flapped from big tears.

"Looks like we'll be a while before we need the gear,
anyway," Land then said. "Know what's going on?"

"They apparently took some hits when they approached the bridge," the operations captain said. "According to the sitrep, a few of the trucks got dusted with
small-arms fire, no one hit. I guess the cargo is no worse
for wear. But they are held up until a unit can get the
bridge cleared."

"Looks like folks that lived here before left in a
hurry," Burke said as he began picking up trash.

Carlos joined him in the work.

"Skipper," Gunny Wilson said to Land, "I'm going
on a prowl for some hammers and nails, and whatever
other tools and material I can scrounge."

Land nodded his approval, and watched the Marine
jog up a path that led from Finger 4 to the headquarters
compound on the hilltop. Then, seeing the gunny glance
back, Land shouted to Wilson, "Get some paint, too."

Master Sergeant Reinke walked down a path toward

the entrances of two large fighting holes ringed with sandbags stacked three high and two bags across. Land and the operations captain followed him and talked.

"Hooch is a little ratty," Land said, "but we can fix that. Hard to beat these firing positions, though. From here, we can control a decent part of this hill face. Plus, camping on this finger we're out of the way, and have plenty of room to set up our sniper classes."

"Good area, but there's one downside," the operations captain said.

"What could that be?" Land asked.

"Front row seats for the Apache," the captain said.

Land gave the Marine a puzzled look. "Apache?"

"I'll let your Intel guys fill you in; I don't want to rob their thunder," the captain said. "Right now, I need to catch my ride up to Phu Bai. But I will tell you this: She's the devil."

The captain took several steps up the path toward headquarters, then he turned toward Land and said, "And I do mean the devil."

Several hours later, the snipers finished their cleanup. Carlos Hathcock had rebuilt the screen door, straightened and reattached the hinges, and nailed it back in place. Burke and Roberts had policed all the trash and cleaned the hooch. Reinke and Wilson fixed screens and repaired holes in the roof while Land divided his time with each project, overseeing the work, and repainted the sign that stood to the left of the hooch's front door.

With a small can of red and another of yellow paint that Gunny Wilson picked up after someone had left the two cans sitting unattended next to a new sign at the supply tents, Land lettered in yellow over a red background 1st MARDIV SCOUT/SNIPER UNIT AND SCHOOL.

While they waited for the truck, Land and his Marines further busied themselves stacking sandbags around the rear of their hooch. Its back door faced outward on Finger 4, toward the rice fields and jungles below, vulnerable to enemy gunfire.

When the truck carrying the remainder of their gear

finally arrived, a lieutenant from 26th Marines intelligence section stepped off its running board, where he had hitched a ride from the headquarters area.

After a sweaty handshake, Land and the lieutenant examined area maps while the snipers unloaded their equipment and set up their cots, cabinets, tables, and workbenches.

The intelligence officer pointed out enemy strongholds, places like Charlie Ridge, Dodge City, and Happy Valley. Then he went into detail about the Apache.

He showed Land on the maps her more frequent operating areas, and graphically described several of her torture techniques. He told of a civilian contractor she had captured. She had tied a basket on his head in which she enclosed several hungry rats.

The lieutenant concluded the horror story by telling of the two South Vietnamese soldiers she had tortured all night and, that very morning, had left tied to the trees below their hooch, skinned.

"Get her and you can write your own ticket here," the lieutenant said.

Jim Land said nothing. He just stood with his arms folded, quietly watching the setting sun.

"Downside all right," he muttered under his breath.

WITHIN THE MONTH, LAND COMMENCED THE FIRST scout/sniper class. All six of the Marines instructed the students, assigned there from various battalions throughout the 1st Marine Division. They divided teaching chores according to each sniper's best skills. Carlos Hathcock focused on marksmanship development and individual tactics.

A critical part of Hathcock's shooting fundamentals involved a marksman's thorough familiarity with his rifle and his ability to adapt the various firing positions to accommodate his body, and still provide himself a solid platform.

"Snapping-in," as Marines called it, provided Carlos's students the opportunity to develop an intimate familiarity with both their rifles and their shooting positions.

While leaves from Maine to California turned golden and red, everything remained a dust-covered green in Vietnam. The heat waves rippled across the valley as twelve sniper students sat in a line on the edge of Hill 55's fourth finger. Here men with empty rifles, contorting their bodies into various shooting positions, trained their sights and dry-fired the weapons. They sought stability. Smoothness. Trigger control. A snap with no bounce.

Below, in the fields, Vietnamese farmers had begun cutting and thrashing their rice crop at dawn. After binding the base of a bundle of rice stalks, the heads heavy with grain, the farmers and their families cut the plants and laid the bundles along the rows where they worked. Others then gathered the bundles, which they carried off several at a time. The workers suspended the bundles in flat wicker baskets tied at each end of long poles, which they balanced across their shoulders. They brought their loads to the edge of the field. There, holding a handful of the stalks at a time, women standing behind a small, foot-powered thrasher, stuffed the plant heads into the machine's snout. Squatting below it, other women scooped the harvested grain into large pots. Nearby, women and older children poured rice into cloth bags that they then sewed shut with string and piled into a cart pulled by a water buffalo.

Through the morning, the Marine sniper students watched through their rifles' scope sights as any worker would walk to or from the road. As the farmhand moved, a rifle would follow him. If he stopped, so did the weapon's muzzle.

"Remember to breathe, relax, focus your aim, and at the same time, squeeze," Carlos said to a student who held his scope's crosshairs on the chest of one field hand. As the man carried a load of rice bundles, the sniper student gently titled his rifle down and to the right, keeping his sights fixed on his target until the trigger snapped the firing pin forward.

"That looked pretty good," Carlos said. "How did it feel?"

"Felt fine. Really steady, Sergeant Hathcock," the student answered. "But that guy looks a little ticked. He's waving his hands and pointing up here."

Carlos took the student's rifle and trained the scope on the man below. He could see him talking to another farmer, both wearing flat, cone-shaped hats woven from straw. While one of the two workers began walking up the road toward a cluster of huts, the other put the pole and baskets back on his shoulder and returned to the field for another load.

"Don't worry about it," Carlos said as he handed the rifle back to the student. "It ain't like we're really shooting at 'em."

Then Carlos took several steps backward and spoke in a loud voice to all twelve sniper trainees. "I want you to pick out one man, woman, or kid down there, it don't matter, and follow your sights on 'em, and let that trigger break while they're on the move. Remember, trigger control."

Carlos paused for a moment, and added, "Most of the time when you take a shot at the enemy, he ain't gonna stand still for you. So you have to get used to moving those crosshairs with the target, and still keeping good trigger control and a solid position."

After taking a long drink of water, Carlos sat on the ground in a modified cross-ankle position. He tucked his rifle into his shoulder, his sling taut on his arm, and joined his students, snapping-in on the farmers below.

Before lunchtime, the workers suddenly left the field, leaving the thrasher and hundreds of rice bundles unattended. First, they gathered on the road. Then, as a group, they walked back to their village where two South Vietnamese police jeeps waited.

All dozen sniper students and Carlos had kept their

scope sights focused on the people, watching and still snapping-in, as they proceeded along the narrow road-way.

"I think we may have a little problem," Carlos said to himself, when he saw two police vehicles. So, when Gunny Wilson tromped down the path after lunch, his face slightly flushed, Hathcock had a good idea of what troubled his supervisor.

"Before you say anything, Gunny," Carlos said as Wilson stopped in front of him with his arms crossed, "we have no ammunition loose out here, and I personally made sure every rifle chamber was clear."

"I don't doubt it, Sergeant Hathcock," Wilson answered. "But the colonel had Captain Land standing tall after a village chief and four RVN cops had chewed his ears about you guys pointing your guns at their people."

"We were just snapping-in, Gunny," Carlos said. "They need practice on moving targets. What else are they going to be able to aim at?"

"Just snap-in on the barrels," Wilson responded. "Keep your rifles pointed away from those farmers. Captain Land said so. If those students need practice on moving targets we'll take 'em off the hill someplace. Sight in on the VC."

Carlos knew better than to try to argue the point any more. As the gunny departed, Hathcock walked to the side of the sniper hooch and rolled back two fifty-five-gallon barrels, painted white with rows of black circles and silhouettes stenciled from top to bottom, all around each of them. He set the steel drums thirty feet apart. When the students returned from chow, Carlos divided the group, six men each, around the painted barrels.

"Next time you put your crosshairs on a moving target," Carlos told the Marines, "you'll have rounds in your chambers. It's gonna be Homer the Hotdog in his black pajamas at the other end. So, now is the time to get solid and hard. Don't waste it because you're pointing at a gas can."

* 　 * 　 *

EACH MORNING BEFORE CLASS, CARLOS AND BURKE visited the 26th Marines S-2 office on their return walk from breakfast. The snipers hoped to get news of a VC avenue that would provide them with the opportunity to initiate their students. Pop their cherries, as the instructors put it. A well-traveled path would offer the snipers several positions and enemy targets.

Finally, the opportunity came. The gunnery sergeant, whose shaved head glistened in the morning sunlight, told Carlos and Burke about an area southeast of Hill 55.

"It's a wide, clear area several miles long with a big bend south about dead center," the gunny said. "You've got heavy cover on both sides that connects to some pretty hot areas. The past few days, we've had sighting reports of several VC patrols crossing at different spots."

"Sounds like just the thing we're looking for, Gunny," Carlos said, and hurried to the sniper hooch to report his news to Captain Land.

HUMIDITY FROM THE NEARBY SEA AND THE EARLY morning's cool air left layers of fog creeping along the hillside, clinging in the ravines and channels that had eroded from the top. Along the higher parts of the valley, the fog spread thin in a translucent veil, a sheer white shroud caressing the ground and trees. Where the earth fell to gullies and other low-lying places, the fog rolled thick, white, and heavy. Puffy as marshmallows.

In a silent procession, each man draped with camouflage, their skin painted green and bush hats pulled low above their eyes, Carlos Hathcock and John Burke led their twelve sniper students along a down-sloping trail. Passing the last line of green-painted hooches, the snipers followed the path toward the picket lines and listening posts that guarded the wire surrounding Hill 55.

On a flat area approaching the wire, Carlos gathered the snipers in a U-shaped formation, to inspect them and their equipment. He made sure the men had taped covers on their scopes to keep the wet air from condensing water on the lenses. He checked ammo pouches, canteens, and packs. Then he asked if anyone had questions. Were they clear about this day's mission, their shooting partner, and which instructor the two of them would join in the field? Were they certain of the positions of their primary and secondary rally points? Could they find them in a panic?

Satisfied, Hathcock waved his right hand forward with his index finger pointed down the trail, signaling the men to move ahead.

One by one, as the camouflaged Marines, sporting bush hats and hunting rifles, passed the watching sentries, Carlos could hear voices muttering from the sandbag-protected holes.

"There goes murder incorporated," he heard one man say to a watch-post partner. "Cold-blooded fuckers."

Carlos knew his students had heard the various comments, too. The words had humiliated him because he never considered himself cold-blooded. He had compassion. He had never murdered anyone either. But he could deal with it. Don't let the bastards wear you down.

What worried him was that some of his students might enjoy such comments. They might boast about it. Murder incorporated. Cold-blooded fuckers. Macho and hard.

A bad attitude for a sniper.

"Form me a school circle," Carlos whispered to the man behind him after the group had cleared the last security perimeter and entered a thicket of chest-high bushes. The student passed the word to the next, who passed it to the next.

They squatted in the fog where the slope of Hill 55 turned flat and joined the valley. Although not a man to make speeches, Carlos knelt in the center of the circle, and spoke from his heart.

"You probably heard the comments those troops made about us as we walked by them a while ago," Carlos began. "I don't know if it's the first time you heard anybody say that about you or not. Maybe you, yourselves, have said it. But you better know right now, we don't commit murder. We are not murder incorporated. We ain't cold-blooded either. Every single one of you has scruples. I have scruples.

"Anybody we draw down our sights on and squeeze off a round at is the enemy. We make sure. He has to carry some sort of military equipment or a rifle. Something to make you absolutely certain he's a bad guy. It ain't murder. Killing that VC will prevent him from killing your fellow Marines.

"Your units chose you, and we screened you with several things in mind. One principle we looked for in each one of you, and what we keep looking for, is you must value human life. You never take one casually.

"I don't like being called murderer or cold-blooded. I'm not either one. Just remember, those guys don't know any better. It's up to you to teach them better.

"We're just cogs around a big wheel. We're no higher on the food chain and no worse than any line trooper out there. We just do a different kind of job. We're another tool of the battalion, just like a radioman or a supply clerk, or a rifleman in a fire team."

Carlos stood slowly and carefully looked above the brush that had hidden their school circle.

"We're gonna move out two by two in intervals," he whispered to the men. "We are in Charlie's country right now. So it's heads-up time. Life and death. From here on this ain't practice. It's real.

"Remember, slow and deliberate movement. Pay attention to your cover. Most important, pay attention to what's happening out there. Smell it, taste it, feel it, and hear it.

"Charlie is paying attention. He can smell a cigarette a mile away. You got on flu-flu juice or deodorant, he'll smell you. Break a stick, talk, cough, sniffle your nose, he'll hear it. Move without thinking, jerk or twitch, slap at a bug, and he's gonna see you. And then he'll do his level best to kill you.

"Don't forget, control keeps you alive. Let your fear, your wits, or your discipline get out of control, and Charlie will use it against you.

"We are the aggressor. We are the hunter. Charlie is the squirrel. And we're gonna get him. One shot, one kill."

Land, Reinke, Wilson, and Roberts had gone ahead of Carlos, Burke, and the class. They waited along the route where each instructor would pick up a pair of students as they passed. From that point, the three Marines would stalk to a preselected hide where they would spend the day watching a likely avenue.

At day's end, at a designated time, Land had instructed that each team would retreat south of their original route and join the other teams at the primary rally point he had chosen and had coordinated with the regiment operations section. Once the students and instructors had regrouped, they would patrol their way back home.

Carlos Hathcock had taken the last team from the group. A sergeant and a corporal. John Burke had taken the next to last team, two lance corporals, and moved to a hide at the edge of the clearing, 1000 meters to Hathcock's east. Their main rally point lay directly south of Gunny Wilson, who had the middle team. The route home looped far south from the way they had gone out.

By nine that morning the fog had disappeared, and the foliage that surrounded Sergeant Hathcock and the two students had long ago dried. Now, as the sun climbed high in the east, its heat sent swarms of gnats hovering in the shade of the bushes and trees.

The corporal who took his turn behind the spotting scope right of Carlos slapped his ear.

"Fuckin' bugs!" he grumbled. "Feels like they're gonna crawl in my head and eat my brain."

Carlos said nothing. The gnats swarmed his ears, too. And the sergeant's to his left as well. He made a mental note.

Two hours more. The heat cracked the shades of green greasepaint on the snipers' faces. They still had seen nothing.

"Shouldn't we move to a better spot?" the corporal whispered to Hathcock. An hour ago he had traded spotter duties with the sergeant, who now peered through the green, foot-long, 20-power spotting scope.

"Shhhhh," Carlos whispered. He made another mental note.

Five more hours passed. The three Marines had not moved. They had heard no shots from any of the other teams. Nothing moved except a breeze from the west. Yet Carlos considered the day very successful so far. It taught an important lesson in patience. Sometimes a sniper might lay in one spot a day and a night, and see nothing.

Slowly, Hathcock moved his canteen to his mouth and sipped water. The sergeant followed suit in the same manner. He would make a good sniper, Carlos concluded. However, the corporal was trouble.

He was a good marksman and very smart with tactics, land navigation, and with fire and air support coordination. But his mind wandered. He lacked the discipline to remain still.

The slowly strengthening breeze swept through the wide stretch of fields and tree lines that extended below the small rise where the three men lay. It had taken away the gnats, but large flies now dive-bombed through the branches above the snipers.

"Fuckin' bugs," the corporal muttered under his breath. "We seen nothing but bugs. Fuck this shit."

Carlos shifted his eyes at the corporal, then back at the grass growing across the flats. He watched how it now bent under the pressure of the more rapidly moving air. The sergeant to Hathcock's left carefully turned the focus adjustment on the spotting scope, reading the mirage. He gauged a windage estimate from the angle that it boiled its heat waves upward.

Laying his hand next to the ground, hidden well below a line of grass that grew in front of the three men, the sergeant showed four fingers and pointed left, signaling that the sniper should consider four minutes left windage. Carlos judged the adjustment needed was double that, but said nothing. He watched the corporal turn the knob on the right side of his rifle scope, six minutes left.

The sergeant slowly panned the spotting scope right and left, carefully searching for movement, a flash, anything that might signal an approaching enemy. Carlos had watched the sergeant work, feeling pleased with this student, when he noticed that the Marine had suddenly frozen in place.

Following the spotting scope's line of sight, Carlos saw what had stopped the sergeant. Hidden well in the shadows, beneath low branches, a man dressed in black squatted.

Carlos thought to himself, "Okay now we're gonna find out who guessed the wind right."

Very softly Carlos whispered to the corporal, "Slowly and deliberately, start scoping the tree line on the far left. Don't shoot yet."

Like oozing tar, the corporal glided his rifle's aim leftward, searching the trees. When he saw the man squatting, he fixed his aim on the center of the target.

Carlos raised his binoculars and looked closely at the man.

"He's got a rifle," Carlos softly whispered. "Don't shoot. Not yet."

Like a deer, the man suddenly sprang up and ran out of the trees, an SKS rifle in his hand. Crossing fifty yards of clear area, he then disappeared into an island of bushes and tall weeds.

"It's okay," Carlos whispered. "He can't go nowhere without us seein' him. Not unless he's got some tunnels in there. Besides, the direction he's goin' he'll find five other sniper teams waitin' on him."

Discipline had now taken hold of the corporal. He was on the rifle. He wanted this shot.

"Keep watchin' those trees where old Homer ran out," Carlos whispered to the sergeant, who had turned the spotting scope after the running VC.

Just as Carlos had finished speaking, another VC, and then another, and then three others broke from the tree line and entered the thicket where the first man had disappeared.

"They're heading east," the sergeant whispered to Carlos. "Bet they're gonna join an ambush back near the base."

They were the first words the sergeant had uttered since the three Marines had crawled into their hide.

Carlos smiled.

"Before you shoot," Carlos whispered to the corporal, "let's see what cover they aim to get to next."

Ten minutes later, the first man darted from the trees, ran 100 yards, and then dove behind a paddy dike. He raised his head for a moment, searching his surroundings, and then waved to his comrades.

"We got 'em now," Carlos said.

Spread several yards apart, running single file, the remaining five guerrillas darted from the trees to join their point man.

"Shoot the last one out," Carlos whispered in his most relaxed tone. "Take your time."

The corporal's rifle cracked its shot, and the last man fell backward. Then he got up.

The others kept running, and with his own Winchester rifle Carlos shot the fourth man in line. The sergeant fired within a split second, as well, and blew dust behind the third man.

The last man, who had fallen backward, ran past his dead comrade when the corporal fired a second shot, dropping the soldier.

"They're gonna try to get as far away from us as fast as they can," Carlos said. "Let's fall back from here and try to get around behind them. Set up in a new hide, in case they come back this way, or send company. This much shooting, they know exactly where we are right now."

Cautiously, the three snipers moved westward, and then followed the forest cover north for a quarter mile. From their new position they could see the trees that stood out from their previous hide, and the island of tall foliage where the six Viet Cong had hidden.

"We'll keep a watch to the left, where they first came out, in case they got friends," Carlos whispered. "But we gotta keep our eyes peeled to the east, too. They could try to swing back."

The shadows from the trees overhead the snipers now stretched across the land in front of them when they heard two almost simultaneous gunshots, east and around the bend in the tree line from their previous hide.

"Bet that's Burke," Carlos whispered.

Ten minutes later, one more shot echoed farther east.

"They keep running into our folks," Hathcock thought as he checked his watch and nudged his two students.

"We better get moving to the rally point," he whispered. "We'll be walking back up the hill in the dark otherwise, and we don't want to be doing that."

The sun cast long shadows at sharp angles when Carlos and his two students reached the rendezvous site. They were the last to join the group. Two by two the Marines set up a patrol formation and pushed toward home, crossing the wire in the twilight.

"I kind of feel sorry for those poor gooners," John Burke said to Carlos that night. He lay on his cot, his back propped against his seabag, wearing a T-shirt and trousers, rubbing one bare foot with the other.

"Why's that?" Carlos asked, sitting on the side of his cot, writing in a notebook.

"They never could get across those flats," Burke said. "Every time they broke out of the trees and tried to run across, somebody shot at them. Finally, those last two just quit putting their noses out."

"We did put a dent in their game plan, I suppose," Carlos said as he continued writing, never looking up from the page.

Three of the sniper students logged kills that day, Carlos claiming the fourth.

Their class's first test against the enemy proved successful, Hathcock concluded. Yet the misses still bothered him. He wrote more in his notebook, and Burke began to snore.

"Windage and range estimations," Carlos mumbled to himself, still writing. "We're gonna have to find more time to concentrate on those two items."

During their subsequent missions, after several days of range finding and wind guessing, the twelve students' percentages rose dramatically. In total, Land, his men, and their students recorded seventy-two kills in less than a month.

By early November, the first class of students had departed Hill 55, and returned to their units, veteran snipers.

4

The Frenchman

"MONSIEUR METZ, SIR," A VIETNAMESE LAD, WHO looked no more than sixteen, said in the local French dialect. "We're going home tonight, yes?"

"Yes, Huong," the man who called himself Philip Metz answered.

He stood on a concrete floor in a brick and iron building across the Cambodian border, washing his hands in a deep metal sink. Behind him, on the cold, hard floor, four naked bodies lay side by side. Blood running from their opened throats flowed into a metal drain set into the concrete.

"I am finished for now. We will leave as soon as it is dark," he continued while wiping his hands on a brown-stained piece of cloth that at one time had been part of a flour sack.

The building in which the man had just washed his hands supported a rust-streaked metal roof and a wide front porch that extended the full length of the structure. Two separate doors, flanked by tall iron-barred windows, led inside. At one time it had served as a plantation overseer's house, typical of those built in French Indochina by white western colonists during the early 1900s.

On the cool concrete floor of the porch, eight Viet Cong guerrillas, dressed in black shirts and shorts, and wearing rope-soled sandals, sat in a circle. At each man's side lay his rifle. They spoke in soft voices, sipping tea and eating rice with a fish and vegetable topping. From a platter in the center of their circle, the soldiers nibbled six-inch long rolls made of a nearly transparent thin noodle-pastry wrapped around vegetables and meat and then fried. Before each bite, the men dipped the inch-thick rolls in a golden sauce in which floated pieces of very hot red pepper and finely chopped chives.

A teapot steamed on a hibachi nearby where an old woman waited. She watched the men eat, ready to respond to them should any need arise.

Philip Metz walked through the door to the left of where the men sat eating, and stepped to the porch's edge. As he leaned against a support post, he lit his dark brown calabash pipe.

He had come to Indochina when he was barely more than a boy. At fifteen, he had left his home in Chartres while most Europeans spoke of their concern about Germany's chancellor, Adolf Hitler, but did little more than speak.

Hungry and homeless in Paris, surviving on his wits, he came to loathe the wealthy and bourgeoisie. In time, he found others who shared his newfound leftist fervor. They subscribed to the philosophy of Karl Marx, despised Stalin, and passionately defended Lenin. At night, in the Montmartre, they gathered in side-street cafés, drinking wine and decrying capitalist greed.

Angry for change, Metz and several friends sought to join the emerging Communist party in Paris. They found, however, that it was littered with the very wealthy and bourgeoisie that they had come to disdain. Philip found that these noble elite, politically liberal pigs would sleep their days in the Georges V Hotel, and then at dusk, ride limousines to Montmartre where they could slum away their nights being fervent, fashionable Communists.

Philip Metz and two of his friends left Paris, disgusted. The three men took a train to Nice where they sailed to Cairo, working as deckhands. There, an Egyptian rubber merchant hired the French trio to work as supervisors at his plantation in Cochin China.[1]

When the Japanese invaded that region, his two friends fled to Australia, but Philip remained at the plantation. There he joined guerrillas in a resistance effort, subsidized and equipped by the Allied Forces. British SAS agents accompanied them, and helped to arm, organize, and train these underground fighters.

Throughout the war, Philip helped to rescue and spirit to safety many British and American pilots who crashed in the jungles. Although they shared a common enemy, Philip could not support their political beliefs. He would remain neutrally cool whenever any of these men tried to befriend him.

When the war ended, and the British invited the French to return and resume control of their Indochina colonies, Philip chose to remain with the guerrillas. This army, led by Ho Chi Minh and a former teacher from Cochin China, Vo Nguyen Giap, had expended some of the weapons and ammunition that the Allies provided while putting up a token fight against the Japanese. However, they managed to stockpile the bulk of these weapons for the inevitable revolution they saw coming.

During the next eight years, their Viet Minh[2] resistance bloodied the French badly. Loyal to the Viet Minh, Philip put on a façade of allegiance to his native

---

[1]South Vietnam.

[2]The League for the Independence of Vietnam, the chief political military organization that battled the French for independence between 1946 and 1954.

France. Its soldiers there regarded him as a patriot and hero, having endured life in the jungles, fighting the Japanese. As a result of their regard and trust, officials frequently invited him to their parties and formal gatherings where military officers often discussed with him *la sale guerre*, this dirty war.

For years, he freely traveled the country, listening to boastful officers while taking note of French military strength, movement, and other activities. Then he faithfully passed the information to his Viet Minh comrades.

By 1953, the war was going poorly for the French. They asked Philip to join in their efforts to infiltrate the Viet Minh. He graciously accepted their offer but then promptly deserted.

Deep in the mountains southwest of Da Nang, Philip began living a comfortable yet primitive life in a plantation villa, sheltered by a thick jungle canopy, overlooking Cambodia. There he became useful, interrogating French soldiers and pilots, captured by the guerrillas. If befriending them did not work—trying to convince them that they were now safe with a fellow Frenchman—then he resorted to torture.

He always stripped his victim naked. Then he would stand the man before him and openly admire his sexuality. He would tell the man that he really preferred young Oriental boys, because of their smooth skin and willingness to please. Their small, hairless genitals excited him. However, a well-endowed Frenchman, covered with black, coarse hair, could be exciting, too.

As he approached the naked man, he would reach into his right pants pocket and take out a straight razor, folded inside a yellow-stained ivory handle. While he talked, he tumbled the closed razor through his fingers, sometimes pointing it to the man's face to impress a point. He made sure his victim saw the implement and fixed his eyes to it.

Philip would smile and gently glide the razor's handle down the man's chest and then up his inner thigh. Delicately he would follow with his left hand, caressing and fondling him.

Disgust often sent the prisoner into a rage.

This delighted Philip. He would smile and fondle the man even more, and dare him to resist. They nearly always did.

Guards would tie the prisoner onto a wooden seat with his legs spread and his ankles strapped to the rear legs of the chair, leaving his penis and testicles fully accessible and vulnerable. The guards bound the man's arms and hands to the chairback and then soaked him with their urine.

"Some people enjoy this kind of bath very much," Philip would tell his victim, still tumbling the razor in his fingers. "Although sexually stimulating to me, I also find urine a remarkably efficient conductor of electricity. Wouldn't you agree?"

Metz always waited to see the man's reaction. He knew that the talk of electricity evoked wild speculation of what horrifying torture might await. Often, if the prisoner was an inexperienced soldier, he would immediately crack from no more than the soaking. The victim would cry and offer to cooperate.

Once satisfied that the prisoner had said all he could, Metz would take the straight razor, flip open its blade and slice the man's throat. He considered it personally hazardous to allow any of these men to live.

Through the next twelve years, Philip had elevated his interrogation skills and his thirst for masochistic pleasure to what he considered an art form. He sought to make a prisoner talk, not from brutality or excruciating physical pain, but from the mental games he loved to play. It satisfied his deep-seated need to feel dominant. Powerful. Masterful.

However, there were those who withstood his mental torture. These men then experienced his expertise at inflicting profound pain.

When the Americans entered the war, business for Philip picked up considerably. Almost weekly, the

Frenchman had work to perform just across the border in the plantation house the Viet Cong had converted to a way station on the Ho Chi Minh Trail. In addition to providing shelter and storage, it served as a temporary jail to hold prisoners bound for transport northward, and to restrain others for the Frenchman to interrogate at his leisure.

The air smelled sweet from the cool dampness brought on by sunset. Philip gazed into the peaceful evening as he smoked his pipe. A sense of calm always welled within him following a successful interrogation.

His boy companion came to his side, carrying a small rucksack. He reached inside it and took out a chocolate disk wrapped in foil, taken from an American C ration. He offered the treat first to his mentor, and when he refused it the boy pulled the foil away and took a bite.

"American chocolate mixed with rice cereal," the Frenchman said to the boy. "They are very good, yes?"

"Yes, Monsieur Metz," Huong answered.

The Frenchman drew smoke from his pipe and let it gently drift from his mouth and nose, listening to the sounds of the frogs and night birds singing in the darkening jungle.

THAT SAME EVENING A GRAY HELICOPTER LAUNCHED from an airfield near Pleiku, hidden deep in Montagnard[3] country.

The chopper followed a dirt and gravel roadway that led through the mountains toward the South China Sea coast, intersecting with Highway 1 north of Na Trang, but not quite at Phu Cat.

Its pilot, a stocky man with shaggy gray hair, wearing a red St. Louis Cardinals baseball cap, flew the craft

---

[3]Montagnards are native inhabitants primarily of the southwestern mountainous region of Vietnam near the Cambodian border. These aboriginal people live communally in longhouses set on stilts, and today work chiefly as woodcutters.

low, zigzagging across the rivers and other areas where enemy forces might hide. He pushed downward on the UH1E Huey's collective,[4] set at the side of his seat, while giving the bird maximum power by twisting the checkered metal handle on the collective bar, much like a biker would turn a motorcycle's throttle. He lightly grasped the cyclic[5] control, set between his legs, delicately maneuvering the aircraft as it raced just above the treetops.

His copilot, a dark-haired man wearing a khaki cap with a long green transparent bill, rode in the right, front seat keeping watch for any movement on the ground that might signal trouble. Both men wore revolvers in shoulder holsters over green flight suits that bore no markings.

Air America, a quasi government civilian air service manned by contract pilots, paid the men an exceptional salary compared to what pilots back home made. These contractor airmen typically possessed a thirst for adventure, and a good deal of greed for a fat paycheck. Few, if any, sought this hazardous job as an act of patriotism.

Two other Americans rode on this flight, seated on the gray cloth and tubular aluminum bench that stretched across the rear of the chopper's cargo and passenger space. Buckled in jump seats facing the American passengers, two South Vietnamese men, wearing khaki trousers and shirts, clutched automatic rifles that they pointed out the open side doors.

The helicopter had just crossed a river that cut deeply

---

[4]Collective controls the angle of attack of the main rotor blades. The control is a bar extending up at an angle from the floor of the helicopter at the left side of the pilot's seat. A pilot operates it in coordination with the cyclic and the floor peddles to control the aircraft.

[5]Cyclic controls the altitude of a helicopter, used for turning and tilting. It is a stick that comes straight up from the floor between the pilot's legs. It is fitted with a pistol grip at the top, which also contains a trigger, a toggle, and buttons that control such things as radio microphone switch, weapons firing, sling-load release, and trim control.

through the land when the pilot and the Vietnamese man in the left jump seat saw a white stream of smoke shoot up from the trees toward them. The pilot banked hard left, trying to dodge the small rocket. The trail of smoke traveled above and just behind the helicopter's cabin, missing the main body, but the explosion sent debris and shrapnel into the engine and rotor head.

The console set on the floor between the pilot and copilot suddenly began sounding alarms and shining orange lights behind gray rectangular buttons. Similar buttons set in rows between the two instrument panels and on the overhead glowed as well.

"We're going in," the pilot called through the headsets.

Drawing back hard on the collective, the pilot attempted to flare out his auto-rotation into the trees, slowing the bird's descent rate to soften the impact.

Branches shattered the Plexiglas front of the aircraft, and broke off the still-turning rotor. The tail section remained in the trees while the body fell to the ground, buckling its skids on impact.

Smoke billowed into the cockpit, and raw fuel spewed from the auxiliary bladders installed against bulkheads behind each end of the wide backseat.

"Get out! Get out!" the pilot screamed as he leaped out his side door, the cabin still shuddering from impact. The copilot bailed from his side as well, and the four passengers scrambled away just as the fuel caught fire. It happened in split seconds, nearly instantaneously.

"We better get far away from here as fast as we can," one of the CIA field operations officers told the others. "The guys who fired that rocket gotta be beating feet this way. Those smoke signals will take them right to us."

The two Vietnamese carrying the automatic rifles had already begun leading the four Americans away from the crash site.

"Stay on their tails," the copilot shouted as he ran

after the two Vietnamese. "You gotta keep up 'cause they're not slowing down."

As they ran behind the Vietnamese scouts, the sounds of automatic rifle fire caught their attention, urging them on to greater speed.

"They're running a recon by fire[6] around the crash," the pilot said breathlessly to the men who now ran several yards ahead of him. "They'll be on our trail pretty quick."

---

[6]Reconnaissance by fire is a term describing the act of shooting heavy fire in all directions and into all possible hiding places around a suspected enemy site. "Hosing down the area" was a term Marines often used to describe the same action.

5

The Riviera

"GET UP, BURKE," CARLOS SAID SO CHEERFULLY that it nearly sounded like singing. "Found something exciting for us to do this week while we're off from teaching school."

Lance Corporal John Burke sat up from his cot, where he had dozed and read much of the morning. A paperback copy of *The Deep Blue Good-by* lay spread open, pages down, on a nightstand that he had fashioned from an ammunition crate. Two other John D. MacDonald mysteries, *Nightmare in Pink* and *Bright Orange for the Shroud*, lay beneath the first of the Travis McGee series.

"Exciting?" Burke asked. He turned his head at an angle and closed one eye, looking back at Sergeant Hathcock. "Fun and exciting, or scary and exciting?"

"Probably both." Hathcock shrugged as he sat on his cot and began unlacing his boots. "We've got a bunch of small unit patrols that're gonna start over near the beach and back to the hills down south a ways."

"Like around Que Son, Cam Ne, and the Riviera?"

Burke said, letting Carlos know he, too, knew of those areas. "They sound more scary and exciting than fun."

"Scary if you do something stupid," Carlos said. "We ain't gonna be that."

Carlos lay back on his cot and picked up one of the Travis McGee books and began thumbing through it.

"These any good?" Carlos asked, steering the conversation away from the scary and exciting.

"So far," Burke said, picking up *The Deep Blue Good-by*. "I just started reading them. Lance Corporal Hull over at the Public Information Office let me borrow 'em. He said that he really liked them."

"What're they about?" Carlos said, closing the book and reading the cover of *Bright Orange for the Shroud*.

"About a private eye that's not a private eye but does investigations and stuff like a private eye," Burke said. "He's pretty cool. Lives in a boat called *The Busted Flush* down near Fort Lauderdale, Florida. Bahia Mar, says here on the first page."

Carlos laid the book back on the stand and lit a cigarette.

"Never heard of it," Carlos said, blowing smoke.

"Me either," Burke said, "and I'm from down in that part of the world."

Carlos quietly smoked his cigarette while Burke returned to reading the book. Then Hathcock dropped the finished butt in a red-painted can half-filled with sand, sat up on his cot, and looked at Burke until his partner stopped reading and looked back at him.

"So, when do we go?" Burke asked.

"We've got a ride headed that way tomorrow morning," Carlos answered.

Two days later, John Burke stood on the damp sand of a wide and curving beach. He opened his jungle utility jacket and let the wind blow across his sweaty T-shirt. His bush hat fluttered behind his back, hanging from the string looped around his neck, and he raised his arms like the wings of a great condor to let the wind cool him.

Carlos Hathcock and his partner had spent this first day stalking among the sand hills and low dunes that bordered the beach and extended miles inland. Tall grass grew in clumps on these hills, providing the snipers ample hiding places where they could watch the narrow avenues that wound among the high piles of sand. So far this day they had seen nothing.

"You know, anybody a mile away can see you out there," Carlos called to Burke.

"There is nobody within a mile to see me," Burke said, still holding out his arms, feeling the sea air.

Pulling a wrinkled package of Beechnut chewing tobacco from his back pocket, Carlos took a pinch of the dark brown leaves and tucked them inside his cheek. He held the red and white pouch up for his partner to see, offering him a chew. Burke shook his head no, and then walked toward the barren dune where Hathcock lay sheltered at its base.

"We get skunked on the first day out, is not a good sign," Burke said, buttoning his shirt.

"We ain't skunked yet," Carlos said, and glanced over his shoulder to see where the sun stood in the sky. "Looks like at least three hours of daylight left. I'll bet if we move on south toward Chu Lai we'll see something."

"That's five or six miles, Sergeant Hathcock," Burke said.

"Probably closer to eight or ten, so we better get moving," Carlos answered.

The two snipers had walked barely half the distance, following the higher contours of the dunes, staying away from anything that looked like a path, when the crunch of a mine exploding inland stopped them. Both men dropped to their knees and began crawling to the top of the highest dune around them when they heard shooting.

"Ambush," Carlos said.

"Not that far either," Burke added.

"Which way you think Charlie will flush?" Carlos asked Burke.

"Out here?" Burke answered. "Anyplace else I'd say west. They go west here, and they hit Highway 1, villes and more of our patrols. Either north or east."

"I say they flush west, circle right, and angle northeast," Carlos said. "Once they're far enough up, they'll cut back west, toward home. That's what I'd do if I had just ambushed an American patrol out here, where they get thick as flies on dung the closer you get to Chu Lai."

"So, what are we going to do?" Burke said. "We're due east of that ambush. We beat feet at 'em?"

"We go back where we were," Carlos said. "If we're gonna get a shot, we have to skedaddle. They'll be scootin' but they got a whole lot more ground to cover than we do. Let's go another set of dunes more toward the beach, and then hotfoot it to a place where we can get up a little higher anyway. Gotta be hidden and breathing slow before they get near us."

"Wonder if that patrol's okay?" Burke said, looking toward the west.

"Shooting didn't last long," Carlos said. "Had to be either a hit-and-run, or somebody stepped on a mine and the rest of the patrol shot at nothing. It's happened, but odds are they had VC turn loose on 'em and high-tail it."

Burke nodded, agreeing with his sergeant.

"I'm concerned about anybody being hurt, too," Carlos continued, "but they got a corpsman, radios, and a lot more people. There ain't a thing we can do for them but cure our own curiosity. We can do more good hittin' the hamburgers that might have ambushed that patrol. Besides, I don't want to get skunked first day out."

An hour later, Hathcock and Burke lay hidden among large clumps of grass growing at the top of a high sand hill. The two snipers focused their watch to the south and southwest.

The wind gusted inland from the choppy seas straight over their backs and toward the enemy's likely direction of approach. Both men remained still and silent, knowing that even a voice spoken in a normal tone could ride the air currents an astonishing distance.

Nearly two hours had passed and the sun rested just above the mountaintops to the west when Burke spotted the first man. He carried an old Chinese rifle across his back and had appeared from the north. Obviously, this lone guerrilla had not attacked the Marine patrol.

Carlos had laid his scope sight's reticle squarely on the man's back when he first appeared. Although he could easily shoot this one Viet Cong, the sniper rifle's loud report would carry for miles. Certainly, no other Viet Cong or patrol on the run would approach after hearing the shot. So Burke and Hathcock waited, and watched the lone soldier walk along the sides of the sand hills' slopes, rather than in level bottoms that wound between them.

"The place has got to be littered with mines," Carlos thought, watching the soldier avoid the more likely channels where a person might walk. He thought about the ambush earlier in the afternoon, how it had begun with an explosion. Boredom and complacence—not a shot heard all day—may have steered that patrol down the easy path.

Carlos thought about Burke earlier that day, standing with his shirt unbuttoned, his arms out like a large bird, cooling himself in the wind on a wide open beach. What a foolish act, brought on by both their complacency and their boredom.

"It won't ever happen again," Carlos said to himself. He still held his sights on the Viet Cong soldier, who had now stopped and squatted on the slope of a dune, half-hidden in the grass.

"Hmm," Carlos whispered under his breath. "Looks like old Homer, there, is waiting to meet up with somebody."

Burke smiled.

As the distant mountains began to eclipse the sun, the wind fell to a breeze, sending much cooler air across the backs of the two snipers as they lay hidden. From their vantage point, they could see well above the hills in the distance, although most of the troughs remained hidden.

However, from the point where the Viet Cong soldier waited, 400 yards in front of them, the Marine snipers had a clear field of view for several hundred yards.

Carlos still felt concern that if he fired only one shot, the remaining soldiers might possibly reach cover, and then maneuver in a circle behind his and Burke's position for a counterattack.

"Should I shoot as many as I can and let them identify my position?" Carlos thought. "Or should I make one shot, sit tight, wait for them to move, and hit them again?"

Neither choice seemed a good one. He had anticipated just hunting stragglers, one or two Viet Cong sneaking through the sand hills and dunes from the American patrols. He could take his shots, slip out of the hide, move to another. If this platoon had more than five or six men, he knew he and Burke would face a much higher risk than he had ever found acceptable.

"Scary and exciting," he whispered to Burke.

Burke knew exactly what Hathcock meant. The sand hills provided too much cover and room for a platoon to maneuver on them. Furthermore, if he and Carlos tried to move out low, and stay well-hidden, they risked the mines that possibly lay in their path. Perhaps holding this hill until dark offered the best chance of getting out alive against any significant number of VC.

"If there is a bunch," Carlos whispered, "we got to drop as many as we can. Four or less, and it is one shot and wait."

Carlos glanced down at the M-14 that Burke carried.

"When was the last time you zeroed that stick?" he asked under his breath.

"Two days ago," Burke said softly. "It's within a foot at 700 yards. I'll hold a little low here."

"Don't hesitate if there's a bunch," Carlos warned.

"I'll be cranking this bolt as fast as I can, too."

Carlos hated the close distances and ample cover that this place presented. Any sort of patrol through this land that Marines had come to know as the "Riviera" faced high risk. The sand and soft soil easily hid mines. The maze of troughs winding and crossing among the hills and dunes offered plenty of room for a VC ambush to hit-and-run, and then hit-and-run again.

Hathcock decided that after today, he and Burke would hunt farther south and more west, where the terrain better suited a sniper's long shot.

Clouds spread orange and purple across the sky as the sun disappeared behind them. Grayness lay across the land beneath when the first Viet Cong guerrilla appeared in the distance.

The man who squatted raised his hand. Then the man approaching came forward and squatted, too. Shortly thereafter, two other men appeared, one behind the other, edging along the sandy slopes, working their way to where the two now waited.

Three more VC appeared in the distance, each well separated from the other.

Carlos looked at Burke and nodded toward his M-14, affirming that he expected the lance corporal to shoot as well.

The man who walked at the head of the group of three, joined the other four squatting while the second man walked fifty yards ahead, and the third man remained about fifty yards behind them.

"They mean to sit here a bit," Carlos whispered, "right in the back of our shooting gallery."

Burke offered Carlos a slight nod, agreeing.

"You shoot the one standing guard up-front, he's the closest shot, and I'll take the guard in the rear," Carlos told his partner. "Then start working on their circle from the right and I will from the left. They'll either run at us or over the top of that hill. I'm hoping on 'em taking a chance for the hill."

The shot from Hathcock's rifle had just broken the

evening's silence when Burke's followed so closely that it sounded nearly like a single report. Both snipers found their marks, dropping the two Viet Cong standing sentry.

When the first shots struck their targets, the remaining five soldiers scrambled to their feet, rifles in hand and ready to fire. The men at first thought that a squad might have enveloped them, attacking their flanks. Their immediate reaction to that idea sent them running straight at Hathcock and Burke.

"Here they come," Carlos said as his second shot struck the soldier on the far left. That man had just stood up and tried to run when the bullet dropped him dead.

Burke caught the man on the far right as he sprang to make his dash. He had launched himself in flight when the shot struck him squarely in the chest. It stopped him in midair, and the momentum sent the dead soldier plowing facedown in the sand.

The remaining three guerrillas opened fire toward the two snipers and ran for cover behind a small dune on their left flank.

"Hold 'em and squeeze 'em," Carlos said to Burke, dropping his third man.

Simultaneously, Burke hit his third, and before the last man could disappear behind cover, Burke settled his M-14's open sights on the man's back and killed him, too.

"Seven rounds, seven dead VC," Carlos said. "Not bad for beginners. That just proves my point that there is nothing on the battlefield more deadly than one well-aimed shot."

While Carlos jotted notes hastily in his logbook, Burke scanned the hills and lanes surrounding their position, searching for enemy patrols advancing toward them. Certainly, the gunfire had alerted any Viet Cong within earshot that some Americans still lurked here in the fast-closing darkness.

Both snipers knew well that each minute they remained on this hilltop brought potential disaster closer.

Throughout the night, the two Marines silently crept westward, carefully moving to the higher hills and more accommodating hunting ranges that lay beyond Highway 1.

By midday, the sniper team had turned southward, and now rested in a shady hide below the crest of a hill that dominated several miles of open rice land, cross-hatched by hedgerows and tree lines. Carlos knew that country well. He had patrolled it frequently as an MP during his first five months in Vietnam.

They took turns catnapping while one of them kept watch over the flat land and dry rice fields covered in stubble from a crop recently harvested. If nothing crossed the openness that outstretched beneath the hill where Carlos and Burke hid, the two Marines had decided to remain in their well-hidden seclusion through the night. Secretly, each man hoped that nothing would cross their sights this day. They were very tired.

At midnight, raindrops fell against the thick jungle canopy above the two snipers. Soon water began to drip and run off the broad leaves and limbs above the men, showering them. The splattering drips from overhead awakened Carlos Hathcock, and he looked to see if Burke had remained awake.

He should have known better—both men kept their discipline high while on patrol. Yet Burke had walked out of the cover of the dunes and onto the beach this afternoon, exposing himself to the enemy, if one had been around to see him.

How did they know an enemy had not seen Burke, and told others about it? Perhaps they had moved from that place at exactly the right time, Carlos considered.

Perhaps the enemy patrol that they had wiped out with seven shots had not earlier attacked the Marine patrol south and west of them, but had come to that place to hunt the two snipers. It was possible, Carlos thought.

Rain clattered overhead and thumped the ground

around the two men, laying a mask of noise over them. Carlos liked that. Dampness made the sound of their walking disappear by softening the dry mulch under their feet. It washed their dusty, dry world, and made it different and strange. Rain makes all places strange, even places where you live.

The cooling downpour brought out smells of fertile soil and decaying leaves and wood. The freshly cleaned air carried a sweet aroma. It reminded Carlos of the earthy fragrance of the black, moss-filled, composted soil that his grandmother had used to plant her geraniums in large, red clay pots that she then set on her front porch in the spring, and in which the flowers bloomed bright red and pink and white.

Burke had covered his and Hathcock's rifles with a poncho that he had unstrapped from its carrying place beneath his pack. With raindrops dancing across his back, the lance corporal looked through the rear lens of a spotting scope, holding his right hand above the front lens to keep off the water while he searched the dark fields below them.

"Can you see anything at all?" Carlos asked.

"Barely," Burke said. "You get any sleep at all?"

"A bit here and there," Carlos answered. "How are you doing?"

"Pretty good, really," Burke said. "Amazing what a few short naps can do."

"You want to close your eyes awhile?" Carlos asked.

Burke did not argue. He could still use more sleep. The young sniper handed Hathcock the spotting scope laying belly-down in the wetness with his head on his hands, and closed his eyes. In a moment his breathing deepened and slowed.

Mud and water oozed beneath him and rain splashed on his back while he thought of his sister and dreamed of home. He wondered if she or anyone else in his family would understand? His life made a difference here. He cared little for the politics, but he cared greatly for the Marines he had come to regard as closely as brothers. Could they understand that? Few could, unless one had also been a Marine.

The start of a snore two hours later caught Carlos's ear and he nudged Burke. The young lance corporal raised his head. The rain had stopped.

Now a steamy dampness filled the still night air with wisps of fog that slowly snaked along dips and ditches. The clouds had long since disappeared, allowing the moon and a sky filled with bright stars to light the puddled land below the mountain where Hathcock and Burke now searched the countryside for movement.

"Two o'clock," Burke whispered.

"No, three-thirty," Carlos whispered back.

Then Burke pointed his finger toward a tree line far across the flat land, where a figure sneaked among the shadows.

Carlos moved his eyes to the right and saw the figure, too, his knees crouched and waist bent forward as he stepped. He held a rifle in his right hand, and kept looking over his shoulder, as if talking to someone at his right. Then as suddenly as he had appeared, he vanished among the shadows and trees.

Two hours later, gunfire and explosions echoed from the east. In that same direction an orange glow, alternately darkening and brightening, shone above the trees.

"That's no sunrise," Carlos whispered. "You can see signs of that farther to the left, way up from what I bet is a pretty good-sized fire. Ten to one that's a truck convoy out of Chu Lai headed for Da Nang on Highway 1."

"That lonesome Charlie that we let slip by probably had company," Burke said. "And that's their work."

"A bunch of company, looks like," Carlos said, still watching the pulsating glow beyond the eastern trees. "They come back this way, probably in about an hour, and we're gonna be able to see 'em with the daylight, even in those trees."

*   *   *

LITTLE BY LITTLE THE SKY BRIGHTENED, AND THE SUN quickly rose above the tall forests, casting orange light on the flat land beyond the shadows of the trees and hills. In the hour that passed, water droplets from the night's rain—that had earlier covered the leaves and grass and rice stubble—dried. Now only large puddles remained, and they shone like odd-shaped mirrors scattered across the open fields, reflecting blue and white among the soft green and yellow and brown that surrounded them.

Heat sent white clouds, scattered like popcorn, across the horizon, rising in puffy billows that would later tower over the land and send evening thundershowers across the mountains.

Beneath the leaves and trees and broad-spread ferns the Marine snipers lay silent and motionless. Beads of sweat slid in small rivulets down their cheeks and foreheads and the backs of their hands as they methodically searched the world below them with a telescopic gunsight and a spotting scope.

Carlos pushed his heel against Burke's ankle, drawing his attention with a nudge. Without taking his eye from his rifle scope, Hathcock pointed his finger left, directing Burke to the flicker of movement behind the distant trees to their southeast.

"Got 'em," Burke whispered as he followed several more dark forms stepping swiftly behind the tree trunks at the forest's edge. "They're staying behind the trees pretty much."

"We'll lose 'em if they stay in that particular cover, since it curves south," Carlos said, "but if they want to keep going west, where we saw old Homer the Hotdog last night, then they got to break out across those flats to get in these trees down front and to the right."

"Bet they're not heading south," Burke said, knowing that most VC strongholds lay more west and northwest of their position.

"Good bet," Carlos said as he saw the first guerrilla dash from the forest's cover and run along a trail on the top of a paddy dike.

Quickly a second, a third, a fourth, a fifth and then a sixth and seventh and eighth black-clad soldier followed the first, all of them now running on the dike.

"Bingo," Carlos said, dropping the last man who had run out of the trees. "If ther're any more behind these folks, they're gonna be turning south now."

The remaining seven VC ran as fast as they could push their legs, seeing their comrade tumble dead. They kept on the trail atop the dike, knowing that if they stepped off in the rain-soaked bog of the rice fields at either side, they would not have a chance to escape at all.

"Go ahead and take the leader," Carlos told Burke, who immediately shot, missing with his first round and sending a rooster tail of mud and water skyward.

"Damn," Burke said, missing his second shot, too. Taking aim with open sights on an M-14 at targets 1,000 yards away would frustrate even the best marksman.

"Damn is right," Carlos said. "It's the BAR Team."

"BAR Team?" Burke responded, after finally dropping the lead runner.

"Browning Automatic Rifles," Carlos said, shooting the next runner at the rear of the line. "Five women with BARs. Gave us fits while I was an MP at Chu Lai."

"That's them?" Burke said, missing again.

"That's them," Carlos said, killing one of the women who had several bandoliers of .30-caliber ammo draped from her right shoulder across to her left hip.

"Shit," Burke said, missing again and watching one of the women running with a BAR finally make it to the trees, where she quickly began to fire toward the two snipers.

"Try to get another one before she gets her range figured out," Carlos told Burke.

The lance corporal's next shot took down a man running with an SKS semiautomatic rifle in his hand. He veered left and splashed into the mud, gliding down like an airplane crash-landing.

Carlos killed a second woman with a BAR, but watched the remaining pair on the dike run to the trees and join the third BAR Team member, who now sent bursts of automatic fire into the ground and rocks below Hathcock and Burke. With each burst she walked her gunfire closer to their position. Seconds later, the other two women joined the shooting.

Both Marines slid on their stomachs behind the large trunks of trees growing at their right and left just as several bullets glanced across the ground between them. There, Carlos and John lay quietly until the shooting stopped.

After several moments of silence, the sniper duo carefully slid from behind the trees and finally caught a last glimpse of the three women as they disappeared behind a distant low hill.

WHILE THE TWO MARINE SNIPERS HUNTED THE COUNTryside northwest of Chu Lai, the four Americans and their two Vietnamese scouts, who had crashed the previous day, continued to push eastward, trying to elude the Viet Cong and make their way to friendly lines.

The six men had not stopped pushing themselves since the previous afternoon. Their only rest came during the few moments that they paused whenever they drank water, usually from a clean-looking stream or spring-fed branch. They had no canteens, no radio, no map, no compass. Worst of all, the group had only the four side arms the Americans had worn—two .38-caliber revolvers and two .45-caliber semiautomatic pistols, with two spare loads apiece—and the two rifles that the Vietnamese scouts had carried, each of them with four additional loaded magazines. All total, the six men had 234 rounds of ammunition: 27 rounds for the two revolvers, 27 rounds for the two pistols, and 180 rounds for the rifles—hardly enough to stand up against even one small firefight.

By noontime the second day, the four Americans had little strength left, pressing onward purely on adrenaline. However, the two scouts never slowed their pace. To survive one had to keep up. To live, one had to run.

Each of the men knew very well that by now many Viet Cong patrols combed the countryside looking for them. Rather than moving due east, the scouts ran north, then east, then north again. By that tactic, they hoped to avoid ambushes set up anticipating a more directly eastward route of travel. With no radio, however, the odds still lay clearly with the VC.

"Don't worry about me," the pilot told his copilot, who slowed because the older man had begun to fall back.

"I'm going to ask if we can't take a break," the copilot said to him. "I can barely go any farther myself. Surely the VC are not pushing as hard as we are."

"Bullshit," the pilot said. "You know better than that. Keeping the pace, we have a chance. We stop, we die."

"Hold up," one of the field agents called to the scouts.

The two agents squatted where they stopped and looked back at the two aviators who now walked toward them.

"No, we go," a scout called to the Americans. "*Didi mao! Didi mao!*"

"VC, they come fast," the other scout said, pleading to the Americans. "They have many look for us now. They maybe take you prisoner. Maybe. But they kill us for sure. We go, hurry. Please."

"We see American patrol soon," the first scout added. "Maybe ARVN. One more day anyway we reach Hoi An, Bong Son, maybe An Lao."

During the night, they crossed the treacherous An Khe Pass, several miles north of where Highway 19 made its descent toward Phu Cat and the seacoast. The

U.S. Army base at Qui Nhon offered the most attractive refuge. However, the six knew that the VC had easily considered this, too. Surely, they would look for them in that southeasterly direction. Turning around just after they had escaped the crash site, trying to skirt the VC force that had shot them down and making an attempt to reach the Army compound at Pleiku that first day seemed too risky as well. Certainly the VC had anticipated that possibility, too. Following a stair-step route northeast offered the least likely chance for encountering enemy units. That route crossed rougher country, required covering a greater distance, and only led to sparsely populated outposts.

Considering the insignificance of their weaponry and the few rounds of ammunition that they had, the long, rough route was their best chance.

However, as their fatigue had grown, so did the noise they made, and their alertness dulled.

"Let's get a move on," the copilot said. "We can't lose those scouts."

"If we can find the bastards," a field agent said. "They're way the fuck in front of us now."

As the four men ran, they could hear brush crashing ahead of them.

"For two guys, they are making a lot of noise," the pilot said, stopping to listen more closely.

"You guys wait here," an agent said, "I'm going to take a look-see. If it's our friends, I'll whistle."

The pilot collapsed in a fern and leaned against a small tree. His red baseball cap dripped sweat from its bill and had salt rings covering its crown. When he pulled out his handkerchief to wipe sweat from his gray and black hair, two gunshots cracked the air less than 100 yards ahead.

Startled, the pilot jumped to his feet to run, just as the copilot and remaining field agent dove for cover. In that instant, several bullets spit through the branches, one catching the pilot in the throat and breaking his neck. He died before he hit the ground.

"*Chu hoi*," the copilot shouted from where he hugged the ground. "*Chu hoi! Chu hoi!*"

"Fuck!" the field agent said, and spread out his arms and legs.

"Highway engineers," he whispered to the copilot. "When they ask, we tell them that."

In seconds, several hands yanked the two men to their feet.

"American?" a little man with gray and black hair said. He wore a black shirt and pants, and had a black-and-white checkered scarf draped around his neck. His teeth shone white with gold trim on their edges, and he missed none of them. He had the look of an intellectual, not a rice farmer. He spoke with the eloquence of a well-educated man.

"What happened to your escorts?" he asked the copilot. "Our information says six of you, two Vietnamese."

"We lost them a while back," the copilot said.

"I see," the little man said.

He looked at the copilot, feeling his flight suit and studying his shaggy hair. Then he looked at the field agent, examining the khaki trousers and utility vest over a khaki shirt that he wore.

"Neither of you are military, is that correct?" the little man asked, looking at both the Americans.

"Highway engineers," the field agent said.

"But he is a pilot," the little man said, taking the sleeve of the copilot's flight suit in his fingers. "You are both armed. I know pilots wear revolvers, but why would a highway engineer carry a .45?"

"Everybody carries guns here," the agent said. "You know that."

"Yes," said the little man. "I also suspect that so many armed American highway engineers and so little highway work to do indicates other motives. Intelligence, perhaps?"

The little man spoke to the soldiers who held the two

Americans, and they immediately began binding their prisoners' hands behind their backs.

"You are very lucky that I encountered you," the little man said. "Most others would simply have killed you on the spot. They don't know any better. They don't want the trouble of escorting prisoners.

"Unfortunately, because of the weapons you carry, and because I suspect that your work is other than highway engineering, we must take you into custody.

"I am Colonel Ba. I command the People's Liberation Army in this district. I realize you have run many miles with little rest, but unfortunately we have little time to offer you for recovery. Please follow my men now."

Hearing the gunshots, the two Vietnamese scouts circled, and at a distance watched the two Americans leave with their captors. They counted more than thirty black-clad guerrillas. The enemy soldiers carried an array of automatic and semiautomatic rifles, and several mortars and butt plates. Many of them wore green canvas packs. No doubt these were filled with mines and other explosive devices.

The two scouts followed the well-armed VC patrol until they clearly understood their direction of travel. Due west, skirting well to the north of Pleiku. Swiftly and silently, the two scouts then returned to their northeasterly trek.

6

Farewell, Jacques

"Top! Top!" Gunny Wilson shouted as he ran toward the sniper hooch, orange dust flying from beneath his heels and his opened utility shirt flapping behind him. "The skipper and Sergeant Hathcock killed the Apache!"

"Slow down, Jim," Master Sergeant Donald Reinke said, starting up the Finger 4 trail to meet Wilson, who had just left the Operations hooch in a mad dash. "What happened?"

"They got the Apache!" Wilson repeated, nearly breathless. "Captain Land and Carlos."

"No shit," Reinke said as he met Wilson, and then turned to walk with him back to the sniper hooch. "You know anything about how?"

"I was at Operations, checking sit-reps, and listening to radio traffic on the com, when I heard the skipper call Fire Base Ross for an artillery mission," Wilson began. "They spotted the Apache and her platoon, and the captain put a salvo of H-E's[1] in their mess kit. That

[1] High-Velocity Explosive rounds.

must have killed a bunch of them, but apparently missed the Apache. So Carlos nails her when she hotfoot it up the trail."

IT WAS LATE AFTERNOON WHEN LAND AND HATHCOCK finally stepped from the UH1E Huey that had picked them up from their morning patrol at a remote landing zone and now let them off at Hill 55. They had stalked through the countryside southwest of Hill 55 since well before daylight. The pair of snipers was hot, dirty, but happy as they headed up the path that led home.

"Good news travels fast, I guess," Carlos said to his captain after the third man to pass the two Marines had offered them another "good job" compliment.

"Everyone is glad to be rid of her," Land said. "Now, I wish I could forget what we have seen of her work."

The two men remained silent until they neared the top of the hill.

"Me, too, sir," Carlos said. "I keep remembering that Marine from the cooks and bakers patrol—the one she tortured all night and then cut off his gonads. Seeing that poor guy screaming and bleeding all the way to the wire, and dying there. As long as I live, I will never forget it.

"I thought about him today when I dropped her. That's why I shot her twice, to make sure. I never ever felt good about killing anybody until now. But today, I feel like drinking beer and dancing around the fire. Is that wrong?"

Land smiled.

"No Carlos," the captain said after walking several more steps. "I think what makes you feel good is not killing the woman, but knowing you have stopped her from torturing anybody else. I feel good about it. Nothing wrong with that."

Reaching the hilltop, Land stopped across from the Operations hooch where the trail branched to Finger 4.

"I need to check in here for a few minutes, Carlos,"

Land said. "You're welcome to tag along."

"No, sir, Skipper," Carlos said. "I can still get to the mess tent and catch late chow if I hurry. If you don't mind, I'll just dump our gear at the hooch and then see if I can get a hot meal for once."

"Just one thing, though, Carlos," Land said, smiling. "If you get back and I'm still gone, wait for me before you start telling tales about today. I probably ought to be there to help keep your story straight."

"You don't have to do that, sir," Carlos said, shuffling backward toward the sniper hooch, so that he could still see his captain's face while he laughingly spoke. "I ain't never told no fib in my life."

Then Hathcock turned, still laughing, and jogged down the trail.

AN HOUR LATER, JIM LAND SAT, EATING C RATIONS BEhind the sniper hooch, his legs astride an empty ammunition crate turned on its end. The captain had just scraped the last bite of cold beef stew from the bottom of a can when Carlos sauntered up.

"Sorry you missed hot chow again, sir," Carlos said as he took a seat on another of the empty wooden boxes. "It wasn't that great, though. Just hot. I think all that they do anyway is open a bunch of C rations and pour 'em in a pot."

Master Sergeant Reinke cleared his throat to get Captain Land's attention.

"All right, Skipper, now that our star has finally graced us with his presence, tell us about it, sir," Reinke said.

"Go ahead, sir," Carlos said, lighting a cigarette and taking a sip from a can of Sprite that Burke had handed to him. "I'll make sure you keep your story straight."

The dozen students attending sniper school, and several other Marines, mostly from neighboring work sections, sat with Land and his colleagues this evening. The men, a mix of enlisted Marines and junior officers, sat on ammunition crates, upside-down buckets, and other makeshift chairs, crowded together in a circle, their eyes trained on Land. They, too, wanted to hear how the Apache had met her end.

"Correct me if I am wrong, Carlos," Land began.

"Oh, I'll be sure to do that, sir," Carlos interrupted.

"I guess I asked for that." Land chuckled. "Looking at it in retrospect," he continued, "it was sort of an accident.

"Carlos and I had set up in a hide before daylight, and we saw little to nothing all morning. We took turns, as usual, on the spotting scope and then on the rifle.

"So then it comes time for my shift as sniper, and I said, Carlos, it's time to trade.

"He whines back at me, 'Oh, no, Skipper, just another minute.'

"About that time old Nguyen Schwartz comes slipping out of the trees with an AK-47 in his hands.

"Carlos sights in on him, and I tell this knucklehead here to pass me the rifle. I'll shoot him.

"Carlos says, 'No, no, I'll get him.'

" 'Let me have the rifle, damm it,' I said.

"Carlos pulls back on the rifle and says, 'No, Skipper, let me shoot him.'

"In a few seconds, Carlos and I are wrestling over the rifle. Rolling around in the weeds. And old Nguyen Schwartz sees us and takes off.

"By the time I finally got the rifle away from Carlos, Charlie was long gone.

"After a while, here comes a whole band of VC snooping and pooping, and I think that they are looking for us.

"Of course, we had moved our hide. So we watched them search around our old spot. Since they are all in this little cluster, I had Carlos read out the grid coordinates, and I called in a fire mission. I figured we could just bombard the shit out of them.

"The salvo lays in, and wipes out most of the platoon, except for a couple who took off running. A woman and a man."

Carlos laughed. "We figured out she was a woman about the time she rolled up her britches' leg and squatted down to pee. She was far enough away from the others that she didn't get hit by artillery, but I'll guarantee you this, she dang sure wet her pants."

"That's right. She jumped straight up, right in midstream, and took off running, still squirting piss," Land said, laughing so hard he could barely talk. "That's when we recognized her as the Apache.

"The other was old Nguyen Schwartz himself. The same VC that had watched Carlos and me wrestle over the rifle. That's when I realized that this guy must have been a scout for the Apache, and he had actually led her to us.

"With the shells landing on their position, old Schwartz takes off up the hill like he's got blue flames shooting out his ass. Then the Apache gets so screwed up she runs right at us.

"Meantime, Charlie dashing uphill suddenly remembers that we are somewhere down below, and tries to warn her. But old Hawkeye Hathcock, here, dumps her wet butt first. Now she's writhing on the ground, so Carlos cranks another round downrange and finishes her.

"Old Nguyen immediately turns, beats feet up the hill, and Carlos drops him, too.

"So, I call it kind of a freak accident—him seeing Carlos and me fighting over the rifle, and then bringing back the Apache and her gang. It couldn't have turned out better even if we had planned it."

"It don't matter how we did it," Carlos added, "the important thing is, we got her."

"That's right," Land said. "She's history."

"Fuck-an-a-skippy," an ITT Marine said, pounding his fist into the palm of his other hand with a loud pop. Several other of the neighboring Marines joined in his exclamatory expression of celebration, congratulating the snipers.

"Now, to bigger and better things," Land followed, holding one hand up, asking for silence.

"Yesterday, I briefed you on that operation fixing to happen down south. Well, I finally have some details for those of you going."

"Rio Blanco, sir?" Gunny Wilson asked. "I heard some word on that today while I was up at Operations, listening to you guys on the radio."

"That's right, Operation Rio Blanco," Land confirmed, spreading out a tactical map with a laminated clear-plastic overlay on which the captain had drawn arrows and unit symbols with red and black grease pencils.

"We will operate off of Hill 263," the captain continued, pointing with a ballpoint pen, "and patrol along the north side of Song Tro Khuc valley, here, about twenty-five miles below Chu Lai. We will directly support the four ground force companies, Bravo, Charlie, Delta and Mike, 7th Marines, and provide supplemental forward observation and fire support coordination for the two reinforced artillery batteries assigned from 11th Marines.

"It is vital to our personal safety that we remain on the north side of the river when patrolling on our own. If we venture south of the river, we must be attached and in coordination with the unit whose mission puts them over there. We must also coordinate our movements through S-3[2] with the ROK[3] Marines' Dragon Eye Regiment, and that ARVN division. What's their name, Top?"

"Lien Ket 70," Master Sergeant Reinke added.

"That's right," Land said. "It's one of the local ARVN divisions that operates down in that country."

John Burke sipped from a can of Orange Crush and

---

[2] Operations section.
[3] Republic of Korea.

noticed Carlos cracking a smile. The area Land had circled on the map included some of the same places from which the two of them had returned only days earlier.

"We know about three boom-boom honeys we might run across down there," Carlos said, grinning.

"Boom-boom honeys?" Wilson said with a smirk. "What were you guys really doing down there, Sergeant Hathcock?"

"B-A-R boom-boom, Gunny," Burke said. "As in Browning Automatic Rifle–type boom-boom honeys. Sergeant Hathcock calls them the BAR Team. There used to be five, but we retired a couple of 'em the other day."

A day and a half later, Captain Land, Carlos, Burke, Roberts, Wilson, and eight sniper school students scrambled from the side door of an H-34 helicopter atop Hill 263. As the captain and twelve snipers jogged toward the 7th Marines compound there, the men could see the many channels and islands of the Tro Khuc River, below, and the wide, flat valley that spread from it. It looked like an excellent hunting area.

Master Sergeant Reinke and the four other students had remained at Hill 55 where they manned the sniper command post and supported 1st Battalion, 26th Marines.

MORE THAN FIFTY MILES SOUTH OF WHERE THE SONG Tro Khuc flows past the city of Quang Ngai, the two Vietnamese scouts who had survived the helicopter crash lay hidden in a thicket. They had lost count of the Viet Cong patrols that they had eluded. By now they had walked nearly two-thirds the width of their homeland, still managing to remain free.

Silently, they watched from their cover of leaves, branches, and thick grass as another enemy patrol passed less than twenty yards away.

The two scouts had spent the past week eating mostly bird eggs, grubs, worms, and bugs. All of it was raw since they didn't dare build any cooking fires.

Now beneath the cover of the thicket, they nibbled bugs and worms that they had gathered by dragging their fingertips beneath the dead leaves and debris that covered the ground. Throughout their ordeal, the men not only remained alert for the Viet Cong, but they kept their eyes open for any protein-rich morsel that they might snatch and eat. Like horses, the Vietnamese scouts grazed on the move, slept on their feet, and never stopped smelling the air and listening for danger. For them, survival meant becoming more animal than man. Following primitive instincts. Quick-witted and ready as jungle cats.

Sounds of gunfire froze the men to the ground beneath their heavy foliage cover. The enemy patrol that had passed them no more than fifteen minutes earlier had either sprung an ambush or had stepped into one. In either case, the two Vietnamese scouts felt a sudden surge of joy. Friendly forces, whether American or Vietnamese, though presently in battle, were nearby. Perhaps their rescuers held the ground below the small rise, just ahead, that gently sloped its backside downward to the flatlands and rice fields where Highway 1 cuts its way northward.

How, though, could they make contact without their potential rescuers shooting them first? The two scouts were dressed in civilian clothing not uniforms. With rifles in hand, any friendly patrol could easily mistake them for Viet Cong.

Silently, sliding on their stomachs, the two men eased themselves to the top of the rise, hoping to see the forces below them that continued their fight. But too many trees stood in their way.

Certainly their brethren had these VC pinned. It seemed obvious to the scouts that if the VC had attacked the Americans or ARVN below them, they would have hit-and-run. The enemy guerrillas had too few men in their party to sustain a long-held attack against the typically superior numbers and firepower of their opposing forces. To be saved, the scouts had to put faith in their assumption, and gamble their lives on it.

Now, only sporadic gunfire echoed below. The two men waited. Listened. Smelled the air and looked for movement. They did not want to encounter a retreating enemy force this close to redemption.

Finally, silence.

"Chu hoi!" one scout shouted, letting his voice carry downhill to the flats in the still air of this day.

More silence.

"Americans! Don't shoot!" he now shouted.

Still silence.

Careful to move behind cover, the two Vietnamese men, holding their AR-15 carbines, ready to fire should they meet Viet Cong, crept down the gentle slope.

"We ARVN scouts!" one man shouted, now closer to what he and his comrade hoped was a friendly patrol.

"We need help!" he called through the trees.

"Throw your rifles ahead of you, and then lie facedown with your arms spread out," an American voice called back to them.

"Yes," both men cried. "Yes, please help us."

NEARLY NINETY MILES WEST OF WHERE THE TWO SCOUTS happily walked homeward with a patrol of U.S. Army Rangers and Vietnamese Popular Force volunteers, Philip Metz stood in the doorway of his plantation home, smoking his calabash pipe.

He wore a white bush shirt and khaki trousers, and stood barefooted on the polished wooden planks of his front porch. The sweetly scented smoke from his pipe drifted toward the lush green trees and bushes that surrounded the large lawn that extended 100 feet outward and encircled the home.

Grass-covered ruts from a narrow, infrequently used road cut through the forest that surrounded Metz's home, and stopped at the side of his house. Tall weeds grew in the road's center, between the now-faint tire traces. Few vehicles had passed along this route since the days of World War II. Then, they were mostly square-nosed old trucks and cars with hand-cranked starters and wooden-spoked wheels with thin rubber tires set in a narrow track under their chassis. Now, though, only random vehicles carrying cargo or troops made their way through this overgrown country.

Once in a while, a truck carrying supplies wound its way along Highway 19 from Andaung Pech or Lomphat, Cambodia, and turned northward, following the Ya Krong Bolah River, along its west bank, to a place where the waterway makes a wide arching bend toward the east, nearly halfway between Kontum and Dak To, Vietnam. There, the truck turned westward, along the Ho Chi Minh Trail. Nearly ten kilometers farther, the narrow, faint road that led to Philip Metz's house branched northward through the jungle.

From his home, one could easily reach Laos or Cambodia, and the Viet Cong way station that also served as a holding facility for prisoners of war bound for Hanoi, in a day's or a night's walk. Metz frequently made this trek on foot, whenever his Communist allies needed his talents as an interrogator.

As Philip Metz stood on his porch, enjoying the fragrance of the evening and the smoke from his pipe, he could hear the whine of the truck's engine as it climbed its way to his house. He smiled, because in addition to the regular fare of canned goods, sacks of rice, flour, beans, and other supplies, he knew the truck carried a long awaited gift from France somewhere within the tarpaulin-covered load.

Perhaps, finally, with today's shipment, he would receive the two cases of Beaujolais Villages wine a friend in France, a former lover, had sent to him. This man, whom he had first known in Paris as a youngster, had visited him nearly a year ago in Muang Mai, Laos, an ancient city on the Sekong river, once called Attopeu, which lay on the southeastern side of the Plateau Des Bolovens. The two men had remained devout Communists since those early days in Paris.

When his friend departed from their year-ago reunion, he promised Philip that he would send as much of the delicate red wine as he could, once he had arrived home. Four months ago, Philip had received a letter from this friend, written a month earlier, stating that he had managed to ship him two cases of Beaujolais by air freight to Bangkok, but then it had to travel overland across Cambodia, which could take a few weeks or even months. He had carefully packed the twenty-four bottles in two large wooden boxes, surrounding each bottle tightly with straw.

Philip had always preferred the delicately tart yet slightly brut flavor of this fine red wine of Beaujolais. He had difficulty finding any sort of wine here, though. He mostly drank poor quality Oriental versions derived from grape juice shipped in railway tank cars from central and eastern Europe, then corked in green glass bottles with poorly printed labels featuring flying cranes or snowcapped mountains as trademarks. They reeked of formaldehyde with a bitter bite that left one suffering a dull headache if consumed on an empty stomach. In his remote setting, even a bottle of Chianti represented to Philip a fine and rare delicacy to savor slowly. Thus, twenty-four bottles of Beaujolais seemed an unthinkable joy.

Certainly, he would save them for his private time, to sip quietly and enjoy alone. They were too rare and fine in this world of jungle fever and unappreciative palates to share with anyone else.

"Huong, come quickly," Philip said in the southeast Asian-French dialect. "I can see the truck coming."

The Vietnamese youngster ran out of the house to the porch where the Frenchman stood barefooted. The boy stopped momentarily to slip on his sandals, which he had left by the front door, and then handed his mentor the pair of brown leather ankle-high boots that Philip preferred to wear.

Metz had finished tying his laces, and had stepped onto the grass when the truck pulled to a stop at the side of his house. The vehicle had a three-ton capacity bed, covered with a green canvas tarpaulin. Although Yugoslavian-built, the Viet Cong had painted the truck's cab, front, and frame a medium shade of robin's-egg blue with bright red trim, and red lettering on its door. American aircraft making the excursion to Vietnam's western border, to hunt along the Ho Chi Minh Trail, seemed less likely to bomb a blue, civilian-appearing truck than one painted dark green with a red star on its door.

The driver and his helper wore white shirts and tan cotton shorts. They carried no weapons on them nor in the truck. Should anyone question the two men, they could easily pass themselves off as Vietnamese civilian delivery drivers, and the nonmilitary cargo as simply a restock of food and supplies for their village. Such trucks were common traffic, even in the remote reaches of Vietnam.

"*Bonjour, bonhomie*," Metz said embracing the driver, a man who had made this delivery every month for several years. "You have for me something special today?"

"*Oui, Monsieur Philip*," the driver said, smiling at his friend, and leaned into the cab of the truck where he had carried the two wooden boxes.

Handing each case carefully to his assistant, the driver called to Philip, "At long last they have arrived. You have asked for the last three trips, and I was always sad to tell you not yet. Today I am happy to tell you they are here."

"We will open one bottle and you must join me in a toast," Metz said, smiling as he pulled loose the wooden top to one box and tore the straw packing from one of the dark brown bottles, exposing its brightly colored floral label.

"No, thank you, sir," the driver answered. "This is too fine a beverage to waste on such as me. You have waited so long for them as well. I could not."

"As you wish," Metz said, laying the bottle back in its place, and then gently carrying the box inside his house. He knew the man would not accept such an invitation, because of his inferior station. However, Metz felt it poor form not to offer, since this man had acted so carefully to carry the prized cargo in the front seat with him.

"I have this letter for you, too, sir," the driver said, taking an envelope from inside the cab where he had carried it tucked behind the sun visor. "Colonel Ba, himself, said I should make sure to hand you this personally."

"You have done your job well, my friendly man," Philip said, taking the envelope and pulling loose the flap with his finger. He took out the gold, wire-framed spectacles that he carried in his trouser pocket inside a brown, hard-shell leather case.

After studying the message carefully, he looked at Huong. "My boy, I must prepare to travel one day after tomorrow."

WHILE PHILIP, HUONG, THE DRIVER, AND HIS ASSISTANT loaded the new month's stores into the large pantry built next to the kitchen, Jim Land sat in the tent that had been set up for Operation Rio Blanco's intelligence section. There he listened quietly to a civilian field officer from the U.S. Mission in Da Nang, who had moments earlier stepped from a gray, unmarked helicopter that now waited on the landing pad at Hill 263.

"Sergeant Carlos Hathcock and Lance Corporal John Burke should get here any minute," Land said. "As far as I am concerned, they are the best sniper team in the country today."

"This mission is vital to the security of nearly every operative we have in I Corps and II Corps. I cannot emphasize that enough, Captain," the field officer said. "That's why we asked General Walt for the best he had. Colonel Herman Poggemeyer, Walt's G-3, told us if anyone had the people capable of accomplishing this mission, it would be you. We have no room for failure. No second chance on this."

Land looked outside where he saw Hathcock and Burke walking toward the tent, their rifles shouldered and packs on their backs. Hathcock carried the captain's pack in his left hand.

He looked back at the field officer and then at the major who had summoned him a half-hour earlier from the sniper detachment's headquarters tent, where a group of them had been eating.

"They won't fail, sir," Land said. "I would have no problem putting my life in their hands."

"I'm glad you have that kind of confidence in them, Captain," the field officer said. "They will have the lives of a lot of our people in their hands."

"Ready to go, sir," Carlos said, stepping inside the tent and handing Land the pack he carried. "You might check to be sure we got everything you need, Skipper."

"Change of skivvies? Spare socks, bootlaces, shaving kit?" Land asked, shouldering the pack.

"Yes, sir," Hathcock answered as the group of men began walking from the tent toward the landing site where the gray helicopter waited. "We also threw in your binoculars, knife, and some peanut butter, cheese, John Wayne crackers, and hot sauce, too. You already had quite a bit of suff in there as well."

"Thanks. That'll more than work," Land said.

"Huong, please hurry," Philip said, sitting on the side of his bed, pulling tight the laces on his brown leather ankle-high boots. "I must be on time to rendezvous with the colonel's patrol. It is a long walk to accomplish by sunrise."

"I am just finished packing your kit, sir," the boy answered.

"You did remember to fill my tobacco pouch, too, Huong?" Philip called to the boy.

"Oh yes, sir," Huong answered. "I placed it next to your pipe, on the table by the doorway."

"Thank you," Philip said, standing and walking into the living room where he found his pipe and tobacco.

Huong handed the Frenchman a soft leather valise with two small handles at its top and a long strap that Philip draped over his shoulder.

"I will be back in two or three days, Huong," Philip said walking to the porch steps and stopping to light his pipe. "Take care that you do not burn down the house while I am away. If you do happen to catch the house afire, though, please save my boxes of wine."

"Please be cautious, sir," Huong said as he watched the Frenchman disappear into the darkness.

Metz started down the faint, narrow roadway that led from his house, enjoying the sweet smell of his freshly lit pipe tobacco. He wore khaki trousers and a white bush shirt. A straw hat, its brim worn ragged in several places along its edge, hung over his back on a cord coupled with a wooden ball slide, which he could snug under his chin to hold the hat on his head should the wind blow. He would need the hat tomorrow to protect his balding head from being blistered by the sun.

His mix of gray and black hair lay shaggy and well past his ears, nearly touching his shoulders in the back. Huong had trimmed it seven months ago. The square, level lines that the Vietnamese teenager had cut in his hair left Philip embarrassed to remove his hat. It took the Frenchman many brushings and much more work with his ivory-handled straight razor and turtle-shell comb before he finally succeeded in returning his hairline to its natural, tapered look. He vowed never again to allow the boy near his head with scissors.

*　　*　　*

CARLOS AND BURKE LOOKED OUT THE SIDE DOORS OF the single-engine Huey, watching the black jungle below them as it rushed past at 160 knots only a matter of feet beneath the helicopter's skids. Neither sniper knew why they had to shoot the white man, only that it was extremely vital that they do it.

"Kind of tall, a bit portly, shaggy gray hair, somewhere in his fifties," Carlos repeated to himself. "Can't be too many like that around. Be hard to hit the wrong guy."

A colonel had briefed the two snipers the day before at a remote base, somewhere west. Concrete block hooches and showers had impressed the two Marines who got to lay in real beds with real mattresses last evening.

"They want us to kill a white man," Burke said to himself, wrinkling troublesome furrows along his brow as he watched the dark world skim past his feet. "I have never even looked at a white man through my rifle sights."

After making its short flight, the Huey settled into a small clearing just past the crest of a hill that would lead the two snipers down a gentle slope, through the jungle, along a narrow stream to a spot where they could fire 500 yards across a clearing and kill the Frenchman. They did not know his name, what he had done, nor why the CIA wanted him dead. But both snipers knew it was important.

They lay silently in the jungle until the helicopter had cleared the treetops and the thumping sound of its rotor blades faded in the distance. Neither man spoke. They knew what to do and set out on their mission.

A second chopper landed an hour later on a hilltop two kilometers distant from where the two snipers now lay. Jim Land, a four-man reconnaissance team, and a CIA field officer, who wore tiger-striped utilities, a camouflage ranger hat with its brim pinned up in the front, and had a bushy walrus mustache, quietly picked their way off the hill's crest and hid themselves in a blind of rocks and brush. Already the black shapes of the mountains and trees began to show depth and detail against the now light gray sky. In a matter of minutes, the first rays of sunlight began to creep across the jungles.

"Either your man is real good or dead back in the woods. I never saw a sign of life from the time it was light enough to see. He's well-hidden or not there," the man said in a cold tone.

"He's there," Land said. "When that Frenchman heads down that path, you'll see. The bastard's good as dead."

"You better hope so. Otherwise a couple of folks will be wishing they were dead."

"What are you talking about?"

"This Frenchman. He's a professional interrogator for Charlie. One of the best. I think he's a little funny, too, you know, sadistic sex, likes little boys. They say the bastard gets his rocks off fuckin' up people."

"Where you get all this?"

"Just take my word for it. That son of a bitch is bad."

"Charlie has a couple of our people down there waitin' to meet ole' Jacques. We don't want ole' Jacques to get there."

"Why don't you go in and take them? You know where they are?"

"Can't."

"Your man is the key to this. He has to kill the cat."

"Spooks," Land thought to himself.

"I HOPE THAT INFORMATION IS GOLDEN," THE COLONEL who had briefed Land and the two snipers said to the field officer from Da Nang as they sat in his office watching the day brighten.

"Our guy personally carried the message to the Frenchman," the field officer said. "He is one of our earliest infiltrators, and has never let us down. It's gold."

"That copilot is no problem, but if they break our

field coordinator, all these operatives, including your messenger, have had it," the colonel said, looking at his watch. "I hate to consider where we would be standing in this mess if those two scouts had not made it out. Us assuming all were KIA."

"I hope that Marine is as good a shot as they say," the field officer said, looking out the window at the orange-trimmed clouds above the sunrise. "He misses, then we have no choice but to go with the air strike."

PHILIP STOOD IN THE SHADOWS WHERE THE FAINT TRAIL he followed broke from the jungle into the long clearing. He hesitated there until he could see the seven black-clad guerrillas waiting for him at the long meadow's opposite edge. He stepped into the sunlight and waved to them.

"Good timing," the Frenchman said to himself, seeing his escort walk into the sunlight, too, waving at him. He took the brim of his straw hat with his fingers and lifted it onto his head, pulling the wooden slide up snugly under his chin. He waved to them again as he strolled forward, along the path that led across the clearing.

Birds sang in the forests at each side and now behind him, so Philip felt comfortable that no danger likely lurked there. An absence of normal wildlife sounds, no birds singing, quite often signaled the presence of a predator, which in wartime commonly meant men.

He paused a moment and lit his pipe, pulling the sweet smoke into his mouth.

The leather valise bounced lightly against his left hip as he strolled toward his comrades. He held the bowl of his calabash as he bit on the stem and waved again with his free hand, signaling all was well.

Suddenly, a powerful force struck the Frenchman's chest with a loud bang. He saw his own blood gush and spray into the air around him as he was knocked off his feet. When his back slammed against the ground,

Philip opened his eyes wide. He wanted to run. He tried to catch his breath. Then he realized a gunshot had mortally wounded him. His world went forever dark.

The crack of the rifle shot echoed across the tall grass that covered the long clearing, and rolled into the trees. Its surprise shattered the peaceful morning and the seven soldiers immediately fell to the ground beneath the grassy blind. They lay there a moment, listening for another shot.

Then the men crawled on their bellies, spreading out so that each rifleman was fifty feet or more from the next. Cautiously, the leader raised himself to his knees. He saw nothing and heard only silence. Not a bird sang. Nothing.

Suddenly, he heard the flutter of wings followed by branches breaking on the slope of the hill more than 500 yards in front of his patrol. He immediately raised his automatic rifle to his shoulder and held back the trigger, sending a burst of AK-47 rounds into the brush and trees.

His six comrades stood and joined his gunfire, as the sound of an approaching helicopter came from beyond the far ridge. Then a second Huey made a sweeping turn just above the treetops on a hill far to the left.

Machine-gun fire erupted from the second aircraft, sending dirt and grass into the air around the guerrillas. Several of them fired back at the helicopter while the leader focused his rifle on the two men he now saw running up the hill toward the first chopper.

He shouted at his comrades to direct some of their fire at the escaping men dressed in green camouflage, who also had themselves covered with leafy twigs and clumps of grass.

Seeing his bullets fall short of his target, the patrol leader raised his rifle's muzzle high, arching his fire now onto the helicopter. He had emptied a second magazine of ammunition at the escaping men and their aircraft, and had just slammed a third banana-curved container into the well of his rifle when the second Huey tilted toward them and turned. A Marine leaned precariously out of the bird, laying his weight at an angle behind an M-60 .30-caliber machine gun that he had tied to the top of the helicopter's door with long straps, and again opened fire on the Viet Cong.

The seven men dove for cover as the chopper raced down the slope and flew low over the clearing between the black-clad soldiers and the first helicopter, which now lifted away and disappeared beyond the ridge. Again the men fired as the second aircraft turned, swept up the hill, and disappeared, following the first.

Philip lay with his empty eyes opened wide, dilated, and clear. Their irises left only a thin brown line around the edges of their crystal black pupils. In them, the reflection of the sky and drifting clouds grew dim as the Frenchman's tears dried and specks of dust settled on the now-sticky surfaces of his eyes.

The shadows of seven men spread over the dead man's body. After a few moments, the shadows disappeared.

7

Spook Central

THE CRUNCHING OF HEAVY FOOTSTEPS ON THE gravel walkway outside the Quonset hut door aroused Carlos Hathcock from his afternoon nap. He turned his head to see Captain Jim Land trudging toward the screen door, looking tired and dirty.

Outside helicopters flew nonstop, beating their whirling wings through the humid evening air, churning a rhythmic *whomp, whomp, whomp,* while cargo planes, running up their turbine engines for takeoff, droned in the background. The Marine sniper found it curious that with all that noise he could still hear a man walk across pea-size rocks that covered the path outside the hooch where he and his partner slept.

When Hathcock and Burke had returned to the air facility this morning, they had immediately taken advantage of the hot-water showers, located in a concrete-block head facility behind their Quonset hut. Clean and refreshed the duo then found an all-ranks, all-services club of sorts in a nearby hooch.

There, a civilian-looking pilot wearing khakis and a

St. Louis Cardinals baseball cap had shown them his gratitude for eliminating the Frenchman by giving the two men a six-pack of cold beer he had taken from a decal-covered, gas-operated refrigerator with *Playboy*'s 1966 Playmate of the Year taped to its door. It stood next to a Formica-topped, plywood bar, also festooned with decals that ranged from Flying Tigers Airways to the Dallas Cowboys.

By three P.M., both Marines had finished the six-pack and used up the dollar's worth of games the man had left on the pinball machine. With no money and no beer remaining, they returned to their soft beds in the Quonset hut where they slept until the sound of crunching gravel awakened the sergeant.

"Sir, got some showers out back, and these racks feel mighty good," Carlos said to his captain in a sleepy voice.

Burke leaned on his elbows and said, smiling, "Skipper, we ought to move down here, they have lots of room. We could cover the whole TAOR[1] by just jumping on one of these choppers outside. They could drop us off, we shoot some VC, they pick us up, and we kick back here. What could be better!"

"Not a thing, Lance Corporal Burke," Land said. "Take advantage of it while you can. However, I have to head back tomorrow morning. You two need to get going as well, once these people here finish with you. So enjoy.

"For now, I'm going to take advantage of the showers and those racks."

Carlos waited for his captain to disappear to the rear half of the hut, where he had located a bed and a locker. When Hathcock heard the screen door at the other end of the hut slam shut, he smiled at Burke.

"We play our cards right, we might squeeze a couple of extra days here," he said.

"I could hear those wheels turning as soon as the

[1]Tactical Area Of Responsibility.

skipper said he was leaving tomorrow," Burke said with a smile. "What do you have in mind?"

"We go back to that club tonight and listen to what the boys here have to say," Carlos responded. "I'm hoping that some of those spooks will be in there, and we can let them know we are in no hurry to take off, if they have some more business for us. Skipper has plenty of snipers up at 263, anyway."

"Besides," Burke said, grinning, "we might get some more free beer."

"I have a feeling that even if we did have money, we still couldn't buy a drink there," Carlos said cheerfully.

JIM LAND HAD JUST BEGUN SNORING WHEN HATHCOCK nudged him.

"Sir, we're going over to a hooch a few doors down and check out this pool table they got there, if you need to find us later," Carlos said.

With a groggy moan, Land acknowledged the sergeant's report, and quickly fell back to sleep. Later that evening, the captain awakened and recalled what Hathcock had said to him.

"Bet I could get a cold drink there," Land said to himself as he tied his boots and walked outside. He stood a moment and looked both directions. Then he heard the sound of the Beatles singing *Love, Love Me Do*, coming from a green-painted sea hut with a rusty tin roof, three doors down.

When he stepped inside, he saw Hathcock and Burke seated at a round table with two in civilian clothes drinking beer and playing spades with a dog-eared deck that featured a naked woman spread-eagled on the cards' backsides.

"Skipper," the man with the mustache and bush hat from the morning's mission called to Land. "Let me buy you a drink."

Land smiled and walked to the bar where the field

agent popped open the door to the old Survel refrigerator.

"Name your poison and keep your money," the man said. "It's no good here."

Carlos looked up and smiled at the captain.

Land shook his head, grinning back. He could almost read his two men's minds. "See what we got you?" he thought.

"I'll just have a 7UP," Land told his new friend who leaned against the open door of the beer-packed cooler, twisting the end of his mustache with his right thumb and index finger.

"Shit, Captain," the agent said. "I thought you Marines were hardcore."

"I have an early flight," Land responded, "and I'll need all the brain power I can muster to deal with the situation back there."

"Your pilot's probably sitting shit-faced in the corner, Skipper," the man followed. "You sure you won't have one beer?"

Land shook his head as he took the cold, dripping can from the fellow. Carlos and Burke laughed loudly as their two opponents threw down their card hands.

"Sniper team wins again," John Burke exclaimed, writing down the score.

Against the wall an old Wurlitzer jukebox with red and blue lights behind chrome grillwork churned as it extracted another 45-rpm record from the two rows of plastic disks stacked inside it. A young pilot with shaggy hair punched in his selections.

As the sound of Paul McCartney singing *Yesterday* filled the background, Land settled onto an easy chair across the room, and quietly sipped his cold soda while watching his two men enjoy their respite from the filth and sadness of war. The melancholy Beatles song sent sweet memories drifting through the captain's mind. He thought of Elly. He thought of his son. He thought about how time had flown so quickly since he had gotten here from Okinawa, and that now he looked forward to going home. Six months in Vietnam after a half-year on Okinawa made up this overseas tour. He loved his people here, and his job, too. But he loved his wife much more.

It was already well past ten o'clock, yet Carlos and Burke continued to laugh and play cards. Quite unusual, Land considered, since both snipers notoriously went to bed early and rose every morning long before the other men. He didn't want to consider the possibilities, but he knew that the two Marines bore some watching.

"I am going to bed," Land said to the snipers as he stood and tossed the empty soda can into a large metal trash container set on the floor at the end of the bar.

"Two points," Carlos called to him. "We're right on your tail, sir."

"Take your time," Land said.

"That's okay, sir, we got to go hit the rack now, anyway," Hathcock said casually. "That colonel here wants to talk to Burke and me first thing tomorrow. It's really not much of anything, sir. Nothing you need to get concerned about. I'll be sure to tell you if it's anything at all important."

Land smiled. He had already smelled the fish, and now began to consider delaying his return. The captain felt an obligation to be with his men if they were going to meet with a colonel. However, Brigadier General W. A. Stiles, commander of Task Force X-Ray, counted on Land's prompt return and his status report at the operation's headquarters on Hill 263.

"I expect to see you both or at least hear from you tomorrow before noon," the captain said, walking out the door.

"Yes, sir! Don't worry about us, sir. We'll keep you informed, Skipper," Carlos said a bit too happily.

He had taken the ". . . at least hear from you tomorrow . . ." part of Land's instructions to mean there was some additional flexibility in his and Burke's return time.

By seven A.M., Jim Land had rejoined his sniper platoon on Hill 263, and prepared to brief General Stiles while Sergeant Hathcock and Lance Corporal Burke sat at a conference table looking at several large photographs of three different Vietnamese civilians: an older man, balding with gray streaking his hair; a middle-aged woman; and a younger man, perhaps in his late twenties. All three had friendly smiles.

"One of these hotdogs is a spy?" Carlos said to the man with the thick mustache, who sat left of the colonel.

"These are the three government employees that our counterintelligence team at Tan Son Nhut Airbase has narrowed its investigation down to," the agent said. "All three hold what we consider sensitive positions within the facilities engineering office there in Saigon. Each of them makes regular trips up this way every other week or so. Also, they all happen to be visiting family in Pleiku right now."

The colonel interrupted. "You gentlemen don't need to know many details other than we believe one of these nice, gentle-looking faces belongs to a spy. We want you to confirm for us which one. Or which two. Or maybe all three."

"Why can't you tell by just following them?" Burke asked.

"We can't follow them everywhere," the civilian intelligence officer answered. "Besides, our watchdogs managed to spook the whole trio. They won't make contact with the other side as long as they believe we have surveillance on them. So they will have to meet up with their VC controllers at a place where our tails cannot follow."

The colonel pulled a fourth set of photographs from an accordion folder, and spread them on the table.

"Like this place," he said, pointing to one of the color aerial photographs of a beige stucco house with a wide front porch, a tin roof, and green camouflage netting draped across much of the structure.

"Just tie a bell around the cat's neck," the man with the mustache said. "We do not want you to shoot anyone. Stay out of sight, both going in and coming out. Avoid encounters with anyone at all costs."

DANG QUANG PHUNG SIPPED WARM TEA WHILE READING a very thick book at a hotel in the center of Pleiku. The building sat diagonally across a large corner lot. It had a great curved front wall made of glass, above which Dang sat in its second-floor restaurant, by a window that overlooked a stone-covered patio built atop the lobby roof. From this vantage point, the young Vietnamese architect could see much of the city and watch Pleiku's two main thoroughfares where they intersected in front of the hotel.

Although just twenty-five years old, Dang had designed the blueprints for much of the construction at Tan Son Nhut during the past two years. In that time, the French-educated artist had also studied the locations and structures of every building and bunker that the facilities office oversaw.

Occasionally, Dang looked up from his book and gazed casually at the streets. Below, he could see a police jeep and its two white-helmeted patrolmen parked near the corner, pretending to count traffic. The Viet Cong spy then observed two Americans with short-cropped hair, wearing sports shirts and slacks, who sat at a table, drinking 333 beer in the open-fronted bar across the street. Besides these four, Dang also noticed the Vietnamese man who sat near the restaurant's main door, chain-smoking Winston cigarettes across the aisle from the bar, and watching him from the side of his newspaper. So Dang sat quietly and read the heavy hardcover volume of Marcel Proust's *Remembrance of Things Past* that he had bought in Paris just before his college graduation.

As he sipped warm tea, this devotee of art, architecture, French literature, and Ho Chi Minh pondered the philosophical meaning of Proust's phrase, "*Les seuls vries paradis sont les paradis perdus.*" The only true paradise is paradise lost. It was Dang's favorite declaration from this French classic, the longest novel ever written.

Works such as Proust's great novel and Victor Hugo's *Les Misérables* had impassioned him to oppose injustices beset on the poor, and to seek a greater share of power and wealth for common people. His Utopian, liberal passions had connected him to the idealistic pragmatism of Ho Chi Minh and Vladimir Ilyich Ulyanov Lenin. Thus, he came home to Pleiku a Communist, and convinced his older brother to embrace the philosophy as well.

WHILE DANG SIPPED TEA AND READ, WATCHING THE people who watched him, Carlos Hathcock and John Burke sat on the wide-back bench of another gray helicopter. It was already afternoon.

Their chopper took a quick dip below a ridge, and touched down for a few seconds while the two snipers jumped off into a stand of shoulder-high grass. Quickly, the pilot turned the craft southeastward and flew away. It dipped twice more below ridge lines, and then many miles farther away it landed in a clearing and waited several minutes. The helicopter launched again, and flew eastward, and eventually home.

In the cover of the thick jungle that canopied much of the hillside where Burke and Hathcock had disembarked, Carlos unfolded the map section that would lead him to his objective, and to the two men's return rendezvous point for their flight home.

"Gotta be Cambodia," he told Burke. "We skirted Pleiku too far back, and there ain't a thing I recognize on this map."

"I have to tell you, Sergeant Hathcock, I feel funny about this whole thing," Burke said. "Did you tell Captain Land?"

"Not about this," Carlos said. "Besides, I couldn't if I wanted to. It's secret. All he knows is we hung back there for a little recreation and recovery."

"So, the only people that we know for sure know about us being out here are the colonel and that CIA guy?" Burke asked.

"Far as I know. And those two pilots that dropped us off," Carlos added.

"Skipper will sure be pissed if we get in trouble out here," Burke said.

"You know that won't happen," Carlos said smartly. "These hamburgers ain't smart enough to catch us."

Then he looked at Burke and grinned. "But we ain't gonna take any chances either."

The two snipers began creeping silently through the jungle. They planned to move ten kilometers over the next mountain and up the next ridge, where they could observe the stucco house at a close distance without being seen.

DANG CLOSED HIS THICK BOOK AND GENTLY PLACED IT inside the leather satchel he had set on the floor next to his chair.

The chain-smoking watchdog folded his newspaper when Dang stepped through the doorway and made his way down the stairs to the hotel lobby. The young architect climbed into a cyclo taxi parked at the hotel entrance and gave the driver directions to his father's house.

As the driver peddled the three-wheeled, bicycle-driven carriage with its rickshaw-style passenger seat away from the hotel, Dang glanced across the street at the two Americans. They casually finished their beers, stepped away from their street-side table, and began window-shopping as they strolled up the sidewalk in the same direction Dang traveled.

The police jeep pulled away from the corner and turned left in front of the hotel. Another police jeep passed him as he rode toward the edge of town where his family's small farm had been for three generations. Dang's older brother would take it over once their father had passed away.

He had chosen to ride home in the cyclo so that the watchdogs could keep close track of him. He wanted to keep them fully occupied with him, especially tomorrow when he would return to the hotel and wait while his brother took their father's old Land Rover north on Highway 14 to Kontum, and then west on a rugged back road that forded the Ya Krong Bolah, on through Plei Nong and northwest another eight kilometers, along a faint trace, to the stucco house.

There he would deliver the four rolls of film that contained detailed drawings of new facilities and defense structures on and around Tan Son Nhut Airbase. While there, his brother would pick up another box filled with dragon fruit,[2] a delicacy that once grew in abundance in the forested mountains west and south of Pleiku. Since the war began, the fruit had stopped growing. Now, one could only obtain dragon fruit from eastern Cambodia, where war and defoliants had not destroyed the fragile plants that produced it.

People in western Vietnam considered dragon fruit sacred. They believed that it would only grow where peace and happiness prevailed. If the plants refused to produce their unique fruit, it meant that an evil time had come upon them.[3]

As night fell, Dang sat with his father, mother, brother, and young sister, looking at old photographs.

---

[2]A mangolike fruit that resembles the apples from the prickly pear cactus, but is much larger and has no needles. It is typically six inches in length and three inches in diameter with a red leathery skin on which triangular, leaflike appendages grow, similar to the tips of leaves surrounding the artichoke. The fruit's interior is white with tiny black seeds throughout the meat, which is very juicy and delicately sweet.

[3]Several years after the end of the Vietnam war, dragon fruit reappeared in the countryside south and west of Pleiku. Today it grows in that region in abundance.

His father especially liked a portrait Dang had taken of his sister. He had taken it just after he had returned from Paris and she had enrolled in a Catholic high school in Pleiku. The white audsai[4] she wore, her long black hair that hung straight nearly to her waist, and her smooth, narrow face and large black eyes gave her a look of angelic innocence.

Gazing up from the photo, Dang smiled at his sister, who now held her four-month-old baby at her breast. He then turned his eyes toward his brother, whom he loved dearly, and thought of what he must do tomorrow. His risk was great. It posed a serious threat to the safety of his father, mother, sister, and his infant nephew. People they had never known watched them now. But they especially scrutinized Dang. And he now used it to his advantage.

WHILE DANG SAT WITH HIS FAMILY, A TIGER'S ROAR echoed from somewhere in the valley below the ridge where the two snipers hid. The big cat sounded far enough away that it presented little real threat, but close enough to hear and to raise concern in the minds of Carlos and John. They lay quietly listening to it. Perhaps it called a mate. Maybe it celebrated a kill. More likely, the animal called out caution to all who might trespass here tonight.

Oil lamps glowing inside the house cast a dim orange light through the front windows and across the wide porch where Hathcock and Burke could clearly see a dozen Viet Cong guerrillas squatting barefoot in their dark outfits, talking and eating. The snipers were so close they could hear the men's voices and words. A

---

[4] A very attractive clothing ensemble worn typically by young women and girls in Vietnam, commonly students. Usually made of fine silk in white or light pastel colors, the outfit includes flowing pants worn under a top that features a long panel that hangs to knee length in front and in back, and is open at the sides to the waistline.

black dog ran loose in the front yard, barking incessantly.

"He knows we're here," Carlos thought. "Probably smells us. If he comes a-hunting, we'll have to catch him with a K-Bar. I hate killing a dog, but he'll probably wind up on their dinner spit tomorrow anyway."

One of the men threw a sandal at the dog and swore at him. A person did not need a translator to know that the barking irritated the men. An old woman hurried into the yard, caught the dog by the scruff, and tied a short rope around his neck. She disappeared with him behind the house and the dog quit barking.

The tiger roared once more. Voices from the porch followed. "Thank God for the tiger," Carlos thought. Burke laid his head on his hands and closed his eyes. He would relieve his sergeant in four hours.

LIGHT FOG ROSE FROM THE GROUND IN THE VALLEY, laying an eerie cloak over the predawn world. John Burke nudged Hathcock with his heel.

Carlos slowly raised his head and saw the dozen guerrillas in their black shirts and pants—wearing sandals made from tire treads—slip through the fog, rifles in hand. The twelve soldiers followed a trail that led up the ridge, passing within fifty feet of where he and Burke lay hidden. Each man in the Viet Cong patrol carried a large pack strapped to his back.

"Not just a short patrol," Carlos thought. "They're heading east, and we're going to have to deal with them when we leave here."

The guerrillas passed so close to Burke that he could smell their body odor drifting up the hill on the slight breeze. As he watched the dark shapes creep slowly past him, the words and melody of one of the many Beatles songs that the young pilot had kept playing on the jukebox replayed over and over again in his mind. "How ironic," he thought.

He knew he would always remember this moment

and the black-dressed enemy coming so close to him. "Baby's in black" now had a whole new meaning.

IT WAS JUST AFTER NINE O'CLOCK WHEN DANG climbed inside the Land Rover and his brother drove him to the hotel. He had arranged to meet a friend he had known since grade school, who now served as an artillery captain in the Army of the Republic of Viet Nam.

He hoped to point out the people watching him, and would ask his friend if he could find out why. He would be very convincing in proclaiming his unyielding loyalty and diligent service to the Republic. Why in heaven's name would they be watching him? What had he done to deserve such scrutiny? He was only a simple architect.

Dang Quang Phung embraced his friend, who waited in uniform at the corner, in front of the hotel. He had not yet seen the watchdogs, but he knew they were there, watching him greet his old schoolmate.

JOHN BURKE CHECKED HIS WRISTWATCH. STRAIGHT-UP noon.

He and Hathcock both heard the distant whine of a jeep-type vehicle climbing through the rocky roadway that led across the low part of the ridge where they lay hidden. Carlos trained his rifle to his left limit, looking to see what approached.

A dark green four-wheel-drive carryall dropped its square snout over the ridge, into a washout of rocks, slamming its front end into the boulders and then lurching forward. Carlos could see the four men inside toss into each other as the vehicle struggled down what may have once been a road but now more closely resembled a stone quarry.

He withheld the laughter that erupted inside him. "Every one of those hamburgers has got busted kidneys," he thought. "Bet they wished they walked now."

John Burke put his spotting scope on the vehicle as it approached and saw that the four men wore tan uniforms with red cloth sewn to the epaulets on their shirts. He could see gold devices pinned in the red. "Four officers, NVA, company grade," he concluded, and then looked at Hathcock.

"Some sort of lieutenants or captains," Carlos whispered, and Burke nodded.

When the carryall finally stopped in front of the house, the four officers climbed out, stretching their legs and arms. They laughed as they stood around rubbing the circulation back into their thighs.

"These jokers act like they're back on the block," Carlos mused in his mind. "One thing for sure, we are someplace where they don't think they have anything to worry about. We're probably way the heck across the border in Cambodia."

He worried a bit more now about what Burke had asked earlier, regarding who knew they were out here. "Long as we get home safe, and no one is the wiser, we best just keep on moving back to the operation where we belong," Carlos concluded.

Nearly an hour had passed when the snipers heard the noise of a second vehicle climbing its way along the rocky roadway. In a few minutes the front end of the brown Land Rover bounced over the ridge, dropping into the washout with a bang. One man occupied the all-wheel-drive utility sedan.

"Bingo," Carlos whispered as the vehicle chugged down the slope and then parked in front of the house.

Both snipers trained their scopes on the man as he stepped from the driver's seat.

"That eliminates the woman and the old man," Carlos told himself. Then he glanced at Burke who had the spotting scope, which had twice the magnification that Hathcock's telescopic rifle sights possessed. The sergeant studied the expression on his partner's face and it confirmed his conclusion. This man was none of the three suspects.

He was young, perhaps late twenties, but he had a thin build and narrow face. A completely different look from the photo of the young man who had a round face and stocky build.

"A complete and total waste," Carlos thought as the man disappeared inside the house.

Ten minutes later the man walked out the front door, carrying a cardboard box. He bowed to the four officers and they waved good-bye to him. Moments later the brown Land Rover bounced up the rocky roadway and disappeared over the ridge.

The four officers went inside the house, and Carlos decided to wait.

DANG OFFERED TO BUY HIS FRIEND ANOTHER GLASS OF Johnny Walker Red Label scotch whiskey. Two bar girls had joined the young men and drank their mostly water cocktails slowly, trying their best to entertain their clients and glean more from the large stack of 500-piaster bills that the civilian gentleman carried in his wallet.

As the two men sipped their whiskey, Dang glanced at his watch through the corner of his eye. In another half-hour he would be sure that he had given his brother ample time to have returned home. A woman and a man watched him in the bar across the street from the hotel where he sat with his friend. Outside another police jeep waited.

His leather satchel with Proust's novel inside had kept the watchdogs' interest.

Dang had pointed the police jeep out to his friend, as well as another man in the hotel, and now the couple at the bar. His friend had a difficult time believing him, until the young architect took him for a walk two blocks over and one block down, and then back to the hotel, and then across the street to the bar. Throughout the trek, the observers kept them in sight.

"We should go to my father's home," Dang suggested. He knew his friend would argue. He would want Dang to accompany him to his apartment and have more to drink.

"I will share a taxi with you to your apartment," he told the young Vietnamese officer, "but I will just make sure you get home safely. I must be at my father's home before dinner. However, you are most welcome to join me. The family would be excited to hear your stories of how you are beating these rotten Communists."

The ARVN artillery captain considered the offer once more. He missed home cooking since his parents had relocated to Na Trang, where they felt much safer. However, he had been drinking most of the day and did not want to risk embarrassing Dang's family with his drunkenness.

"We have both consumed too much spirits," he told his friend. "You are welcome to come to my apartment and drink more with me and stay the night. Perhaps these lovely ladies would also enjoy accompanying us?"

Dang smiled. Perhaps he might. However, he must first inform his father of his plans.

"You and I shall go to my father's home and tell him that we have made plans, and I will be with you tonight," he said putting his arm over the captain's shoulder. "I am sure these ladies will wait here until we return."

"I will sit in the cab, though," the Army officer said.

"That will be fine," Dang Quang Phung[5] said. "I will speak to him only briefly. Perhaps my brother will join us, too."

---

[5]Dang Quang Phung remained a Communist spy at his Tan Son Nhut post throughout the war. In a 1994 interview, Dang claimed that during the 1975 collapse of South Vietnam, his detailed knowledge and expertise as a South Vietnamese government architect enabled Viet Cong and North Vietnamese forces to lay in artillery, mortars, and aerial bombs with great accuracy at Tan Son Nhut Airbase, the nearby Defense Attaché's Office Compound, and other key facilities in Saigon. After the war's end, Dang received a pension from the new government, and moved to the countryside northwest of Saigon, near Cu Chi, where he resides today.

Long shadows faded into the early evening grayness as the two friends hailed a taxi.

AT THE SAME TIME, THE FOUR NORTH VIETNAMESE Army officers bounced in their carryall as it climbed across the rocky ridge and disappeared from Hathcock's and Burke's sight.

"That was our spy," Carlos whispered in Burke's ear. "Colonel won't like the news, but that's all we can tell him. I think the only person down there now is that old woman. I expect the show is over."

Throughout the remainder of the night, the two snipers picked their way quietly down the back of the ridge, across the valley, and over the next mountain. At its base, a narrow stream cut through the ground, eroding the soil from beneath the tall trees that grew along its banks.

Hathcock and Burke had just begun to feel their way toward a place where the ground had broken from the steep walls of the wash and offered them a means of crossing without having to drop ten feet to the water, when footsteps above them froze the two Marines in place.

"Ah yes, our friends in black," Carlos whispered in Burke's ear. The lance corporal nodded and pointed to a tree just below them. Half of its roots dangled over the embankment, offering not only handholds down, but a hiding place as well.

"Snakes and scorpions," Hathcock thought as he slipped down the roots with Burke. "Probably full of 'em. All kinds of nasty critters, I'll bet."

Less than ten yards upstream, the first of the twelve Viet Cong slid down the cut in the wash and splashed in the water with a thud. A man above him muffled his laugh. Another guerrilla whispered something to the others, and then the next soldier slid down to the creek.

John and Carlos had pulled themselves up into the mass of roots that emerged beneath the tree's base, and hung suspended like giant sloths among the tangle of dangling wood, debris, and mud clods. Ants and other biting bugs began to sting the two men as they held their lives in the grips they maintained with their hands and legs.

Ten feet below the two Marines, the water cascaded across fallen logs and rocks that had once lain on the ground by the tree. Floodwaters had taken away the soil and left the heavy objects piled in a jagged mess. If either man dropped, he would most likely impale himself or break an arm or leg. Their only way out was back up.

Carlos felt the muscles in his arms begin to tremble as the Viet Cong continued to slowly cross the stream, one man at a time. The weight of his pack pulled against his shoulders, and he asked God to please hurry the soldiers on their way.

One by one, he counted silhouettes as they emerged into the skyline on the far side of the deep streambed. He could see the packs still on their backs, and believed confidently that these were the same men he and Burke had watched leave the house this morning.

After the twelfth guerrilla disappeared, the snipers waited for what seemed another eternity to be sure no one else followed the patrol. Then, like spiders on a ceiling, the Marines crawled their way back through the roots, and climbed out of their precarious hiding spot.

At the top, Carlos and John saw the distraught looks on each other's faces, and then began to fight laughter. Burke clamped his hand over his mouth and shut his eyes.

"Never again," he thought.

HELICOPTER BLADES CHOPPING THROUGH THE MORN-ing air awakened the two snipers as they lay in a hide, catnapping. They had placed themselves well back from the clearing where they would meet their ride home. They crept forward to a place where they could dash to the Huey as it dipped into the landing zone, even so they would only have seconds to fall inside its open doors. Suddenly anxiety swept over the duo as they heard breaking twigs and thudding feet somewhere behind them.

"They're coming to greet our ride," Carlos told himself, looking for a hiding place. Nothing would do. He looked at Burke and whispered, "Let's get going."

Both men dashed into the clearing as the gray helicopter appeared at the treetops and then dropped into the tiny meadow. A crewman inside waved at the snipers to come ahead just as bullets began to snap past their ears and pop through the waist-high grass.

Several rounds blew through the Plexiglas windscreen in front of the pilots, and Carlos could see the helicopter begin to tilt forward, lifting the heels of its skids.

As it rose from the grass, both snipers fell into the door, clinging to chair legs and straps as the bird lifted away. Only their arms, shoulders, and heads were inside. The lone crewman in the back began to pull against their pack straps and shirts while Hathcock and Burke kicked and scrambled, and finally slid onto the helicopter's metal floor.

"Cheated death once again," Carlos said, lifting his eyebrows, trying to raise a smile from Burke.

"Bug-bitten and scraped up, our clothes all torn. Hell the whole Viet Cong Army right on our heels, shootin' everything they got at us. I guess we cheated death, all right," Burke said, finally grinning at his partner. "But not by much."

8

Hunting White Feather

IT WAS MIDAFTERNOON WHEN THE GRAY HELICOPTER landed at Hill 263 and the snipers hopped out. They had met with the colonel and the intelligence agent to break the news that the man they saw meet the NVA officers was none of the three people in the photographs.

Identifying the Land Rover helped, but not much. There were many like it in this country, especially in the rough territory south and west of Pleiku. Most of the vehicles were refurbished and pieced together from those left behind by the British and the French, like the one owned by Dang's family in Pleiku. Nearly all were either brown or green.

"It's about time," Gunny Wilson said, seeing Hathcock and Burke step into the doorway of the general-purpose tent where he sat behind a small green field desk. "Our two prodigal snipers have finally returned to the fold."

He looked over their filthy faces, torn clothes, and tired, aching bodies. "You don't look like you could take much more R and R. Probably a good thing you got back here where you can go to work and get some rest.

"Might be a good idea to grab a rag and a bucket, go over to the water bull[1] and clean a layer or two of that crap off your scuzzy bodies. Also, it wouldn't hurt to get into some serviceable utilities before the skipper gets back."

Ten minutes later, the two Marines stood in their shower shoes, slopping cold soapy water from a bucket over their bodies, washing away the grime from the previous day and night. Countless red sores covered the two men.

"Looks like chicken pox," Burke said, gently scrubbing his chest with a washcloth. "Reckon we ought to put something on them?"

"My grandmother used to dab baking soda on my ant and chigger bites when I was a kid," Carlos said. "I don't know where we'd find any of it around here."

"You have a problem with me seeing the doc at the aid station?" Burke asked. "I reckon he might have something we can put on them. I'd hate to get sick from these stings."

Hathcock thought a moment, and considered the hazard of having raw sores or open wounds in the field. He had seen some of the bad infections prevalent here. Even an innocent-looking insect bite could become a serious enough problem to take a man out of action. He knew that in some cases a Marine could go on report or even get a court-martial over not taking care of his body.

Carlos recalled that in Hawaii a couple of the competitors on his intramural shooting team had fallen asleep while sunbathing, and as a result of their carelessness suffered severe blisters and sun poisoning. Not only did the men get dropped from the team, but wound up receiving nonjudicial punishment of a month's restriction and a $100 fine.

---

[1]A water trailer, also sometimes called a *water buffalo*.

"Whatever he gives you," Carlos said, lightly washing his many bites, "be sure to get two of them."

SEVERAL HUNDRED MILES SOUTH OF WHERE THE SNIPER duo washed themselves, General Tran Van Tra, Commander in Chief of the People's Liberation Army, sat on a stool in an underground command complex northwest of Saigon. Tran served as Commander in Chief of the Viet Cong forces throughout the Vietnam War and beyond its end in 1975. The general held equal status with General Van Tien Dung, the commander of the North Vietnamese Army, and was subordinate only to General Vo Nguyen Giap, Commander of all Communist forces, and to Chairman Ho Chi Minh. Following the war's conclusion, General Tran led Vietnamese forces into Cambodia, defeating the Khmer Rouge after their invasion of Vietnam.

The middle-aged man cleaned his wire-frame spectacles with his handkerchief, and concentrated on controlling his anger while his chief of staff told him details of what he termed the Frenchman's "assassination."

General Tran hooked the glasses onto his ears and adjusted them on the bridge of his nose. He ran his handkerchief over his head, wiping away sweat from his thinning gray and black hair that he combed straight back. The stocky man who stood five feet, four inches tall, sat quietly in the dim orange light of a kerosene lantern and considered what the colonel had just told him.

"Do you believe these assassins are the same two Americans that our people have identified in the Da Nang and Chu Lai combat zones?" Tran asked his senior assistant.

"Colonel Ba is positive and I believe so, too," the chief of staff answered. "He recognized them from three other engagements. Furthermore, one wears a white feather in his hat, just as the one at Da Nang and Chu Lai."

"This whole platoon of men has become a significant problem," General Tran said. "Not only do they disrupt operations and morale, but have succeeded in penetrating security and killing several key leaders. These two assassins are especially troubling. Intelligence sources in Da Nang have suggested it was just these two men who held and annihilated the company of regular Army replacements a few weeks ago in the Ca De Song Valley below Dong Den Mountain."

"It is difficult to imagine that only two men could assess such a victory," the colonel said. "Nearly 300 soldiers and officers died there. Many from the artillery barrage, but a significant number from direct fire."

"The Americans claim it was just these two men," General Tran said. "Whether or not this is so remains immaterial in light of the impact it is having on our morale. Many of our soldiers have heard this story and regard it as so.

"This fellow who wears the white feather has killed some of our most effective leaders and soldiers.

"Have any initiatives against this problem been pursued?"

"None specifically address it, General, sir," the colonel answered.

"I want it established as a priority," General Tran said. "I want the commander for that district to report to me, and discuss his proposals for initiatives that will eliminate this problem."

Once the colonel had left the general's small underground chamber, Tran Van Tra slapped his hand against the clay wall as he looked at a map showing the disbursement of his main forces throughout South Vietnam. The death of the Apache troubled him. And, despite the fact that he held little respect for the Frenchman, knew him only by reputation, and felt little grief at his loss, this man's death nonetheless troubled the general. Philip was a man protected by one of his best field commanders, Colonel Ba. These snipers had not only penetrated their deep security, but had killed the Frenchman in the presence of that revered leader.

SEVERAL DAYS HAD PASSED SINCE HATHCOCK AND Burke had returned from their intelligence adventure into Cambodia. Since no one had said anything about it to either sniper, Carlos concluded that Gunny Wilson had likely said nothing to Captain Land or anyone else about his and Burke's haggard appearance when they reported home. Wilson had asked them nothing about it since then, either. As far as anyone was concerned, the two snipers had spent an extra day down south and nothing more. Carlos and John felt satisfied with that, too.

Two days after Thanksgiving, Operation Rio Blanco ended. While Jim Land returned to Hill 55 with the majority of snipers, he left Burke and three others with Sergeant Hathcock to support the units that remained on Hill 263 to counter any resurgence of enemy strength.

"Carlos," the captain said, looking at him squarely, "I expect you to properly supervise these men, and not get so absorbed in any hunting expeditions that you lose track of your greater responsibility. I expect situation reports from you every two days."

Hathcock obeyed his captain at least for the first four days. Then business picked up so rapidly that he assigned his two teams out around the clock. Carlos hardly slept. He picked up all the slack, providing sniper support to units by himself.

In two weeks, the endless demands on his men had taken their toll. Even Burke looked like a walking scarecrow. The men's eyes lay hollow and sunken in their faces. Their mouths turned down and hung open. Long lines cut along their cheeks and out the corners of their eyes. Kids only a month ago, now they looked like aged men.

"You've got to take these men back to Hill 55,

John," Carlos told his partner. "They're used clean up. Can't do anybody any good if they're walking dead."

"What about you, Sergeant Hathcock?" Burke asked. "Have you taken a look in a mirror?"

"You report to Captain Land that I sent you back because you can't do any more good up here," Carlos said, ignoring Burke's questions. "You boys need to get some rest."

"You sure this ain't a mistake?" Burke asked.

The sergeant snapped back at his partner and friend. Fatigue had made his short temper even worse.

Burke pled again for Hathcock to reconsider, or at least allow him to remain at his side.

"Just tell the skipper I will keep him informed," Carlos said, "and that I will be back soon as they get things under control here."

ALL THE CIRCUITS IN JIM LAND'S ANGER CONTROL CENter went red when Lance Corporal Burke reported with his three men and without Sergeant Hathcock. The man had done exactly what he had instructed him not to do. At least he had the good sense to get the completely exhausted Marines out of the field. However, Land knew that Carlos tended to be his own worst enemy, never saying no, always ready to accept more tasks. He had often joked with the sergeant, "You have an alligator mouth and a hummingbird ass."

This time Land hoped it would not get his man killed.

Through the remainder of December, including Christmas Day, Hathcock patrolled nonstop. Many days he depended on ten-minute catnaps scattered throughout the day to fulfill his body's requirement for rest. He considered more than four hours sleep wasteful. It was only on rare occasions that he even got that much sack time.

The sergeant literally met himself coming and going. Returning to the hill with one patrol, he would see a fresh departing patrol and just U-turn at the wire, going back out with the new bunch. He had lost so much weight that his trousers doubled all the way around his waist.

By New Year's, he looked like a stick with sunken eyes and a bush hat stuck on top. His white feather now seemed too large, almost matching his ego and self-confidence. The Marine Sniper truly believed that if he died as a result of combat, it would happen in a situation where he had no control. A direct hit on his bunker, or a stray round from an accidental discharge on the hill. Certainly no Viet Cong or NVA soldier had enough cunning to outfox the fox.

Each day's success, not only surviving but dominating on the battlefield, kept his belief reinforced. He was invincible.

"MORE BAD NEWS, GENERAL, SIR," THE CHIEF OF STAFF told Tran Van Tra as he sat studying reports in a room inside a remote bamboo fortress. "One of the senior Chinese observers has been killed."

"Yes?" the general said, not yet greatly disturbed.

"Our soldiers who witnessed this report that it was *Long Tra'ng du K'ich*," the chief of staff added.

"What news do we have of the initiatives against this man?" General Tran asked.

"We have issued the reward flier, as you instructed," the colonel said. "Three years' pay for either the sniper or his captain should certainly increase initiatives."

"What about direct action?" the general asked.

"Missions directly after this man? Nothing, sir," the chief of staff answered.

"In two days we will return to my field headquarters," Tran said. "Brigadier Le and Colonel Ba should come to discuss this with me. Be sure that they understand that this is not a casual invitation."

The edge to the normally soft-spoken general sent a chill through the chief of staff. The colonel knew that one should not let Tran's quiet, gentlemanly presence mislead him. He hurried to the aide-de-camp, quickly scrawled a message and instructed him to ensure that the communications officer handled the dispatch with his highest priority.

"Gunny Wilson!" Jim Land bellowed as he stormed his way into the sniper headquarters. His voice echoed across Hill 55, causing the hair to raise on the gunnery sergeant's neck. Land nearly broke the screen door when he slammed it shut, so Wilson cautiously peeked inside the hooch before stepping across the threshold.

Land rummaged through the file cabinet, cursing under his breath.

"I need about half a bottle of aspirin to clear this headache a certain wiry, little black-haired sniper has given me," Land growled.

As the captain pulled the lid off the large glass bottle and dumped four white tablets in his hand, he looked at Wilson. Popping the pills in his mouth and swallowing them without water, Land said, "What's the latest on Hathcock?"

"Sir, the last report in on him is two probable kills this morning," Wilson said. "He claims one was a high-ranking Chinese officer—possibly a colonel. They have sent out ground units and air to try and recover the body."

"I am sure it has endeared him even more to 7th Marines," Land said. "I know it must have the enemy thrilled."

"He has patrolled daily since the four other snipers came home," Wilson said, hesitantly, not relishing the task of telling on Carlos. "The gunny I talked to told me that Sergeant Hathcock will come in with one squad, catch another going out, and fall right in with them without even taking his pack off. That gunny's concerned."

"Me, too," Land said in a low voice. "Did you know

that the NVA and Charlie have a bounty out on Hathcock and me? A big one? Several grand?"

"No, sir," Wilson answered.

Then the captain unfolded a handbill that the 1st Marine Division's senior intelligence officer had given him that morning. He spread it flat on the field desk and spun it around for the gunny to read.

"They have our names from a real wet kiss of a story published a couple of weeks ago in the *Sea Tiger*," Land said. "Wonderful headline about Hathcock and company wrecking havoc on Charlie and the North Vietnamese."

"Is this correct, sir?" Wilson asked, reading the translation written in ink below the printed words. "That's got to be, like, twenty thousand dollars?"

"Ballpark," Land said. "Three years' pay. Officers' pay. That's for either my scalp or Hathcock's. Colonel Poggemeyer told me to not even consider extending here. So I'm gone in a month.

"I think it's time for Sergeant Hathcock to pack up and come home. I want you to go and get him—put him under arrest if you have to—but bring him home. I want him standing tall in front of my desk by tomorrow afternoon."

"You want me to arrest him, sir?"

"That's right, Gunny. I want you to hog-tie the little shit, if you have to. But he's coming home. He'll kill himself out there. The dummy won't stop unless I lock him up or Charlie puts a bullet in his head. I'll be go-to-hell if I'm gonna lose him now.

"You had better go and make your travel plans. See if you can get air—maybe a MarLog[2] flight."

THREE DAYS LATER, GENERAL TRAN VAN TRA sat behind an oak desk at his command headquarters. Two

---

[2]An acronym formed from Marine Logistics, used to describe daily resupply/administrative support flights.

flags hung at angles from staffs behind him. On the left sat a banner divided horizontally by a red field on top and a blue field on the bottom, with a large yellow star in its center. On the right was a slightly larger solid red flag with a great yellow star in its center. The flags represented the Popular Liberation Front, for which the People's Liberation Army—commonly called Viet Cong—fought, and the Socialist Republic of Vietnam, for which the North Vietnamese forces fought. He quietly wrote in a journal with a black mother-of-pearl fountain pen.

"Gentlemen," he said, raising his head and screwing the cap on his pen. "Please forgive me for making you wait."

Colonel Ba and Brigadier General Le stood at attention at his door.

"Please come inside and sit," the general said standing and politely gesturing with his left hand toward two chairs positioned across a small mahogany coffee table from a single chair.

The officers walked to the chairs and waited until General Tran had sat down before sitting themselves.

As the general withdrew a cigarette from a blue pack, the two officers likewise took out cigarettes of their own. The aide-de-camp brought in a tea service, pouring first a cup for Colonel Ba, then Brigadier Le, and last General Tran.

"What can you tell me about this problem we have in your combat sector?" the general began. "It seems that with each passing week, I discover that these American assassins become more troublesome. Our latest embarrassment is the assassination of a visiting colonel from the People's Republic of China."

"They use very difficult tactics to counter, sir," Colonel Ba said. "One man, two men, will shoot from more than a kilometer away, and then disappear. It is like trying to capture a puff of smoke."

"In time, sir," Brigadier Le said, "we will eliminate

these men. They will make a mistake, and we will make them pay for it."

"I agree," General Tran said. "In time. However, in that time these Americans will become even more in numbers and operate with greater effect against us. We have lost many valuable soldiers, commanders, visiting officers, and allies. Must we lose more of them until that time comes? Consider also the impact that these guerrillas have on the morale of our units. I am told already that when many of our soldiers hear even a rumor that this American who wears the white feather has been seen in their sectors, they become fearful."

"I must disagree, sir," Brigadier Le said. "Our soldiers may have some anxiety about this insidious threat, but they are not fearful."

"Semantics, my friend," General Tran said. "This man Sergeant Hathcock is a distraction to them. Correct?"

"Yes, sir," Le said.

"Actually, more than just this man," Colonel Ba added. "Any time one of these soldiers kills even one of ours, it becomes very disruptive. The Americans have capitalized on the random nature of this tactic and its psychological impact.

"I agree with you, sir. We cannot well afford the luxury of time in this case."

"When we have a wildfire," General Tran said, "in most cases we find it ineffective to confront the blaze head-on with water hoses. We find that digging wide breaks and setting backfires proves itself the better tactic.

"I have already begun to implement what I hope is a more effective way of countering these assassins, especially the one you call *Long Tra'ng du K'ich*.

"In the north, a fourteen-man platoon of carefully selected soldiers is presently training at a hill identical to that from which these Americans operate. Our commandos will survive and operate mostly in solitaire without the luxury of most types of regular support.

They will live off the land. They will be phantoms in the forests.

"Paramount to their mission is the elimination of this Sergeant Hathcock and this Captain Land.

"We will disburse this elite group throughout the region where these assassins operate. Our men will hunt the two Americans, isolate them, and kill them."

General Tran paused to allow the two field commanders an opportunity to comment. With none forthcoming, he looked coldly at the colonel.

"You will personally command these men, Colonel Ba," the general said. "I give you the best that our forces can assemble. I expect success."

CARLOS HATHCOCK LAY ON HIS COT AND SIPPED WARM beer while reading *The Deep Blue Good-by*. John Burke, now halfway through *Nightmare in Pink*, had finished the first of the Travis McGee novels and had passed it to the sergeant.

Above his head a black and silver clock radio played the latest from Armed Forces Vietnam Radio at low volume. He had balanced the device on the narrow windowsill, securing it with two elastic, boot-blousing garters hooked into the wire screen. Broadcasted from the Da Nang station, Jim Reeves sang his wistful song about hearing the sound of distant drums and beseeching his girl, Mary, to marry him.

Flies buzzed against the door screen and soared inside the hooch, adding an irritating quality to the midday doldrums. They crawled on the sticky residue left on the lips of the empty beer cans that Carlos had tossed into a weathered and tobacco-juice-stained cardboard cookie box.

Gulping the last mouthful of hot beer from another can, Hathcock dropped it in the box and then felt for more beer in the nearly depleted case by the end of his cot. It was his third twenty-four-can package in the sixteen days since Captain Land had ordered him arrested, returned to Hill 55, and confined to his hooch "until further orders." The skipper had given Gunny Wilson money with which to buy the sergeant beer, to keep him on an alcohol-driven tilt and within the camp's confines.

Carlos tossed the book on the floor by his cot. Then he took the piece of finger-smudged paper that lay folded on the ammo-crate nightstand, opened it, and looked again at the pen and ink drawings of himself and Captain Land. He read the translations, again. He thought about the reward. Again. The seriousness of what this handbill represented had stuck in his mind for the past two weeks, ever since his captain had given the flier to him.

Not long after his return to Hill 55, Marines began dying outside their hooches on their way to the privy or the chow hall, struck down by enemy snipers' bullets. A gunnery sergeant had fallen near Carlos's door the very day that Captain Land had shown him the wanted poster with their names and pictures on it.

Hathcock had finally gotten Captain Land to allow him to walk down the finger below the sniper hooch, where he had built a sandbag-reinforced sniper hide. From that position, he had taken a few shots, and had made two probable kills. However, he knew that the only real way to stop this menace, or menaces, was for Burke and him to track this new enemy and kill him.

FAR TO THE WEST OF HILL 55, WELL BEYOND CHARLIE Ridge, Happy Valley, and Dodge City, on a flat grassland two miles across that began just past the downslope of the Annamite mountains, Colonel Ba addressed a dozen lean-faced guerrillas. Each man carried a long, bolt-action rifle fitted with a short telescopic site. The sniper weapons looked similar to many others used by Communist soldiers, except that these 7.62 × 55-millimeter Mosin-Nagant rifles with their 3.5 power PU scopes were new. Each of them hand-fitted and much more accurate than any others like them in Vietnam. Like their rifles, the men looked battle hard, lean-faced, and well-oiled. All of them experienced, efficient veterans.

A short, muscular guerrilla stood at attention two paces in front of the others and faced Colonel Ba, who walked to the end of the line of soldiers and began inspecting each man. After today, the elite platoon would return to the east where they would individually patrol until one of them had brought down the Marine sniper, who wore the white feather, and his captain.

Until today, the men had accompanied Colonel Ba's units as they patrolled near Da Nang and Chu Lai. Two of their group had already fallen.

For the past fortnight, the specially trained platoon had learned the lay of the land, as well as capitalizing on opportunities to inflict damage on the Americans and tax them psychologically. They had made shots that killed a gunnery sergeant, a staff sergeant, and more recently a captain on Hill 55.

Tonight, they would return to the east, fan themselves north and south of Hill 55, and hunt a wide territory, coordinating their tactics to kill Carlos Hathcock and Jim Land. They would live off the land, sleep in trees, in caves, on the ground. They would avoid contact with all other human beings, except when Colonel Ba's patrols checked on their status at prearranged intervals.

Not only did these twelve men feel honored to be a part of this small, elite tribe, but they held opportunity on the tips of their trigger fingers. Whomever among them killed Hathcock or Land would receive a great bounty for the men's heads.

9

Eluding Charlie

LONG SHADOWS CLOAKED THE WESTERN SLOPES OF Hill 55, giving Carlos Hathcock what he considered an edge.

With the sun rising behind him, and the resulting shade cast by the mountain covering where he lay, the Marine sniper could easily see any movement in the valley or among the small knolls and hillocks beyond. Meanwhile, an adversary must struggle to see him, having to face the low-angle morning light and high-contrast darkness below it.

In the still air, he could hear dogs barking outside the huts at the edges of the rice fields. An old man coughed. Another spoke. The smell of burning wood drifted from the farmers' homes as the people who lived there prepared breakfast before another day in the patchwork of rice fields below Hill 55.

Behind him, muffled voices and laughter came from the encampment of Marines who had also begun a new day. Music from radios carried down the slope to Hathcock's ears. Farther back, the whistling, throaty growl of truck engines firing to life mixed with the thumping grind of helicopter blades turning. Their din began to mask the quieter sounds.

Slowly the shadow across the west side of Hill 55 crept away, leaving yellow light that warmed the day as flies swarmed the bushes. The heat dried the thin fog that had only moments earlier lay like sheer chiffon over the cool draws and dips beneath the shade.

Each day had begun the same for the past week that Jim Land had allowed Hathcock to work from the sandbag hide far below the sniper hooch. The captain thought that it kept the restless sergeant occupied while still providing him with relative safety from the enemy. In that time four more Marines had suffered wounds and another had died from the sniper fire that came almost daily now. Carlos held hope that one morning he might get lucky and see the guerrillas that had now claimed the lives of four Americans who had believed themselves safe behind the wire on Hill 55.

Throughout each day, Hathcock munched round crackers spread with cheese or peanut butter from a C ration can. He sipped water and watched and waited. Nothing moved except the unarmed farmers below him.

Jim Land had already packed and sent many of his personal belongings homeward. He had his orders to report to inspector-instructor staff duty with the Marine Corps reserves in the Boston area. Major D. E. Wight had just reported to 1st Marine Division, and now began his check-in process at headquarters on Hill 327, due west of Da Nang, and directly north of Hill 55. Soon, he would move south and join the snipers as their new officer in charge.

By noon, Carlos felt drowsy. He could see Lance Corporal Archer and the long line of his squad snaking its way home from a patrol that they began a morning ago. Surely, if an enemy sniper lurked nearby, he would have taken a shot by now at one of Archer's crew, from 3rd platoon, Company B, 1st Battalion, 26th Marines. They sauntered lazily up the slopes to an entry point in the defensive wire that surrounded the lower reaches of Hill 55.

Carlos watched the Marines, and glassed the countryside, looking for anything that might signal danger to these friends. They were his favorite of all the small units that worked with him.

Although a dark, hulking man of mostly African heritage, Archer's eyes shone pale blue. Because of this, anyone who met him even once remembered him. He had joked with Carlos and Burke that if he ever chose to be a stickup man, he would certainly have to wear sunglasses on a heist.

However, once a person came to know Archer, the quality of the man became far more memorable than his unusual eye color. Although only a lance corporal, he held a sergeant's billet, and performed the job extremely well. He was a fearless leader, bold with inner strength and iron determination. Time and again he proved himself faithful. Dependable. True to his word. For those reasons, Carlos greatly respected the lance corporal, and regarded him as highly as he did Burke, a Marine so close he cared for him like a brother.

A sniper team could find no better patrol to guard their rear security. Archer never let an enemy even come close.

Hathcock smiled. He recalled an afternoon patrolling with Archer only a few weeks ago. An enemy platoon had disappeared into a tree line, and had taken an ambush position beyond a flat of rice paddies, across from the place where Carlos and Burke had hidden. The squad leader offered to move his patrol into the open fields to draw fire, so that the two snipers could pinpoint the enemy for artillery and direct fire.

"Oh, no," Carlos said, laughing. "You'll get somebody hurt doing something like that. Just watch our backs. We'll get 'em."

Archer lumbered near the center of his patrol, several paces ahead of a Marine who had a radio strapped to his back. Carlos thought a man might as well paint a bull's-eye on his shirt as carry a big radio. Radios and pistol belts drew enemy bullets like a magnet in a sack of nails. They represented two of the three primary target objectives a sniper always sought: Deny the enemy access to crew-served weapons, deny him communications, and deny him leadership. Pistol belts and radios represented leaders and communicators. Carlos always took them out first.

Hathcock raised his binoculars and began to scan the valley, hearing Archer's men laugh and wisecrack as they ambled through the gate. They were headed for their hooches where they could finally rest after a full day and a half of patrolling.

Carlos saw a white puff of smoke burst from a clump on the top of a hillock, then he heard the sound of the rifle. Almost simultaneously, one of Archer's Marines screamed. Hathcock looked across the ridgeface and saw one man on his back, his legs kicking. Two of his brothers knelt at each side of him, holding the wounded Marine.

Then came the second shot, and a third.

Another of Archer's men fell.

"I see the hamburger," Carlos said to himself, placing the crosshairs of his rifle scope on the black-clothed shoulder of an enemy guerrilla who lay in a grassy clump on the small knoll across the valley.

In the second that Hathcock squeezed his shot, he saw clods and dirt and grass fly next to the enemy soldier's head. Then nothing moved.

The sergeant squinted through his telescopic sight, trying to see the enemy, when suddenly pieces of rock and wood exploded left of him, sending debris into his eyes. He had no more than turned his head when from the right a second bullet struck, splattering in the sandbag an inch below his elbow.

Then, from the low rise where the first shots came, wounding the two men in Archer's squad, another shot popped and then blew across the valley. Carlos felt the rush of air and heard the crack of impact as the bullet landed in the hillface a foot above his head.

"They shot those men to draw my fire," Carlos said to himself as he curled behind the sandbags and waited for the machine guns behind him, at his right and left, to open on the enemy positions. "Set up three ways, and then suckered me to show myself."

The heavy, cyclic boom of the .50-caliber machine guns, and the more rapid chops of the .30s began to thunder across the valley at the enemy guerrillas. Hearing their reports, Hathcock peeked over the top of the sandbags and watched the red streams of tracer bullets arching to the knolls directly across from him and to his right and his left.

Several Marines rushed down the trail to Archer's patrol and helped carry the two wounded men to safety. With the opportunity to move under the cover that the suppressive fire of the machine guns gave him, Carlos tossed his spotting scope inside the small canvas pack that he carried, slung it and his rifle on his shoulder, and ran uphill, too.

He had no idea how many enemy soldiers had taken positions across the valley, but he did know they had put a lock on his location. No point in sitting any longer at the bad end of a VC shooting gallery.

Breathlessly, he dove over the sandbagged parapet of the gun position just below the sniper hooch where Burke Wilson, and a gunnery sergeant from the 1st Marine Division Interrogator Translator Team had also taken cover. Together they watched for enemy movement.

"Looks like that woman told it like it is," the ITT gunny said. He was a broad-shouldered man who, like others in his staff section, had shaved his head and wore a neatly waxed handlebar mustache.

"Woman?" Carlos said, lighting a cigarette.

"That old gal we took your bullet out of the other day," the gunny answered.

"Oh, yeah," Hathcock said, laying back against the sandbag walls and pulling out his canteen for a drink.

"The one that was cutting those NVAs' hair, and I shot her through the haystack."

"Uh-huh," the gunny answered. "And she told us about the dozen NVA sent here to wax your ass, and the skipper's."

"I picked out three gun positions, not twelve," Wilson said.

"I think I hit the one in the middle, too," Carlos added.

"It was coordinated though," Burke said.

"Yes," Hathcock answered. "I think they actually tried to draw me out for a shot, too."

"I'm going to talk to the skipper," Wilson said. "Tactically, a sniper has the advantage if he is in the offense, and better off if he is partnered instead of alone."

"Not always," Carlos said. "Sometimes alone is better."

"You're safer if you can move around," Wilson told Hathcock. "And better off if Burke here is next to you."

"I won't argue that," Carlos said.

"Me either," Burke added.

AN HOUR LATER, FOUR BLACK-CLAD VIETNAMESE guerrillas crouched next to a small cave, sharing a pot of rice with peppers, oil, and small bits of meat mixed in. The remaining seven of their group carried the body of the man Carlos Hathcock had killed westward. The soldier who led the patrol would inform Colonel Ba of the attack they had carried out, and that they had narrowly missed the one who wears the white feather.

The stocky leader of the group laid against the rockface next to the cave opening and wrote in a small brown booklet bound with cardboard and tape. He described the circumstances of his man's death, the time, date, and his name. He wrote how he had sent a patrol to turn the body over to Colonel Ba and his men, so that they could return the remains to Hanoi, should they desire, for the man's family.

He thought, as he wrote, of the many thousands of his comrades who lay in unmarked, communal graves.

He thought of how close they had come to success today. How his soldier had sacrificed himself drawing *Long Tra'ng*'s deadly fire, so that the others could make their shots at him. It was a good idea, but costly.

It had come to him a few days earlier when the sniper captain had stood in the open, guiding a tour of civilian-dressed news reporters. When Land had stepped in front of the sandbags, showing the reporters the .50-caliber machine gun set up with a telescopic sight, the Vietnamese sniper had fired. His bullet struck a rock below the American, splitting it and sending a shard into the captain's shin. Land had at first thought that the bullet had struck his leg.

The American dove over the top of the sandbags, while the reporters scattered for cover. The sniper simply slid down a trail from the knoll where he had hidden and slipped into a canal. Quietly, as he had done in the past, he allowed the current to carry him away to cover.

"SKIPPER," GUNNY WILSON SAID AS HE KNOCKED ON Jim Land's door. "You have a problem with me letting Burke team with Hathcock, and letting them be a little more maneuverable?"

"I'll allow it, but I want them to remain within the confines of Hill 55," Land said. "It is okay with me for them to move along any of the lower fingers, and to go outside the wire to a point. But they cannot venture beyond the hill itself. That means not across the valley. Not on the hills across the valley."

"That will work, sir," Wilson said. "I think Hathcock will be better off with Burke, and being able to maneuver."

Land nodded and turned his attention back to the

fitness reports he had begun drafting on the sergeants and staff noncommissioned officers under his direction. The captain felt blessed in this job since the reports nearly wrote themselves. He had nothing but the highest quality Marines. The difficulty, however, came with having to rate them against each other, and having to rate Hathcock in particular.

Of course, Land would particularly desire to serve with the sergeant in any situation. Especially in combat. He had found Carlos extremely desirable as a Marine. Always resourceful, dedicated, enthusiastic, mission-oriented. All the pluses a Marine should possess that he would rate outstanding. But what about the independent streak that seemed to grow stronger by the day? What about his fearlessness, reinforced by his attitude of invincibility? What about having to physically remove him from the field for his own safety and health?

Land then thought about himself. Colonel Poggemeyer had restricted him to the hilltop confines a few days ago. More or less to his hooch, after the incident where the sniper had narrowly missed him. The colonel had even ripped up his recommendation for Land to receive the Bronze Star.

The captain appreciated the colonel's concern for his safety, him so close to going home. But was it fair? He was simply doing his job to the best of his abilities. Just like Carlos was simply doing his job. Hazards come with the turf. One cannot do a good job as a warrior unless he accepts the hazards.

Land signed Hathcock's fitness report and looked through the screen door where Wilson stood talking to Master Sergeant Reinke.

"Top! Gunny!" the captain called to them. "Hathcock is off restriction. However, we must keep his situation in the fronts of our minds. Charlie wants Carlos's head."

Both men smiled at the skipper.

"Oh, and by the way," Land said in a casual tone.

"We don't need to mention anything about Sergeant Hathcock's restriction to Major Wight either."

TWO DAYS LATER, CARLOS HATHCOCK AND JOHN BURKE had eaten breakfast when the mess tent opened at four A.M., obtained passwords from Operations, and now stepped quietly in the remaining darkness, finding a hiding place on a low rise at the base of Hill 55.

Well below and left of the old sandbagged hide, Carlos hoped that its slight elevation above the tops of the knolls and low ridges on the other sides of the rice fields would give Burke and him the advantage today. With the two men in place well before daylight, no enemy could know where the sniper team lay.

No sun came with daylight. A gray overcast hugged the world, and as the morning wore on, a mist became a soaking, drizzling rain. Carlos Hathcock smiled. He liked these conditions for a hunt.

So did the North Vietnamese sniper who led the platoon charged with killing Hathcock and Land. Before daylight, he had slithered from thick grass into the stream that fed a canal bordering the many rice fields northwest and west of Hill 55. While Burke and Hathcock had crept through the foliage on the low knoll where they had hidden, the enemy guerrilla had pulled himself along the canal, hugging the bank until he came to the back of a hill, where he moved like a snake to its top and hid.

As the rain began to drizzle, the stocky, dark man hugged close to the base of a bush, minimizing the water that fell. It was a steamy rain, no wind, and fog drifted in and out of the draws and on the low, flat land between them. He opened his mouth, allowing the moisture that beaded and dripped down his face and off his nose to fall on his tongue. He ate nothing. He did not move. He only watched and waited for a target to offer itself to him.

Engines whined through the long day as trucks and

jeeps slid along the muddy road from the hilltop and wound eastward to Highway 1, just south of Da Nang. All day long they drove back and forth, moving equipment, supplies, and Marines to and from the hill and the city. None of the day's activities had offered a single opportunity until three figures appeared on a lower trail that led below several hooches built along the crest of a ridge that extended northwest from the hilltop.

When he began hunting for the Marine who wore the white feather, many soldiers walked along this lower trail. He easily picked shots. Now, rarely did he see a target there.

Carefully, he lifted his binoculars to his eyes and studied the three figures. The man to the far right wore a pistol in a shoulder holster. Two silver bars shined on each collar. The sniper smiled as he took his Mosin Nagant rifle, laid it snugly in his shoulder, rested his cheek on its level stock, and peered through its scope.

Using his toes to adjust where his sight post lay, he maneuvered his body until the sharp tip of the aiming point rested squarely on the captain's midsection. He closed his eyes and opened them to find the sight still on his target.

No expression crossed his face as he applied pressure to the trigger. Calm, peaceful serenity blanketed him as the firing pin released, striking the primer on the 7.62 × 55-millimeter cartridge and sending the 180-grain copper-jacketed projectile out the rifle's barrel, arching above the rice fields at 2,400 feet per second.

It took the captain off his feet, splashing him backward in the muddy path. In seconds a crimson river flowed down the trail as the Marine kicked but could make no sounds and could find no breath for his shattered lungs.

Another officer, a husky one with a square jaw, immediately stepped from the hooch thirty feet above the dying man. The sniper captain. The Communist soldier trained his scope on this new target and prepared to shoot, but at the same time a barrage of machine-gun fire danced up the knoll where he lay. He had to fall back.

As he had done so many times before, the guerrilla slid down the back of the hillock and into the canal where he again pulled himself through the water beneath the cover of the near embankment. Several hundred yards west of the knoll, the sniper stopped to look once again at the activity on the hilltop. Then on the far edge of the rice fields, he saw two figures sneak from the undergrowth and crouch behind a dike. From the long rifles that both men carried, he knew they were phantom hunters like himself.

The guerrilla knew he only had the time that the machine-gun fire from the American positions provided him. Once that ceased, the two hunters would begin their stalk. So he pulled himself along as quickly as he could without splashing.

Rain began to sheet and blow across the wide flatland, and he stopped to see the two American snipers now crossing the field at a dead run, directly to the knoll where he had hidden. They would easily find where he had lain, and the muddy scar on the back of the hillock where he had slid into the canal. Certainly these two hunters would follow him westward. He smiled. Perhaps the missed shot at the sniper captain would in the end garner him White Feather.

Now cloaked in darkness, and well up the slopes far beyond the wide flatland, the stocky brown man climbed to an overlook hidden by granite boulders. Hard rain continued to fall across the country, and he knew that the two snipers would likely hole up until light. So he waited in the shelter and cover that the rocks provided him. In the morning, from his hide, he could easily see them follow the clear trail he had left for them to track. It led to a cave where he had cleared a kill zone at its opening. Before daylight, he would move to the place where he had almost ritually hidden each time he killed an American on the hill, hoping that White Feather would follow him.

Tonight, as the storm pelted the land, he realized that tomorrow this rare quarry could likely fall into his sights, or he into theirs. As he dozed, he thought of that sickening possibility, and how he should avoid allowing his own traps to spring on himself. White Feather had not gained his reputation from being stupid. Unquestionably, he would see the obvious trail and try to flank it. Then the dark man began to smile. He would simply find a new hide where he could see the trap and its flanks.

By this time tomorrow one of them would be dead.

WHEN THE SHOOTING STARTED, JIM LAND HAD STEPPED to his hooch door to see the young captain lying toes-up with his life running down a muddy stream. He jogged to the sniper hooch while machine guns poured lead into the countryside below.

Two sniper teams had gone out today. One had returned just before the attack. Hathcock and Burke remained outside the wire.

Land squatted in the gun position with Wilson and Reinke, searching the world below with a starlight scope. The rain had made looking difficult. However, no sound of gunfire reassured the sniper leaders that their two men were most likely alive, and in pursuit of the enemy gunman.

It was after midnight when Jim Land finally stripped off his wet uniform and fell onto his cot to rest. Fatigue had him withered but not out. Sleep came fitfully.

Carlos and John waited until morning before they crawled from beneath a pile of dead wood where they had spent the night sleeping in shifts and eating peanut butter and John Wayne crackers. They needed light to follow the enemy sniper's trail.

Hathcock had worried that the rain had washed away any tracks or other sign. However, enough skid marks, broken twigs, and grass remained so that he and Burke could easily follow the man's path, which led from the stream up the slope of a high line of jungle-covered ridges and hills.

THE SHORT BROWN MAN WHO HAD SLEPT IN THE ROCKS, moved from his lookout when he saw the two snipers cross an opening through which he had purposefully led them. At a fast pace, it would take them half an hour to reach the area of his killing zone. At a sniper's pace, he anticipated their taking at least two hours, if not most of the morning.

He only sipped water. He had eaten nothing in a day and a half now. He would not eat or disturb anything until he had finished this hunt.

Carefully he crept across the trail he had left, which led to the cave opening and the six-foot-radius kill zone he had cleared in front of it. It might make tempting bait for a typical patrol, but he doubted that White Feather would expose himself in the clearing. But he would certainly approach it, and take a distant look.

After each step, he checked to make sure he had left no tracks, had broken no twigs, had left no marks a skilled hunter might follow. He stepped lightly across a shallow gully and made his way up a steep hillside to the hide he had used each time he had hoped to lure a pursuer by shooting a Marine. From that spot he climbed higher and left until he clearly saw the cave, the killing zone, and much of the trail he had left leading toward it. Now, hidden among granite boulders and densely growing vines, he waited.

Gnats and biting flies feasted on the guerrilla, yet he ignored the discomfort. With the growing, steamy greenhouse humidity that cooked yesterday's rain with today's heat, he knew that the two Americans who now slithered along his trail suffered equally, if not worse. One swat. One sneeze. One groan, and he would have them.

With his binoculars, he studied every inch of ground that led toward the cave. As the day wore toward noontime, the dark man felt anticipation begin to build within him. He focused on the feeling and pressed against it. Impatience could cost his life.

He concentrated on now. He cleared his head of daydreams. White Feather was coming. He had to see him first.

The dark warrior had covered the area above him and on the saddle at the top of the draw with rice. Birds twittered and feasted on it each day. Should anyone approach from behind, the flight of wings would warn him.

By noon, he had decided that the two Americans had gotten wise to his tactic and skirted around him, trying to open his flank. Quietly, he began to work his way uphill.

Then in the middle of the afternoon, birds in the saddle squawked and beat their wings into the air, swarming above the treetops and then drifting to the far right. He calculated that something lay to the left, so he went the opposite direction.

Quietly, he moved down the ridge into another draw, and slipped through tangled vines and thorn-covered bushes. At a place where vines covered rock drop-offs, where down-flowing water had washed away the soil, the dark man slipped. He fell only a few feet, but his foot struck a branch that cracked with a loud *pop*.

In a second, he heard the thudding of feet on the far side of the draw. The sound traveled uphill. He immediately moved down and across, hoping for a shot.

Watching uphill, the guerrilla began to smile. "Of course," he thought. "White Feather is merely trading ends of his kill zone."

The sudden crunch of breaking brush in the saddle told the dark sniper that his quarry truly hid at the top of the draw.

Raising up behind the rotted log where Hathcock and Burke had earlier hidden, the man in black focused his rifle's scope sight on the spot from which the noise had come. It was a mere flash, but enough to see the white feather fastened at the base of the crown of the American's bush hat.

Thoughts of wealth and fame rushed through the NVA soldier's mind as he pulled the rifle's trigger. His excitement caused him to jerk the trigger slightly instead of smoothly increasing pressure. The round went low and to the left of Hathcock.

Burke screamed from the sudden burning he felt on his hip. "Sergeant Hathcock! I'm hit!" The wetness that flowed from the painful spot frightened him.

"Burke, get up!" Carlos snapped, after examining his partner's wound. "That ain't blood, it's water. The bullet just grazed your hip and blew the bottom out of your canteen. Let's go! He's getting away!"

Missing his shot, the guerrilla knew he must put distance between himself and the two snipers. He ran full out into the trees and over the lower slopes of the ridge until he dropped into a deep wash, dug into the earth by many rains. In it, he dropped to his knees and crawled to a spot he knew well. From that place, he knew he could take one last shot, and if he missed, escape.

Hidden in the midst of tall grass, only his head, his hands, and his rifle exposed above the cover of the wash, the dark man trained his telescopic sight up the wide, clear draw where, if his enemy followed, he could certainly see him. It was the Americans' only route to him.

The sun drifted lower and lower to the hilltop, and made seeing up the draw difficult for the guerrilla. He cupped his left hand above his scope, shading out the direct light.

Then, through the weeds, he again saw the white feather contrasted against the dark green camouflage hat. Taking his left hand from the scope, and placing it under the rifle, the dark man laid the sharp point of the sight post directly beneath the brim of the sun-shrouded hat.

He smiled as he squeezed the trigger. Steadily increasing pressure. Waiting for the shot to break.

The NVA sniper never heard the sound of his rifle scope exploding, nor did he even have the chance to comprehend it when Carlos Hathcock's bullet shattered its way through the sight, into the dark man's eye, through his brain, and blasted out the back of his head.

Through his binoculars, Burke had watched the glint, sparkling almost like a mirror. Hathcock realized that no naturally occurring object would reflect the sun like that, so he laid crosshairs on it and squeezed off a round.

With the rifle's report, Burke saw the dark man reel backward. He watched him slam against the opposite side of the gully, his nervous system in a spasm, covering the ground, the bushes, the rocks, and the Mosin Nagant rifle with blood.

Although there was no other sign of an enemy, the snipers took their time, staying behind cover, as they moved to where the body lay.

"Burke, I just had a scary thought. What is the only way a person could make a shot like this?" Carlos asked his partner as he examined the dead man's rifle.

Burke looked puzzled, as though he missed something important. "What do you mean, Sergeant Hathcock?"

"Stop and think about it. He had to be sighting his rifle right at me in order for my bullet to pass clean through his scope and get him in the eye like that.

"Burke, this man was good. He was about as hard as they come. When you get down to it, the difference between me and him is I got on the trigger first."

Carlos Hathcock sat by the dead man and marked a map section where he had made this kill. He took the Mosin Nagant rifle with its blood-soaked stock and the glass blown from its scope, and carried it back to Hill 55.

The two men crossed the wire at midnight. Jim Land lay awake in his hooch when the duo stepped through his doorway and showed him the rifle. Hathcock tagged the weapon, hoping to bring it home, but someone else laid claim to it, and he never saw it again.

Jim Land left Vietnam. However, Carlos and John had plenty more time to hunt. After all, most of the NVA platoon charged with eliminating *Long Tra'ng du K'ich* still remained in the bush. Carlos knew they would be back.

10

Getting Short

COLONEL BA'S NIGHT PATROL FOUND THE BODY JUST after midnight, stiff from rigor mortis. Whoever had killed this man had also taken his map and notebook from his pocket, the small canvas NVA pack in which he carried ammunition and a first-aid kit, and his Mosin Nagant rifle. He dreaded making this report.

Three soldiers lashed the dark man's body to a pole that they fashioned from a young tree they had cut, tying his hands and feet to it, and then taking several wraps around the trunk of his body and his legs to snug him tight. The men did not talk. Their leader squatted and watched them work. His eyes gazed empty and sad.

White Feather killing the guerrilla from the special platoon several days earlier had carried little significance with Ba's men. After all, they realized that he had made himself vulnerable when he shot several times from the knoll. A man that had lain with him had returned fire in concert with his comrades hidden in the two flanking positions. Most average snipers could have made the shot that killed that NVA soldier.

However, this death today would impact everyone. Even Colonel Ba felt demoralized. No easy sniper shot here. This hunt had required great skill, remarkable cunning, and perhaps a bit of luck to eliminate this particular man. He had set the standard for the other men in the elite platoon. They emulated him.

With their leader killed, shot by the man they had sworn to hunt to his death, the confidence they had built from their rigorous training would now erode significantly. This Viet Cong warlord, who held the rank of colonel in the North Vietnamese Army, just as Brigadier Le and General Tran held their respective ranks, felt his legs begin to tremble. Rapidly, the quake moved through his whole body. If he felt panic, what must the soldiers in his command feel?

He watched his men as they finished knotting the ropes that held the dead guerrilla fast to the pole. He studied their faces, their gesticulations, their breathing. Colonel Ba had no doubt that the nervousness that charged him also swarmed within the spirits of his men. They too shook, and breathed fast, and hurried their hands, sweating, their eyes wide, their noses flared.

A solemness swept the ten guerrillas who remained in the elite platoon. Colonel Ba, as they did themselves, believed that no single man or pair of men could match the American who wore the white feather.

Brigadier Le expressed outrage to General Tran at the idea of spreading these men among other platoons. He insisted that persistence with their plan would bring success. After all, their tactics had taken them close to killing the sniper captain and White Feather several times. These ten highly skilled warriors, the best the North Vietnamese Army could select from their forces, would finally claim Hathcock's scalp. He must keep their platoon intact.

"Persist. Persist. Persist," Le stressed to the general, pounding his right fist into his left palm for emphasis each time he spoke the word.

However, Colonel Ba knew better. Brigadier Le was

a hopeless romantic. An idealist among hardened prag-matists. None of these men on their own matched Hath-cock. Ba politely retorted Le's confidence and told General Tran that persistence of the old plan would, with certainty, bring failure. One by one, *Long Tra'ng du K'ich* would kill these ten men, too.

The plan devised by Colonel Ba, the more experi-enced field commander who had risen from a lowly en-listed soldier to his present station of leadership, with great promise to rise much higher, called for organizing ten five-men squads. Each of the ten remaining snipers would lead these squads.

These squads would work in coordination, always prepared to encounter White Feather. Should one team make contact, the others would close with their sup-port. In this way, they could bring the skill and cunning of all ten phantom hunters and forty more disciplined warriors to bare on this illusive and deadly quarry.

Tran Van Tra agreed with the plan, but frowned at the thought of this prospect. How can one man require so much from them? Not only did he kill efficiently, but he caused great internal friction among the Communist forces. His cost of manpower far exceeded the numbers he took out of action.

"SERGEANT HATHCOCK," MAJOR WIGHT CALLED INTO the sniper hooch. "You and Staff Sergeant Roberts pack your trash, and catch a ride south. Got an operation near Phu Cat. You'll bivouac on a hilltop called Duc Pho."

"Now, sir?" Hathcock answered, raising on his el-bows where he lay on the floor.

"Now," the major said.

"What about my partner here?" Carlos said, smiling and pointing with his thumb to John Burke, who lay on the floor across the hooch from Hathcock.

"You and Roberts," Wight answered. "I want Burke to pick up with the new guys we have to train. You're too short, and he needs to get used to working with others."

Carlos looked at his partner and smiled. He put his right hand up, near his face, directly in his line of sight, and held his thumb and index finger nearly together, allowing only a slight gap between them.

"Short," Hathcock said, laughing. "I am so short I gotta use a stepladder to get out of the rack. I can walk under a snake's belly wearing a top hat."

Then Carlos paused and frowned, turning his eyes toward Gunny Wilson, who sat on a stool cleaning his rifle, which he had dismantled, neatly laying the parts on a grease-stained towel he had spread across the top of the field desk.

"No, Gunny, I take that back. I'm not short," Hathcock said, and laughed even harder. "I'm next!"

At Duc Pho, Staff Sergeant Roberts and Sergeant Hathcock spent the remainder of February sitting on a tall hill that overlooked a great flatland bordered on the west by high, jungle-covered mountains, and on the east by the South China Sea. Highway 1 ran north and south directly at the foot of this hill. Behind it, eastward, a patchwork of rice fields faded into sand and the beach. Just across Highway 1 and the western base of the hill, rice fields stretched northward and southward as far as a person could see, and extended westward to the edge of the jungle, and the first steep slopes of the Annamite mountains.

Viet Cong thrived in the mountains and surrounding jungles that edged the thousands of rice paddies. Thus the operation that Hathcock and Roberts had joined included an entire United States Marine Corps landing force.

At the end of February 1967, the force had claimed more than 1,000 enemy confirmed kills, and more than 1,000 listed as probable kills. Carlos Hathcock had gone to Duc Pho credited with sixty-five confirmed kills. He returned to Hill 55 on the first of March with seventy-five confirmed enemy dead to his credit.

Before Duc Pho, his longest confirmed kill was at nearly 1,200 yards. When he returned, he had a new record of 2,500 yards, more than double the distance. Among those longshot kills that he made from the hilltop, a twelve-year-old boy at more than 1,500 yards.

He had pushed and ridden a rifle- and ammunition-laden bicycle from the western jungles and deep valleys between the high ridges to the flatlands below Duc Pho. Carlos first noticed him as he tottered along the far end of a narrow roadway that stretched the length of a dike that divided the rice fields, and then wound into a small village next to Highway 1. As he drew closer, Hathcock realized he carried rifles on the bicycle.

The Marine sniper placed his first shot into the front wheel of the bike, sending the boy and his load spilling across the road. When the boy grabbed a rifle, snapped one of the several banana-curved magazines into it, and began to fire up the hill, Carlos killed him.

The vision of killing the small boy remained vivid with Hathcock the remainder of his life.

MARCH BEGAN DRY IN VIETNAM. THE TROPICAL SPRING season seemed more like July in Georgia for the Marines assigned to the 1st Marine Division Scout/Sniper Unit. Carlos Hathcock now spent most days lying on a cot he dragged outside, wearing only his shorts, letting the sun darken the rest of his body to match his arms, hands, and face.

News of his impact on the Communist forces had finally reached the reporters who covered the war for the world's wire services, newspapers, magazines, and broadcast networks. Hathcock did his best to avoid seeing any of them, and he refused to open his mouth for even the simplest questions. After all, he concluded, it had been an innocent enough looking article in the *Sea Tiger*, a Marine Corps newspaper printed in Da Nang by the III MAF Public Information Office, that had identified his and Captain Land's names and faces to the enemy.

That was last year, too, when he had far fewer kills and a much less notorious reputation.

Yet even in his silence, and the refusal of the 1st Marine Division and the III MAF to discuss snipers, the Associated Press finally put out more ink on Carlos. The short item appeared in many of the larger U.S. newspapers, including the *Raleigh News and Observer*, a major daily that Jo Hathcock had delivered to their home at 1303 Bray Avenue in New Bern, North Carolina.

The story had gone out in February, gleaned from idle-talking grunts, smiling at a friendly reporter who just wanted to shoot the breeze. Not an interview.

Jo Hathcock read the article while Carlos sat at Duc Pho in his mountaintop shooting position. Until then she had believed what her husband had told her. He instructed sniper school students.

Carlos had not lied. He had not told the whole truth either, which was as bad as a lie in Mrs. Hathcock's mind. She wrote him a fiery letter, and enclosed a copy of the newspaper clipping.

The story began:

A SCOUT-SNIPER with the 1st Marine Division in Vietnam earned praise from his commanding officer for "making life miserable for the Viet Cong." Sgt. Carlos N. Hathcock of New Bern is one of several "expert marksmen" credited with killing more than 65 enemy. Firing at ranges up to 1,125 yards, Hathcock and the "crew" have been picking off better than two enemy a day—without a friendly casualty.

Reading the clipping had made the young sergeant sick to his stomach. Yet he still believed the lack of information had been for Jo's own good. He was due to get home in a few weeks, and Major Wight had now begun to keep him inside the compound nearly every day.

He had this tour in the bag. Now all he had to do was stack BBs and wait.

DURING THE SEVERAL WEEKS SINCE WHITE FEATHER had killed the Communist sniper platoon leader, Colonel Ba had incorporated the men into the ten teams. He had them develop teamwork in the western mountains, ambushing Army Ranger and ARVN patrols well south of the country where the American sniper hunted.

With the hot winds of March, he moved them northward to Brigadier Le's headquarters, in the wide, flatland west of the mountains. Fifty men organized into ten small units that operated independently, yet in coordination so that when one struck the enemy, the others could fold in their support.

White Feather might win a tactical battle against one or two snipers, or even three or four. But he certainly had no chance against fifty hardened guerrillas.

CARLOS HATHCOCK AND JOHN BURKE HAD SPENT ST. Patrick's Day in the long valley beyond the first mountain ridges west of Hill 55. The same valley where they had taken their first sniper class in October. They had lain near the head of the long meadow, close to the spot where the students had made their first kills.

Now, as evening approached, the two snipers began to gather their equipment and return to the hill. Another empty day.

For nearly two weeks, enemy activity had subsided noticeably in the areas west and southwest of the snipers' base. At first it had given the Marines quartered on Hill 55 a respite. But after several days of hardly a gunshot or plume of smoke, men at the compound began to get edgy.

In the past three days that Hathcock and Burke had

hunted, they saw only a spotted boar hog that had obviously escaped his pen, and now sought the company of stray sows. He had thrashed his way through the brush behind the snipers, and Carlos had his pistol drawn, ready to shoot, when he saw the source of the noise.

The hog busily rooted his way past the pair, gouging subterranean morsels of tubers and grubs from the earth with his powerful snout. They watched him graze his way across the meadow, eating the grass, then turning the soil to get the roots, too.

"He'll eventually run into a bunch of VC who'll make pork chops and ribs out of him," Carlos told Burke as they watched the hog.

"They deserve him," Burke said. "I would never butcher a big old boar like that. Even if you castrated him and fed him for six months, his meat would still have that foul stink to it. If you tried to make sausage with him, you'd have so much spice and red pepper in it that you couldn't eat the stuff anyway. No, sir. I say let old Charlie have a feast on him."

Carlos began to chuckle, thinking about the hog a day ago. He had just finished fastening the top flap of his pack shut when Burke nudged the sergeant with his toe.

Slowly Hathcock turned his eyes and saw the five men emerge from the same tree line, perhaps the same trail, as had the VC patrol they annihilated here in October.

The sergeant flashed a wide smile at his partner.

Burke laid his cheek against the stock of Hathcock's sniper rifle, letting the scope's crosshairs settle on the back of the last man—a small fellow wearing green shorts and a black shirt. A turtle-shell-shaped, dark green pith helmet tilted on his head. He carried an AK-47, fully automatic assault rifle.

So did the guerrilla walking point. And as Carlos examined the three remaining soldiers with the spotting scope, he saw that two of them also carried the automatic rifles while the man walking in the center position of the line of five held a long rifle with a short scope attached to the top of its receiver.

Carlos looked at Burke, who had already begun back pressure on the trigger, and nudged him. The lance corporal released his finger and glanced up at his sergeant. The white feather in Burke's hat rustled in the breeze.

Hathcock held his palm toward his partner indicating for him to wait. He wanted these men well away from any quick cover. Armed with new rifles and with a sniper at the center position, these men were no ordinary VC patrol.

"Let them get well into the gap, almost to that little island of bushes," the sergeant whispered. "If they reach cover, I want them where I can see them leave, if they decide to do that.

"Once the point man is about ten or twenty yards from the bushes, drop the guy in the middle, carrying that sniper rifle. They look pretty well oiled, so make 'em count. I'll go to work on tail-end Charlie with your M-14."

Burke felt for the white feather in his bush hat, and rubbed it for luck.

Like nearly every Marine on Hill 55, and an increasing number at the surrounding outposts and fire bases, too, John Burke had begun wearing a white feather in his bush hat. It had become the fashion of the men who patrolled the bush to wear a white feather, after the news of the big bounty on Hathcock had spread.

Even officers wore them. And it did not matter if the Marine wore a bush hat or a helmet, he fastened a white feather to the band around the base of its crown.

The gesture made Carlos realize the closeness of his fellow Marines. They had painted targets on their backs to help protect their brother and confuse the enemy.

Hathcock nudged Burke with his heel, and whispered, "Go ahead and turn one loose."

The lance corporal's shot hit the patrol leader in the

neck, nearly taking off his head as his spine popped in two from the bullet's concussion.

Simultaneously, Carlos sent an M-14 round directly into the last man's chest, splitting his breast bone and destroying everything under it.

The remaining three guerrillas dashed for the island of bushes. The same bushes the October patrol had tried to make. The VC opened fire, sending bullets chopping through the brush and over the heads of the two Marines.

"Let's just lay quiet," Carlos said while branches and AK rounds popped overhead. "They'll try to run for it, eventually, and we'll get them. We got a full moon tonight, so let it get dark. Those hotdogs are done."

"They're just wasting ammo," Burke said, and was about to add to his comment when several automatic rifles began chattering somewhere in the distance behind them. The lance corporal's eyes widened and his mouth dropped slightly open. Carlos could read the fear that now began to express itself in John Burke's face.

"Sounds like company," Hathcock said. "I think Archer and his crew may have them tied up awhile in that ambush position they set up to cover our backs."

"I'm just glad they were bored enough to want to come hunting with us," Burke said.

Carlos cracked a smile at his partner. John felt better seeing it. He knew now that his sergeant was not worried.

"Let's keep sitting," Hathcock said. "We're going to get those hamburgers."

Suddenly gunfire opened from the tree line across the meadow, but well west of the island of bushes where the remaining members of the first VC squad hid. Red tracers arched through the evening sky, over the clearing, and chopped their way eastward in the tree line where the two Marines lay.

At the moment the rifle fire walked its way to the Marines' position, the three guerrillas darted from the small thicket and ran westward, trying to join their comrades who had now moved toward the snipers' left flank.

Less than 200 yards south of Hathcock and Burke, Lance Corporal Archer and his eighteen-man patrol began to fall back, closing their rear toward their two comrades, who opened fire on the three running men despite the hundreds of bullets that spattered and popped around them.

Carlos killed one of the guerrillas and John dropped the other two.

"I hope Archer's on the radio getting a little help," Hathcock said, now firing at Viet Cong who moved along the western end of the tree line from the north side of the clearing.

He had no more than finished the words when both snipers felt panic surge through their bodies as someone or something thrashed and ran through the dense brush and trees behind them.

"Keep your fire on them, Burke," Carlos said, turning the M-14 toward their rear, ready to shoot. "Try to keep them from getting around the end and on our left flank!"

Hathcock lay on his back, holding the rifle's stock in his armpit, leveling it waist high for an average height man. In the now-fading evening light, he could see the shape of a person, and then another. He also saw the round steel helmets on their heads and called out, "Archer!"

"Yo, Sergeant Hathcock!" the lance corporal responded. "You two alive?"

"No, we're ghosts talking to you!" Burke growled in a loud voice, still firing at the advancing VC.

Carlos rolled back to his belly and opened fire again with the M-14. He dumped his pack filled with loaded magazines and loose rounds on the ground between Burke and him.

"Hope this little bit of what we have lasts," the sergeant said. "I think all Archer's boys have are M-16 rounds and M-60 belts. And I don't want to be trying to yank rounds out of those machine-gun belts with this bunch coming at us."

Archer slid to Hathcock's left and opened fire.

"We radioed operations when the shooting started," the lance corporal told Hathcock. "I told them we would consolidate and set up a defense with you. I hope I gave the right grid coordinates."

Carlos looked at the Marine and said, "Let me see your map."

He unfolded it and compared it to his own. Then he smiled at his friend.

"These numbers what you gave?" the sergeant asked.

"Uh-huh," Archer said, nodding his head.

"That red spot is us," Carlos said, pointing to Archer's map. "If you read those coordinates, you did good."

Archer smiled.

"We have a little close air support coming, and a couple of choppers with about seventy or eighty reinforcements, after the F-4s get finished," the squad leader said, showing his teeth and raising his eyebrows.

Carlos shot two more Viet Cong, and Burke killed three.

WHEN THE PAIR REPORTED TO TOP REINKE, JUST BEfore midnight, the master sergeant bear-hugged them both. Then he frowned.

"I gotta go let Major Wight know you're back, and alive," he said. "He wants a word with you, Sergeant Hathcock."

While Burke cleaned gear and put it away in the sniper hooch, Carlos and Top Reinke reported to the major, who sat, still in uniform, behind a field desk, writing in the light of a small candle. He looked up as Hathcock snapped his heels together and locked his closed hands at his sides, along his trouser seams.

"You're on restriction, Sergeant," the major said in a quiet voice.

"That it, sir?" Carlos said. "I can tell you what happened."

"That's it, Sergeant," Wight said, again in a quiet voice. "I heard, already. I'll read your after-action report tomorrow."

Hathcock struck his heels together again, took one step backward, then placed his right toe behind his left heel, spun smartly in an about-face, and marched to the door.

"Oh, and one other thing, Sergeant," Wight said. "I don't think it is a good idea to sunbathe on that cot anymore. Those snipers may well have come back to this roost."

"Aye, aye, sir," Carlos said, almost chuckling, and walked to his hooch, where Burke had just finished cleaning the sergeant's rifle and now had the M-14 dismantled.

THAT SAME NIGHT, COLONEL BA KNELT WITH HIS HEAD down, listening to the report from his men. At least one-third of the fifty-man unit had fallen from the American patrol's direct fire, and from the bombs and napalm that followed. When they saw three helicopters land at the bend of the long meadow, the Communist soldiers retreated with their wounded.

Certainly, Brigadier Le would gloat. Ba dreaded seeing him in just over a week.

IN THE FOLLOWING DAYS, HATHCOCK PACKED MOST OF his personal belongings and only used what he absolutely needed during his last few days in Vietnam. He thought of home, Jo, and his baby boy. Some men talked about extending in-country, and continuing their dance with the devil. Not Carlos Hathcock.

He had promised Jo he would not reenlist.

*   *   *

Sweat beaded on Hathcock's brow, and then he felt something cool and wet cover his forehead. He opened his eyes and saw the dim light and a person reaching across his head. He could hardly breathe now. His lungs rattled and hurt with each shallow breath he drew.

He remembered the snake once again. Its green, cold head raising in front of his eyes. Its black and red forked tongue flicking, tasting the air, looking for food or danger. Even when he and Burke hid in the tree roots, even when they had spent three days in Elephant Valley pinning down an entire North Vietnamese Army company—even those times he had not felt the panic, the fright surge through his bloodstream that he had felt when he faced that snake. When he crawled for three days across open ground, with enemy patrols walking within feet of him.

That ordeal had frightened him most.

Only days before leaving Vietnam, at the end of his first tour, an enormous captain, a man who seemed to stand as tall as one of the blackjack pines behind his grandmother's house, and broad as a barn, came to him and had asked him to volunteer to kill one more man. An enemy commander. An enemy commander at his own headquarters. At his own headquarters that lay in the middle of a wide flatland with nothing but grass growing around it for more than 2,500 yards in any direction.

He had to take the mission. Even though they called it volunteering, Carlos knew he had no choice. Who else would they send? Burke? More than likely, since next to Hathcock, he was the best.

But Carlos knew he could not live with himself if he turned down the job and Burke went, and died. No, he had no choice but to go. And he knew full well his chances of getting out alive were beyond any odds-maker's estimation. Less than nothing. Shooting the man presented less of a problem in Hathcock's mind. Escape posed the challenge.

Yet he *did* pull out the miracle. He covered himself with dense camouflage, native grass from the flatland that he gathered in the evening and fastened onto his uniform through small slits he cut with a knife. Then he crawled at the speed a minute hand moves on a clock. Crawled for three days, more than 1,500 yards to his firing point.

He lay there until the enemy commander walked from his headquarters with his aide, both men in full uniform. As this high ranking enemy officer walked away from the large house surrounded by hooches and huts and sandbagged gun emplacements, manned by more soldiers than Carlos could count, he sent a single, deadly shot into the general's chest.

Hathcock had found a low and very shallow draw that led to the tree line. He could hardly discern it, yet he knew that his chances were best if he could quickly crawl on his belly along that low, grass-covered wash to the tree line.

The single shot had left the Communist force tasked with defending this headquarters completely confused. All that they heard was the pop of Hathcock's bullet as it struck their senior field commander. None of them had any idea from which direction the shot had come.

Dozens of uniformed and nonuniformed soldiers swept around the compound several hundred yards. However, they failed to go far enough and this Marine who traditionally wore the white feather, except on this mission, slipped away.

Carlos left Vietnam a few days later.

As he lay in the bed, sick with pneumonia, near death, he tried to smile. He thought of how good it had felt to go home.

11

Home and Back

IT SEEMED LIKE JUST YESTERDAY, YET A LIFETIME AGO, when Carlos Hathcock first set foot on the ground at Chu Lai, Republic of Vietnam. And now the feelings he encountered, as he returned to the place where he began this war, whirled beyond description. The details of stepping on the tarmac at the Chu Lai airfield remained as vivid as though he had done it yesterday, yet so much had happened in this past year. He experienced a lifetime's worth of living and dying compressed into twelve months, and now he felt like an old veteran recalling his past for his grandchildren.

Jo and Sonny had kissed him good-bye a year ago when he boarded a plane at New Bern, North Carolina, and now, in less than a week, he would step off the same cramped, twin-engine Piedmont Airliner, at that same rural coastal Carolina airport and kiss his wife and son again. A lifetime lived between yesterday and today. He felt uneasy about it.

Now the year had come full circle as the sun disappeared behind the hills west of Chu Lai, and Carlos sat on a bamboo chair, looking out across the runways and taxiways.

In the distance, two F-4 Phantoms turned up their engines to a deafening roar, filling the air with black smoke as their pilots proceeded through their pre-flight checks. The roar of the planes dropped to a dull rumble and Carlos turned his head toward them to watch their takeoff roll.

Slow to start, the two planes gained speed and Carlos strained his neck to see the thirty-foot long blue and orange flames that shot from beneath the aircraft tails like four gigantic Bunsen burners. As the pair of 40,000-pound jet fighters turned high and right, departing the air traffic pattern, he could see inside their engines and the fiery hell that churned within them was like thunderous blast furnaces streaking through the late evening sky. The awesomeness of their great power made him feel insignificant.

As he watched the orange lights disappear in the gray darkness, he thought of the men who rode atop the twin kerosene-burning turbines and how fragile they were compared to the engines that rocketed them skyward with 44,000 pounds of thrust. They truly were brave men to harness their souls to such fiery chariots.

Carlos listened as the roar of their engines faded in the distance and fell subordinate to the whistling whine of two A-4 Skyhawk attack jets that settled on the runway, their long landing gear outstretched like the talons of their namesakes as they came home to roost. They had flown close air-support missions this evening, dropping napalm on jungle-covered ridges, burning Charlie as he hid there. Carlos had seen the napalm attacks before, and recalled the foul stench of the flaming jelled gasoline and burning humanity.

Feeling to his side, Carlos grasped the neck of a quart bottle and raised it in a toast to the two Marine Aircraft Group-12 planes as they taxied off the active runway, hurrying toward their aviary of high-stacked oil drums on the edge of the tarmac where Marine mechanics waited ready to service the war birds and prepare them for their next sorties. He turned the two-thirds-full bottle of Jim Beam bourbon straight up and dumped a healthy slug into his mouth. As he gulped the warm, brown spirits down his throat, his eyes filled with tears from the fire that gushed its way to his stomach.

"Ooooh weeee! Mighty fine, yes, sir. Mighty fine," Carlos said to a Marine who sat in a bamboo chair of similar design and who gulped whiskey, too.

The Marine who sat next to Carlos also waited for the eight A.M. "Freedom Bird" to Okinawa. There they would connect with their overseas flight that would return them to Camp Pendleton, California, and release them from active duty.

"Less than twelve hours we ain't gonna be short no more. We gonna be gone!" the Marine said in a whooping laugh. "Just think! We are so short, that in the morning, when we get up, we're gonna have to use a stepladder to climb outa bed."

Half-drunk already, Carlos chuckled. "Yup. I'm so short that I could walk under a snake's belly while wearin' a top hat and standing on stilts."

"Hell, Carlos. We ain't short. We're next!"

Both Marines lifted their bottles in a toast and gulped down another slug of whiskey. "*Ohhhhweeee*, that cat's got a barbwire tail," Carlos said, blowing hard.

"In three days we'll be at Pendleton, a couple of days after that, I'll be home. I figure this time next week I'll be a PFC in the 1st Civ Div."

"What? PFC?" Carlos asked.

"Yup. Proud Fuckin' Civilian!"

Carlos laughed loudly.

"Hell, Carlos. I was thinking about it today and feeling real bad because I have a whole week more to wait before I'm out. But after this year here, I don't think they could do anything to me that would get me down, except cancel my ticket out of here tomorrow.

"As long as we get back to the World, I don't care how many days we stay at Camp Pendleton. At this point I figure I could stand on my head and stack BBs."

Carlos took another slug of whiskey and wiped his mouth with the back of his hand. "Tonight, I'm on a search for oblivion. And I think I'm getting close."

He leaned back in the chair and stared up at the clear night sky scattered with stars that disappeared into the South China Sea.

Both Marines staggered on the flight the following morning—drunk and still happily in oblivion. They felt lucky to be on the plane and alive.

Neither Marine had slept the night before—they drank instead, celebrating their departure from Vietnam. Aboard the plane, they continued laughing and joking, still feeling the effects of the bottle of Jim Beam bourbon and the bottle of Johnny Walker scotch.

Carlos and the Marine sat across the aisle from a major who kept looking at them as though he knew them but could not place their faces. Hathcock noticed the officer watching them and gouged his elbow into his partner's ribs, alerting him to tone down his revelry.

"Major, do we know each other, sir?" Carlos asked.

"I'm not sure, but you look awfully familiar. I'm just trying to place your face," the major said.

"Sergeant Carlos N. Hathcock II at your service, sir. 1st Marine Division Scout/Snipers."

"That's it!" the major said. "Hill 55. You worked there with Captain Jim Land."

"Yes, sir," Carlos said, extending his hand to the officer who shook it, smiling.

"I've heard a lot about you snipers. I don't know how much is true, but I've heard a lot of good sea stories."

The major paused and squinted his eyes. "So you're Hathcock. I've heard about you. Got a lot of kills—most of anyone in-country, from what they say."

"I suppose," Carlos said, feeling uneasy with the direction the conversation had taken. "I really don't put much stock in body count. Confirmed kills, probable kills. I never went after numbers. I just did my job."

"Me, too," the major said as the plane shuddered

under the strain of its engines as it began its takeoff roll. "I had a battery of one-five-fives up in your area. I got promoted and they sent me down here. I worked at the Task Force X-Ray command center for the rest of my tour.

"I don't mean it as an insult or anything, but I don't see how you snipers rate so much hype. It's like you're the deadliest thing since the Cobra, to hear the troops talk. So what's the big deal? You guys do a good job of providing security and I guess a special hit now and then. But for real killing power, you have to agree, a 155-millimeter Howitzer does the best. You want to talk about blowing away VC, I know for a fact that I have killed more men in one day than you have killed on your entire tour in Vietnam."

"Sir, that may be true. And I mean no disrespect," Carlos said, pausing for a moment and looking sternly at the major, "but when you killed all those men, did you look 'em in the eye when you did it?"

The major turned away and said nothing more. It was true that his kills were always distant and done with a great deal of anonymity. He never saw the individual faces of the people his guns destroyed—it was always a grid coordinate, a faraway speck. The idea of watching a man, looking at his face—his eyes—seeing into his soul as the bullet struck him dead had never seemed an issue until the sniper asked him that question. A question that he could only answer, no.

Carlos sat back in the seat, closed his eyes, and slowly drifted into a deep sleep.

He awoke with a jolt as the plane's wheels touched the runway at Kadena Air Base, Okinawa.

His head throbbed with the 86-proof hangover that his all-night celebration had bought. The scorching heat and humidity sent his stomach turning as he stepped down the metal stairs and walked across the concrete tarmac to where the enlisted Marines lined up, four deep, in a formation.

It felt strange to walk across an open area, as though

he stepped outdoors naked and no one cared. There were no sandbags in the windows of the formed concrete buildings. There were no weapons. The walls and buildings had no pockmarks from ten thousand bullets fired by a hidden enemy. There was no rubble of war. It was peaceful. And that made him feel uneasy.

Carlos stood in the formation of Marines and waited for a staff sergeant to call his name. He was glad that his last name started with *H* rather than *W* since the humidity and scorching midday heat that reflected up from the concrete made his hangover nearly unmanageable.

By the time the troop transport trucks reached Camp Hansen, many of the Marines who surrounded Carlos had formed their plans for liberty that night in Kin Village, a bar district just outside the camp gates. There were prostitutes, floor shows, and cheap beer in bars that remained open until dawn. Carlos listened and could only think of lying in the barracks and getting well. He felt awful now.

Flights left Okinawa each Wednesday and Friday morning at eight o'clock. "Freedom Birds" seemed to depart always at eight o'clock in the morning. The twenty-three-hour flight to Norton Air Force Base, California, and then the two-hour bus ride to Camp Pendleton ended well into the night. The out-processing there continued another two days and finally, on a Saturday afternoon in April of 1967, Carlos walked aboard a Boeing 727 bound for Washington, D.C.

He barely made connections at National Airport and caught the last Piedmont Airlines plane headed south that night.

The propeller-driven Convair aircraft taxied to a halt in New Bern at a few minutes past midnight. He sat alone in the back of the plane and looked out the Plexiglas-covered window, trying to see if Jo and Sonny were there to meet him. Floodlights shone from the eaves of the terminal and made it difficult to tell who was who.

No one on the plane had spoken to him; they recognized that he was a serviceman and left him alone. He waited until the pushing mass of passengers had almost all made their way through the doorway on the side of the airplane and then reached under his seat and dragged out his green vinyl satchel with yellow handles and USMC written on the side, and walked out of the plane.

No one greeted him. No one asked him of the battles he had fought. No one cared that he was a veteran returning home from war. He was just another traveler coming home to New Bern that night.

As he walked through the gate, he saw Jo standing there, holding their son and smiling, thankful that her husband had survived and had come home so that they could build a new life. Carlos took his son in his arms and kissed his wife.

The greeting lasted a moment and no one else took notice of him.

He took a sea bag and a vinyl suitcase from the baggage claim and left the airport, bound for his little house on Bray Avenue, a brand-new job with an electrical contractor, and a new life as a civilian.

"CARLOS! YOU BETTER HURRY, HONEY. THEY'LL BE BY to pick you up before you know it," Jo called as Carlos finished dressing.

The smell of bacon, eggs, and fresh coffee filled the small house on Bray Avenue. For Carlos, it was the morning that he had dreamed about while lying in the rain and mud of Vietnam. A reason to come home.

Yet as Carlos pulled the laces tightly around the hooks on the upper portion of his old combat boots, he felt out of place. This was something new. He was starting fresh, just as he had done eight years ago when he left Arkansas for the Marine Corps. Eight years gone in the Corps and nothing to show but a few wrinkles around his eyes.

His new boss hired veterans. He believed in giving them a preference, but Carlos knew that in order to stay on, he had to learn the business of electricity. And the idea of electricity didn't mix well with him.

Carlos dreaded being shocked, and he knew that for electrical workers it came with the turf—electricians get shocked regularly. Thus, each morning, he left for work with uneasiness lurking in the shadows of his mind.

"Your lunch is on the counter," Jo told Carlos as he sipped the last of his coffee and left the breakfast table to meet his ride this Monday morning, his second week of civilian work.

"Bye-bye, honey. I love you," Carlos told Jo as he left the kitchen.

His toddling boy stood at his side, and Carlos rubbed his little blond head. He looked down at the child who clung to his khaki trousers, and marvelled at how much the boy resembled his mother.

"Lucky boy. Looks just like you," Carlos said with a smile. And then joked, "He could have looked like me."

"He's got your temperament," Jo said as a horn blasted in the street. "I'll see you this evening."

As Carlos settled inside the cab of the pickup truck, he thought of the past long weekend. He had taken Thursday and Friday off and had driven to nearby Camp Lejeune where he had watched the Marine Corps' Eastern Division Rifle and Pistol matches. There he met many of his old shooting partners from the Marine Corps team. He again saw that side of the Marine Corps that he loved and missed.

The weekend with his friends had planted a seed of doubt in his mind. In eight years he had anchored many roots in the Corps and now, as he rode down the bumpy street to a house that his boss had contracted to rewire, he thought of what he missed. The daily practice on the firing ranges, the daily jokes between friends, the competition, and the chance to win another national championship.

Before he had shipped out to Vietnam, Hathcock had begun shooting international small-bore competition.

A Marine major named Bill MacMillan had won two Olympic gold medals. That accomplishment by a fellow teammate had made Carlos realize that making the 1968 Olympic shooting team was a goal he could attain.

His mastery of small-bore shooting, however, ceased when he shipped out to war. And today he had almost forgotten that dream until he went to Camp Lejeune and had watched his buddies shoot.

The night that he returned home from the Stone Bay ranges, Carlos told Jo that he missed the Marine Corps already. From the tone of his voice, she knew that the odds of him remaining a civilian and staying out of the war had grown slim.

By nine o'clock in the morning, Carlos had already shed his shirt in the sweltering house. The shrill whine of a circular saw cutting through pine boards drowned out the country music blasting on a portable radio that one of the workers had set in the window. Sawdust filled the air and Carlos already felt gritty from the minute wood particles settling on his sweaty skin.

He sat on the floor and fed stiff copper wires through aluminum conduit. Across the room, another electrician screwed tight the bare ends of wires onto the plugs on the side of an electrical receptacle. Carlos watched a carpenter connect the power cord of his saw to a wall outlet near where the electrician worked. It looked funny to him. Didn't the man know that the circuits were dead, that he would have to use one of the heavy black extension cables from another part of the house?

When the saw started turning and the carpenter began cutting wood, Carlos became alarmed. So did the electrician as he looked up from his work.

Later that night, as Carlos sat on his front step with Jo and Sonny, he told her how lucky he had been to look across the room just as the carpenter plugged in his saw.

When the electrician looked up, he had allowed his screwdriver to touch the outside of the outlet box and grounded the hot wire to it. The sudden shock caused the electrician's muscles to contract. As a result, the screwdriver came hurling straight at Carlos's head. He ducked and the heavy tool slammed into the wall, missing him by inches.

"I think I was safer in Vietnam," Carlos said to his wife as he held his son on his knee and bounced him up and down, playing horsey.

"What does that mean?" Jo responded. "You want to go back into the Marine Corps?"

Carlos sat silent for a moment, looking at his son bounce. He felt a tightness in his stomach wrench into a hard knot with her response.

"Would that be so bad?" he asked. "I'm a competitive marksman and marksmanship instructor. I'm sure not volunteering to go back to Vietnam."

Jo was not surprised and readily accepted her husband's logic. He would always be a Marine, she knew it the day he came home from the rifle matches at Camp Lejeune. And she knew it was only a matter of time before he would confront her with his wish.

"Carlos, I knew what you were when I married you. I have never liked the Marine Corps that much, but I accept it. You are a Marine and you always will be a Marine. Don't feel like you're doing me and Sonny a favor by staying out and being miserable. I want you to be happy because that's what makes me happy."

By June he and his family had moved from New Bern to Quantico where he was assigned to the Marksmanship Training Unit and the Marine Corps' national champion rifle team.

Carlos continued shooting the .300 Winchester magnum rifle at 1,000 yards as well as the M-14 on the

National Match Course,[1] but he also began pursuing the international small-bore (.22 caliber) competition as well, hoping for a chance at the Olympics.

When he arrived at Quantico the Marine Corps matches had already ended. His only chance at making the cut to go to the National Championship Matches at Camp Perry, Ohio, would require his finishing with a medal in the most competitive military shooting contests of all: the Interservice Rifle Championships during July.

It was the first practice day after the July 4th holidays when Carlos came home following an exhausting workout on the 1,000 yard line of the blistering hot range they called "Death Valley," at Quantico's Calvin A. Lloyd Rifle Ranges, and met Jo waiting at the door, holding a letter with a Massachusetts postmark.

"Honey, you got a letter from Captain Land," she called to Carlos as he stepped out of his car.

Hathcock trotted across the lawn to the door, smiling. He had not heard from his friend since he left Vietnam, and he was anxious to read how Land was doing. He tore the envelope open as he walked in the door, stopping for a moment to pick up his little son and give him a bear hug.

He sat in an easy chair and listened to the six P.M. television news. A reporter spoke from atop the Continental Hotel in Saigon. During that portion of the news, he watched intently, hoping to hear of the 1st Marine Division and the war in I Corps.

---

[1]National Match Course consists of firing twenty rounds standing slow-fire from the 200 yard line at an "A" target with a twelve-inch bull's-eye and six-inch V-ring; ten rounds standing to sitting rapid-fire from the 200 yard line at an "A" target with a twelve-inch bull's-eye and six-inch V-ring; ten rounds standing to prone rapid-fire from the 300 yard line at an "A" target with a twelve-inch bull's-eye and six-inch V-ring; and twenty rounds prone slow-fire from the 600 yard line at a "B" target with a twenty-inch bull's-eye and ten-inch V-ring. Total possible score on this course is 300 points with sixty Vs.

Because he left so many friends behind, still fighting in that conflict, he felt an inkling of the anguish that his wife must have had to endure while he served there.

Carlos's eyes and ears were fixed on the television news as he held the unfolded letter, unread, in his left hand. The reporters spoke of escalation and greater numbers of Americans dying in a war that had turned several U.S. college campuses into fields of encounter between protesting students and the "Establishment."

During the commercial, Carlos looked at the letter that he now pressed flat on his lap.

The letter began:

> *Dear Carlos,*
>
> *I'm glad to see that you made it out alive. At first I heard that you got out of the Marine Corps, but now I see that you have made it to the Big Team. You deserve it my friend. You earned it.*
>
> *I can understand you leaving for a while, you were pretty well burned out I'm sure. I'm glad that you got back on your feet and reenlisted. The Marine Corps needs you.*
>
> *I wish this letter could be all good, but I'm afraid that I have some bad news. I got a letter from Major Wight the other day. He said that the sniper program is really working well. Burke got promoted to corporal and went to 1st Battalion, 26th Marines, and took charge of a squad. He was really proud.*
>
> *Burke and his men got assigned security duty up at Khe Sanh and ran into trouble. Carlos, Burke got killed.*
>
> *I don't know any more about it, but I feel sure that he died with valor and not from some dumb mistake. After all, you taught him well.*
>
> *I know that you thought the world of him. I did too. Next to you, he was one of the best Marines I ever had. I feel a great deal of grief about him now,*

and I can imagine the sadness you must feel too. He
was a good, good Marine. We will all miss him.

I hope you stay well, and keep on winning.
Semper Fi,
E. J. Land

Carlos looked up and his eyes flooded with so many
tears that he could no longer read. He walked from the
room and stepped into his backyard and looked as the
setting sun glimmered through the tall hardwood trees
that surrounded his home. He stared at the western sky
and thought of his friend. The best partner he ever had.
And as he stood, looking toward heaven through the
deep green canopy of oak and maple trees, tears
streamed down his cheeks. "What happened, Burke?
What happened?"

12

The Valor of Corporal
John R. Burke

THE DAY THAT CARLOS HATHCOCK LEFT HILL 55 FOR Chu Lai and his flight home, he spoke to Lance Corporal John Burke last, saying good-bye to a man he loved as a brother.

He stood near the tailgate of a canvas covered six-by truck that would take him south. Several Marines rested on their sea bags inside the dark cavern formed by the dirty green cover stretched over tall wooden ribs and anchored to the sides of the vehicle's cargo bed. Sweat streamed down Hathcock's face, and he did not look forward to sitting in the saunalike transport, bouncing down Highway 1 to Chu Lai. Therefore, he stood outside, in the breeze, waiting until the last minute to board.

Burke stood next to him, leaning against the tailgate, talking about the old times, the good times, their last six months together. Several other snipers stood in a small group around Carlos and John. They laughed and swore and spit tobacco juice on the dust at their feet. They slapped Carlos on the back and joked with him about going home, saying things like, "I wish you would hurry up and go. That way I won't be short, I'll be next."

Remaining silent, Burke listened to the others rib Carlos. It was their way of saying good-bye without sounding sad.

"We'll see you back in the World," they would say. They always told their departing buddies that. Carlos knew that he would see them if he happened to cross one of their paths, but usually there was no concerted effort to connect later on. Eight years in the Marine Corps had taught him that.

"Some day we'll all get together," another said. But Carlos knew that odds were slim for that to happen.

"I'll try to make it to the annual Distinguished Marksmen's banquet at Quantico," Carlos finally told his friends. "Most of you guys are already Distinguished, and I expect the rest of you will be Distinguished sooner or later. I'll see you there."

They all agreed that his idea made the most sense.

Burke looked at his sergeant and put out his hand, "I sure hate to see you go, Sergeant Hathcock. We were just now getting to be a tough team."

"Burke," Carlos said, taking his partner's hand and shaking it, "now you take charge. Be the number one gun. Teach a promising, up-and-coming Marine, like I taught you. You're the best sniper I know, and the best partner I've ever had. You'll do well without me."

Carlos shouldered his sea bag and turned toward Burke. "Remember. Every move, slow and deliberate. Don't take any chances. Second place in this shootin' match is a body bag!"

"Don't you worry about that, Sergeant Hathcock," the lance corporal said. "Charlie won't outfox me. I had the best teacher."

"You were the best pupil, Burke. Keep those other boys in line," Hathcock said. "And you keep your head down! Ya hear?"

Burke smiled and his dark eyes twinkled beneath the shade of his floppy bush hat's brim.

"Sure like to see you back in the World!" he said as Carlos climbed up the truck's tailgate and swung himself inside.

Carlos shouted down, "You got my address in New Bern—1303 Bray. You get home, catch a hop to Cherry Point. I'm right there. I'll treat you to a steak and a beer."

"We'll see, Sergeant Hathcock. We'll see," Burke shouted back as the loud diesel engine roared and the big truck lurched forward on its Rough Rider convoy to Chu Lai.

Carlos leaned out the back and put two fingers high in the air forming a V, a symbol meaning victory during World War II and meaning peace in this one.

As the truck rumbled down the hill, Burke waved his arm above his head, bidding farewell to his friend and teacher.

When Carlos dropped back inside the covered cargo bed, and disappeared from Burke's view, the young Marine lance corporal walked back to his hooch where he lay on his cot, opened his *Guidebook for Marines*, and began reading and memorizing key lines.

He was up for promotion and now studied his Marine Corps "essential subjects" so that when he stood before his promotion board in a week he would not be caught without knowing all the answers.

Becoming an NCO was a major step for Burke. It was a rank that separated him from the troops, and gave him the right to wear the "Blood Stripe" on his dress blue trousers. But more important, as an NCO he would take charge as a sniper team leader, just as Sergeant Hathcock had done. As a corporal he could truly be the number one gun.

THE ABSENCE OF CARLOS HATHCOCK HAD BECOME commonplace at the sniper hooch at Hill 55, yet there continued to be the Hathcock stories—exaggerated with time and repeated tellings. Burke felt proud each time someone told a story that included him. The new-bees sat wide-eyed as he agreed that the yarn they were hearing was true because he had been there with Carlos.

Now wearing corporal stripes, Burke walked with a tenderness in his step as he hauled a heavy pack and his rifle down the hill to the landing zone where he would fly north to Quang Tri Province. Both his arms and legs were bruised by his senior NCOs who "pinned" on his corporal stripes with sharp punches to his shoulders, and "pinned" on his blood stripes with equally hard knee jabs to the sides of his legs—a tough tradition practiced among Marine NCOs.

Burke accepted it for what it was—a kind of seal of approval by his superiors and new peers. He now stepped across the line that separated him from the "nonrates" or "snuffies."

The traditional stripe-pinning was a prelude to the more enjoyable "wetting down"—a celebration of the promotion at which Burke treated his friends to a round of beers.

Now a few days since the promotion, the soreness had passed its peak and was leaving his arms and legs, but the bruises were still tender to touch and left him walking a little funny. He had many, many friends, and he wore the several round blemishes of black-and-blue with a certain amount of pride. A day earlier, as he nursed his sore arms and legs, though, he wondered if a Marine could have too many friends.

"You headed to Khe Sanh?" a sergeant asked as Corporal John Burke dropped his pack at the edge of the landing zone.

"Yes, I am. I'm taking charge of a sniper team there."

"Oh yeah? Which one?"

"One with 1st Battalion, 26th Marines."

"I hear they moved into a bad neighborhood up there at Khe Sanh."

"I've been in the worst neighborhoods. Besides, that

neighborhood's gonna be a whole lot worse for Charlie."

The sergeant laughed. "You fellas from Murder Incorporated are hot shit, huh?"

Burke looked at him, feeling the slight cut of his insult, but recalling his lessons learned from Carlos Hathcock and Captain Land. He dug deep inside himself and produced a friendly smile.

"No, Sergeant, I ain't." Burke shrugged, picked up his pack and walked to a small bunker that had a shelter half-stretched overhead to shade the two Marines who sat inside the dusty pit, wearing flak jackets over their bare backs and helmets with catchy phrases and nicknames inked on their ragged green camouflage covers.

"You boys doin' okay?" Burke asked, squatting low and leaning his head beneath the canvas.

"Sure."

"Mind if I squat in your shade?"

"Not at all."

"You Shore Party Marines?"

"Yeah," one Marine said, dusting the leg of his trousers, showing the small red patch sewn there to signify that he was a member of a helicopter support team from Company A, 1st Shore Party Battalion.

"You guys live in this hole?" Burke asked, noticing the personal gear and beds rolled in the corners of the bunker.

"Sure. We're the bastard sons. Since we get salted throughout the division, there ain't enough of us to have any sort of stakes to any one place so so we find us a little place to set up housekeeping and stay out of everyone's way. Bastard sons. Nobody claims us and we're glad. No hassles. Do the job, kick back, nobody bugs us."

Burke smiled. Suddenly he felt very much at home with these Marines.

"I know what you mean," he said, kicking back in the dirt with them.

More than an hour passed as Burke waited in the shade of the bunker. The sergeant squatted in the sun and made no attempt to strike up any further conversation with Burke or the two snuffies in the bunker. It was hot and flying insects seemed to swarm near the grass and bushes surrounding the landing zone; Burke watched the sergeant swat impatiently at them.

"Sergeant!" Burke shouted. The Marine turned his face toward the bunker to see the corporal waving for him to come and sit in the shade, away from the heavy swarm of bugs.

"Thanks," he said. "Those flies were driving me nuts; they don't seem so bad here."

"We keep the place sprayed. They get really nasty at night, but we keep 'em killed out with this stuff," one of the Shore Party Marines said, pointing to a large garden sprayer.

"What's in that?"

"I'm not sure. We mixed up our own recipe from a bunch of stuff we com-shawed from the supply tent and the battalion aid station. Only bad thing is it smells like hell."

Burke sniffed the sandbags where the Marines had sprayed the chemical and said, "Stuff that crop dusters spray on cotton fields back home smells just like that. You reckon it's harmful to folks?"

"Naw. We eat and sleep around the stuff and it ain't bothered us none. Besides, if it was bad, they wouldn't just pass it out to us like that—especially the doc. He wouldn't give us nothin' that would really hurt us."

"Guess you're right," Burke said leaning back again. "It does smell like that stuff they spray for weevils, though. But I guess it all pretty much smells the same."

The sound of rotor blades beating the air roused the two Marines to their feet.

"Time to go to work," one said as both Shore Party Marines bounded out of the bunker in a cloud of dust. Burke looked at the sergeant and then crawled out, looping his pack over his shoulders and taking his rifle by the upper sling and sliding that over his shoulder, too.

The sergeant pulled himself out of the bunker and stood with Burke as a large green twin-rotor helicopter settled to the ground. After several Marines ran down the helicopter's rear ramp, a crewman wearing a white aviator's helmet waved at Burke and the sergeant to come aboard.

As the chopper approached Khe Sanh, small-arms fire opened from the jungle below them. Bullets began popping holes in the thin metal skin of the helicopter, and Burke and the sergeant leaned forward, away from the wall, presenting as little of their bodies to the incoming fire as possible.

The Marine standing in the doorway behind a .50-caliber machine gun turned its fury in return to the fire below as the chopper raced above the treetops.

"Bad neighborhood," Burke thought as he recalled the sergeant's comments back at Hill 55's landing zone.

THAT BAD NEIGHBORHOOD KNOWN AS KHE SANH WAS a series of hills located in the northwestern corner of I Corps along the Laotian border. Hundreds of paths and tunnels branched from the Ho Chi Minh Trail and wound past Hill 881 and Lang Vei, and through the steep mountains of the Khe Sanh area.

These routes carried a constant flow of arms and ammunition to the National Liberation Army, who attacked American strongholds like The Rock Pile, Quang Tri, Cam Lo, Camp Carroll, Vandegrift and Con Tien.

The mountain passes of the Khe Sanh area, though, proved to be the crucial gate into this end of I Corps that faced the DMZ to the north and Laos to the west—the 3rd Marine Division's Tactical Area of Responsibility. They called that crucial gate "The Slot."

One lone mountain among that cluster of peaks called Khe Sanh was Hill 950. On that mountain that overlooked The Slot, a small encampment of Marines defended a combat outpost—one of the toughest corners of the Khe Sanh neighborhood. It was the new home of Corporal John Burke and his snipers.

From Hill 950, Burke and his men ranged out, stalking along the high slopes that overlooked the avenues that the Ho Chi Minh Trail took through The Slot. There, along those slopes, they selectively killed Viet Cong who appeared to be in charge of arms caravans. They also killed the lone Viet Cong who smuggled weapons in carts filled with sacks of rice or stacks of thatching. They killed Viet Cong who pushed bicycles with gigantic baskets loaded with rifles or boxes of ammunition.

Zapping these people along the most obscure, and seemingly most sheltered, lanes made negotiating The Slot an ordeal that the Viet Cong mules did not relish. And when Burke would drop the person who appeared to lead a caravan, often the mules, seeing their leader killed by a silent bullet that came from nowhere, would scatter, leaving their cargo dropped on the trail.

It was the kind of pressure the Viet Cong could not long endure.

Sleep came hard on Hill 950. There were no comforts of home. If a Marine was lucky, his "rubber bitch" did not leak and he could spend a quiet night in relative comfort. But the nature of life in combat does not afford much protection to rubber air mattresses and thus Burke's leaked.

As he prepared for sleep, he blew it as full as it would hold and placed a fresh Band-Aid, taken from his first-aid kit, over the pencil-point-sized hole. But by four A.M. the hard ground and rocks awoke him, and he would remain awake for the rest of the day.

It had come to be a way of life. A thing that he tolerated and on which he did not dwell. Negative thoughts were useless.

Carlos had taught him to accept things as a way of life when one is powerless to change it. But to persevere at what seemed to be any opportunity for improvement.

In every case, a negative thought or outlook meant that one had accepted defeat. That should never happen.

"No matter how impossible the odds, if there is a chance for success then you can win," Carlos had told him.

On June 6, 1967, the Vietnam summer scorched the mountains of Khe Sanh with temperatures that approached 100 degrees. The constant soak of sporadic showers kept the humidity continually above ninety percent. The only relief one felt came from the cool night breeze that lightly brushed the hilltops while the deep gorges and canyons stifled in steamy doldrums.

The snipers' bunker was dug below the crest of Hill 950 and overlooked the likely avenues of attack. Beyond the sandbags and trenches there, several yards of tanglefoot stretched beneath coiled concertina wire and German tape. Burke took his empty C ration cans and tied them low on the wire and dropped a small stone inside each one so that when someone snagged a barb on the concertina wire or the razorlike jagged edge of the German tape, the clank of the stone rattling in the can would alert the Marine standing watch.

Burke told his men that any time they heard that clank, even though it might be a cat or rat scavenging for food, they must roust him.

The sun set at about eight P.M. on June 6 and left the jungle greenhouse hot. Most of the Marines who prepared for sleep pulled their beds—a poncho liner and air mattress—outside, on and around the bunker.

Below, in the jungle, the men could hear the screech of birds and the chatter of other creatures, possibly monkeys. The Marines standing watch listened to the echoes of an animal roaring in the far distant hills beyond The Slot or perhaps in it. And they felt sure it was the sound of a tiger. A creature that none of them had ever seen in this land, but knew that it stalked those jungles there. They had seen the mangled body of a large monkey, half-devoured and left rotting in the steam heat of a long canyon.

And as the Marines who stood watch that night listened to the distant roar, faint and echoing between the rock walls of the tall mountains, another, more frightening sound disrupted the stillness of the night.

Inside the bunker, the field telephone croaked as the Marine in the listening post, next to the wire, hurriedly cranked the handle on his unit.

Burke snatched the receiver, pressed the black rubber button on its side, and spoke.

"Corporal Burke," he answered.

"Got noise on the wire. Several cans rattled."

"Can you see anything in your starlight scope?"

"Nothing."

"Load up and be ready to fall back to your alternate positions. I'll roust everybody here."

Burke felt that familiar tightness build in his stomach, anticipating another encounter with Charlie. He did not like being on the defensive, either. It always seemed the worst end of the fight—no place to maneuver and only two choices of tactics: to hold or to retreat.

Quietly, Burke began waking his men, who quickly pulled on their boots and picked up their rifles. And as he roused his men, the field phone rang again.

"Corporal Burke," he answered.

"Sappers! Looks like they're trying to blow the wire. I see a lot of people out there. They have RPGs and AKs mostly."

"Let them commit themselves to the attack and then turn on the lights with your popups.

"We'll all open on them when you put up those flares."

Burke hurried outside to prepare for the attack when he heard the familiar pop of a rocket-propelled grenade being launched.

"Take cover!" he shouted.

And as he spoke, the grenade exploded in the midst of his camp, wounding several of his men.

He ran to his injured men and began dragging them to the bunker. As he pulled them across the ground, he could hear the heavy bursts of his listening post's M-60 machine gun chewing into the sappers as they hurled their charges at the wire. He hoped the machine gun would hold the attacking enemy until he could get help.

But the wire and machine gun could not stop the sudden onslaught of rocket-propelled grenades as they came whistling into the small outpost.

"Corporal Burke," a Marine called to him in the orange light of the pyrotechnics that now drifted down, burning as they dangled beneath their small parachutes. "Sappers are in the wire!"

Burke knelt next to the bunker with his rifle, and began picking off the Viet Cong who sacrificed themselves to break a hole in the wire with their satchel charges. And as he killed those soldiers, a grenade exploded in front of the Marine who called him.

The explosion sent a large fragment flying, which struck Burke in his hip as he knelt shooting, but the brunt of the grenade struck the Marine who knelt thirty feet away and seriously wounded him.

It was this Marine whom Burke had taken to teach as Carlos Hathcock had taught him. He was an outstanding sniper, too, and John Burke vowed that this man would not die this night.

"Hold on," Burke shouted and ran to the young Marine sprawled in the dirt, crying out from the pain that racked his broken body.

With the care of a shepherd lifting an injured lamb, John Burke picked up his partner and carried him to the bunker's doorway. But before he could get the Marine inside, Burke heard the whistle of another rocket-propelled grenade and set his partner down against the sandbags that surrounded the bunker door.

With a quick prayer, Burke closed his eyes and spread himself over the wounded Marine, shielding him from the shrapnel and explosion.

Burke felt the prickle of more shrapnel embedded beneath his skin as he pulled his badly bleeding comrade inside the shelter.

Many other grenades had exploded within the encampment, and other Marines were left wounded, crying out for help. Burke listened for the sound of the machine gun and as it spoke, belching a deadly stream of fire into the wire, he knew that his priority was to get his injured men to shelter.

As he and another Marine struggled to pull a severely wounded man to the safe haven of the bunker, a grenade exploded at his heels and sent him and the other Marines rolling into the sandbags. He pushed the men inside the underground shelter's crawlway and listened again for the sound of the machine gun.

Burke's heart pounded heavily. He could see his body torn open, exposing those parts that he hoped never to see. He bled from every limb, and knew that with the machine gun now silent, those Marines could fight no longer.

Everyone lay wounded. The end seemed very near.

But with the strength of conviction that he had developed as one of the Marine Corps' best snipers, with the self-discipline and sense of purpose developed from a lifetime of tradition and moral right, he picked up an automatic rifle and hung a dozen grenades on his belt.

"What's going on?" a badly bleeding comrade asked, seeing Burke load down his cartridge belt with explosives.

"Those gooners ain't comin' in here! You boys are goin' home, not to some POW camp. And you're sure not going to get butchered by some bloodthirsty gook! Don't you worry about that! You just keep those rifles pointed out, and don't hesitate to shoot! Help's a comin'. Don't give up!" the badly bleeding Marine said, heaving, half out of breath. Then he charged from the bunker's doorway, screaming.

As he charged toward the dozens of soldiers who now tried to step through the tangle of wire, he hurled grenade after grenade at them.

In his left hand he held an M-16 with its magazines taped end on end. Burke emptied the ammunition from them, one shot at a time, into the soldiers who now fell and scurried and twisted, caught in the wire.

Behind these soldiers, rifle fire erupted, and the familiar sound of the launching of rocket-propelled grenades echoed in the night. But Burke kept charging, killing the enemy, forcing them to retreat off Hill 950.

He never questioned his own motives, but acted according to his beliefs. He reacted from an undefinable virtue common to so many of America's sons who travel to lands with strange names and die there. A sense that makes duty, honor, and courage second nature to them. A goodness that would prompt any of them to soothe the hurt of an injured child or take in a stray dog. To want to feed the hungry and stop oppression. An existence of delicate beauty within their souls that makes them place the lives of others ahead of their own.

For Corporal John Burke, there was no other logical choice. He held hope and sought success, and though he did not live to see it, he won.

Because of his fury, the Viet Cong fled. They did not see Burke fall. They did not look back.

His valor and his love for his brother Marines turned away an enemy who would have slaughtered all of Corporal John Roland Burke's men who huddled, wounded in that bunker.

Because of his ultimate sacrifice, his Marines—the men whose lives rested in his hands—survived.

On April 30, 1968—nearly a year after his death—the Secretary of the Navy, Paul R. Ignatius, acting for President Lyndon Johnson, signed a citation awarding Corporal John R. Burke the second highest medal for valor in the United States, the Navy Cross.

Its commendation read:

2200152   12 March 1968

The President of the United States takes pride in presenting the NAVY CROSS posthumously to

CORPORAL JOHN R. BURKE
UNITED STATES MARINE CORPS
for service as set forth in the following

CITATION:

For extraordinary heroism while serving as a Sniper Team Leader with Headquarters and Service Company, First Battalion, Twenty-sixth Marines, Third Marine Division (Reinforced), in the Republic of Vietnam on 6 June 1967. Assigned the mission of defending an outpost on Hill 950 at Khe Sanh, Quang Tri Province, Corporal Burke's team was taken under attack by a numerically superior enemy force. During the initial assault, Corporal Burke was wounded by an enemy grenade. Ignoring his wound, he administered first-aid to a severely wounded comrade and placed him in a relatively safe position, covering the wounded man with his own body to protect him from further injury. Heeding a call for help from outside the bunker, he unhesitatingly went to the aid of another Marine. While he and a companion were moving the man to the security of the bunker an enemy grenade exploded, knocking him and his comrade into the bunker. Although seriously wounded, he moved the wounded man to a tunnel to protect him from the devastating enemy fire. With all his team members casualties, Corporal Burke unhesitatingly and with complete disregard for his own safety armed himself with grenades, and shouting words of encouragement to his men, stormed from the bunker in a valiant one-man assault against the enemy positions. While firing his weapon and throwing grenades at the enemy positions, Corporal Burke was mortally wounded. By his dauntless courage, bold initiative and devotion to duty, he was instrumental in stopping the enemy attack and saving his men from possible further injury or death, thereby reflecting great credit upon himself and the Marine Corps and upholding the highest traditions of the United States Naval Service. He gallantly gave his life for his country.

13

Déjà Vu, All Over Again

Unbreathable heat. It is, perhaps, the most common arrival memory among Americans who landed in Vietnam during the summer of '69. That and the smell.

Carlos Hathcock got a taste of it early in May as he stepped from the plane to begin his second tour there. What he could see of Da Nang looked much like what he remembered on his few visits to town in 1966 and '67. But beyond the houses, stores, office buildings, hotels, and radio antennae, the hillsides and mountains looked different. Looked dead. Gray. Only broken, naked skeletons of what once stood as thick canopy jungle and forests remained. Smoke plumes rose on several horizons, and the sounds of jets and artillery never stopped. One look, and he knew that the hot months ahead could only get worse.

It was the summer that epitomized the essence of the sixties. Peace, love, protest, free-for-all sex, hard rock, psychedelic dope, and the Vietnam War.

Richie Havens, Janis Joplin, The Who, Ten Years After, Jefferson Airplane, Sly and The Family Stone, Joan Baez, Arlo Guthrie, Tim Hardin, Incredible String Band, Ravi Shankar, Bert Sommers, Sweetwater, Quill, Canned Heat, Creedence Clearwater Revival, Grateful Dead, Keef Hartley, Blood Sweat and Tears, Crosby Stills Nash and Young, Santana, Jeff Beck Group, The Band, Johnny Winter, Mountain, Melanie, Sha-na-na, John Sebastian, Paul Butterfield Blues Band, Joe Cocker, Country Joe McDonald and the Fish, and Jimi Hendrix, one after another, throughout three August days and nights, on a stage surrounded by scaffolding and loud-speakers set on a farm field in upstate New York, enter-tained 500,000 fans, onlookers, hippies, Black Panthers, Vietnam veterans, war protesters, legalize-marijuana ad-vocates, streakers, nudists, kids, and adults. Two people died and two babies entered the world in the midst of that muddy, trampled, garbage-strewn, love-in, three-day rock and roll jam of humanity. Lots of acid, grass, pills, smack, wine, beer, booze, indecent exposure, and public urination, but not a single report of violence. At least no arrests for violence. Mostly dope. Lots of dope arrests.

And in that same summer of peace, love, dope, pro-test, and Woodstock, President Richard Milhous Nixon, continuing a plan established by President Lyndon Baines Johnson and his secretary of defense, Robert Strange McNamara, put 543,400 United States service-men's and women's lives on the line against the Com-munists in Vietnam. It approximated the same number of people who attended Woodstock, and represented the greatest number of Americans committed to combat in Vietnam at any single time during the more than ten years of U.S. involvement in that war.

But Staff Sergeant Carlos Hathcock did not care about politics or Woodstock. Despite not wanting to come back to this land of black-dressed guerrillas and death, he accepted this page of his destiny without com-plaint. He had his duty to perform. Part of his Marine Corps turf, as he saw it.

Two Marines joked in the line ahead of Carlos as they walked from the plane that had taken this load of newbees from Kadena Air Base, Okinawa, to the long, black-skid-marked concrete runway that overlooked Da Nang Bay, once called *Baie de Tourane* until the French left.

Although the world beyond the city looked different now, beaten and worn, a strange feeling of déjà vu gnawed at Hathcock's soul. Familiar. Returning to where he belonged. Like he never really left. He knew the drill. Knew where to find the telephone. Knew who to call.

"Yes, sir, major, this is Staff Sergeant Hathcock. I just landed," Carlos said, speaking on a black telephone at a high counter where a Marine lance corporal stood ready to answer questions of the newly arriving officers and staff noncommissioned officers.

"I appreciate that, sir," Hathcock continued. "I figured on piling in the back of one of these six-by's headed up 327. A jeep would be outstanding. Lot more comfortable on my butt."

Carlos listened intently to the instructions the major at 1st Marine Division Operations told him. The lieutenant colonel in charge of the division sniper school wanted to see him as soon as he arrived at the headquarters compound. They would arrange billeting after discussing what Hathcock would do, and where he would stay during his next twelve months in Vietnam.

"We have lots of places for you here, at Division Schools," the lieutenant colonel said, cheerfully welcoming Carlos. "You're quite a legend, and I know you can do us a great job."

"I would do a better job in the bush, sir," Carlos said.

"Things have changed significantly since you were here, Staff Sergeant Hathcock," the lieutenant colonel said slowly, in a lower voice, suddenly tinged with melancholy. "Morale is in the shitter in a lot of places.

Dope is a big problem out there. Project 100,000[1] has brought us that many problems. I even heard that an entire Army company refused to go on an operation. Most men would give their left nut to be up here. Besides, you paid your dues. You've got a hell of a lot of grass time."

"Sir," Carlos began, "I appreciate what you mean. I wouldn't feel one bit guilty taking a job here either. Nothing to be ashamed about. But, I know I can do the division and the Marine Corps a whole lot more good leading a sniper platoon than up here teaching. Now, don't get me wrong, sir, I do love to teach marksmanship and sniping, but I think those Marines out yonder in the bush need me more. Especially if I can make a difference as a small unit leader."

The lieutenant colonel shifted his eyes downward to Carlos's service record book, which he had laid open on his desk. While thumbing through several pages, he said, "I had a few people already tell me you would most likely ask for line duty. But I still had to give you the pitch because I would honestly like you here teaching. However, if I did that to you, I think you would struggle.

"There is a truck headed for Hill 55 in half an hour, and you can hitch a ride on it. You'll be attached to 7th Marines. I'll make a call to your new commanding officer, Colonel R. L. Nichols, and tell him you're on the way."

Carlos fought back a smile and shook the lieutenant colonel's hand when he offered it across his desk. Then the staff sergeant snapped to attention, took a step to the rear, executed a nearly flawless about-face, and

---

[1] A Department of Defense program initiated by Secretary Robert S. McNamara in the later 1960s in which enlistment requirements, especially individual intelligence and arrest/conviction standards, were significantly lowered to accommodate the increased manpower needs of the armed forces to fulfill its primary national defense missions as well as supporting forces engaged in the Vietnam War.

marched out with his orders and record book gripped in his left hand, under his arm.

THREE HOURS LATER, HATHCOCK SAT IN A CANE-BACK chair on the plywood front porch of a 7th Marines staff NCO hooch, next to a sandy-haired gunnery sergeant named David Sommers, sipping a cold Coca-Cola. The two Marines gazed at the sunset, the distant mountains, and the valley below them.

The regimental sergeant major, Sergeant Major Clinton A. Puckett, had assigned Sommers, the 7th Marine Regiment's career planner and Headquarters Company's company gunnery sergeant, as Hathcock's sponsor.

On the porch beside Carlos's chair lay his new best friend, Yankee—a red mongrel, dingo-looking dog who, according to Sommers, had the ability to forecast incoming artillery and lob-bombs several minutes before anything struck.

Yankee was lying on Hathcock's bunk when Sommers had shown Carlos his new quarters. The dog immediately took a liking to the new staff sergeant. The gunny expressed his amazement, because Yankee rarely liked anyone. He was a cautious dog, usually distant to any stranger. Furthermore, he said that the dog would never before go inside a hooch, even if a person threw a steak on the floor, and the fact that he was not only inside but waiting on Hathcock's rack was even more unusual.

Sommers immediately shooed the dog off Carlos's bed, and the mongrel dashed outside. Then Hathcock had called him back inside to pet him, and the dog trotted directly to him. The gunny told Carlos about the dog's ESP talents, and said there had to be something special about the new staff sergeant for this particular dog to be so immediately comfortable with him.

The rest of that day and into the evening, Yankee remained close to Hathcock. But at rack time, the dog went to his every-night sleeping spot on top of the bunker just outside the staff hooch.

Besides another blistering day of nearly cloudless sunshine, it gave Staff Sergeant Hathcock his first reality check. After an unpleasant morning of waiting, checking into the company, waiting, seeing the sergeant major, waiting, and then finally seeing the commanding officer, Carlos met his platoon. The sight and experience underscored what the lieutenant colonel at division headquarters had told him two days ago.

First, when Carlos walked inside the sniper hooch, he found the former platoon sergeant lying in his rack, reading a magazine, and drinking a beer. The hooch itself had not seen any cleaning in months. The roof looked like a colander and the door tilted off a broken hinge with a flap of screen hanging the other direction.

The sergeant could not tell Hathcock the number of Marines in the platoon, and only knew that the men had either disappeared to goof off, or filled their daily quota of a dozen nonrates to police the hill and burn shitters.

When the staff sergeant finally managed to gather his platoon for its first formation in many months, the sight of them nearly took him off his feet. All of the men needed haircuts. They wore cutoff utility trousers, and either no shirts, slogan-emblazoned T-shirts, or unbuttoned utility uniform tops with the sleeves cut off at the shoulders. Every man had a variety of hardware and jewelry draped around his neck, from peace symbols and iron crosses, to beer openers and beads. Nearly all of them had their heads festooned with maroon, black, or green berets, or bush covers decorated with so many pins and ornaments that they reminded Carlos of a fly fisherman's hat.

By afternoon's end, Hathcock had sent the derelict sergeant packing, had burned the berets, gotten the men into clothing that more resembled Marines, and had managed to have the platoon clean the hooch and surrounding area.

*   *   *

DAVID SOMMERS WAITED IN A CHAIR IN FRONT OF THE staff hooch for Carlos to eat evening chow with him. When the gunny saw the staff sergeant storming up the trail from Finger 4 and the sniper hooch, he grinned at his new arrival.

"I can see by your expression and demeanor that overall you have had yourself a completely wonderful first day," Sommers said.

Hathcock looked sidelong at the gunny and then grinned back. "I've had worse. But it might take me a while to think of one."

"Quite a variety show down there," Sommers said as he stood and walked next to Hathcock toward the hooch-styled chow hall.

"Now, on that count, I have not ever seen worse," Carlos said, and laughed.

"To your credit, though," Sommers said, "they made a hundred-percent improvement just this afternoon. I have never seen that bunch work any harder. And that sergeant never looked worse than when I ordered him to the police tent to hand out toilet paper and brooms until he rotates."

WELL BEFORE DAWN THE NEXT DAY, CARLOS SAT AT HIS desk, looking at his platoon's roster, pairing his snipers into two-man teams. He had chosen a corporal named John Perry, a Marine from London, Ohio, as his own partner.

Carlos had taken a quick survey of the platoon's rifles and knew a difficult road lay ahead for them. They were the same weapons that had been there three years earlier, and their condition suggested that an armorer had done no repairs on them in that time either.

To start his rebuilding program, Hathcock had decided to take the entire platoon outside the wire, and zero the rifles from scratch, while putting his men through a day of badly needed training.

Later that morning, Sergeant Major Puckett fumed. He wanted Hathcock standing at attention in front of his desk, explaining why he had not sent his men to fill the daily police duty quotas, and why the staff sergeant had not answered the telephone when he called. In his final frustration, he sent David Sommers to find the wayward Marine.

In the meantime, the sergeant major sent the former sniper platoon sergeant back to Finger 4. He had taken exception that the staff sergeant had relieved the man without his consent.

At eleven o'clock, a jeep roared to a halt at the small firing range that Carlos had helped Captain Land construct in 1966.

Gunny Sommers casually asked Carlos, "You ready?" He did not have to say more; Hathcock already knew the trouble.

"Corporal Perry, take charge of the platoon and move them back through the wire at fifteen hundred this afternoon, if I'm not back. Spend the rest of the day working in pairs, practicing stalking and movement. Don't get all bunched up and keep your security out."

When the jeep halted at the sergeant major's tent a few minutes later, Sergeant Major Puckett stood outside with his arms folded.

Carlos stepped up to the sergeant major and smiled.

"What can I do for you, Sergeant Major?" he asked.

"Be there when I call you, Staff Sergeant," Puckett growled.

"I got my platoon up early this morning, getting them ready for operations," Hathcock responded. "We've got a whole lot of work to get done. I've got this here list of supplies I need, and I gotta get authorization to go down to Da Nang to get cammies for my snipers. Sure could use your horsepower. Could you help us?"

"When you leave your hooch, I want you to carry a radio," the sergeant major said. "I had several things happen this morning and I needed to talk to you."

"I'll be glad to carry a radio," Carlos said. "You get

me one and I'll carry it. In fact, I could use three or four."

"See the comm chief, he'll sign them out to you," Puckett said.

"Second thing," he continued. "Where were your men who had police detail this morning?"

"I wasn't aware of anyone who had police detail, Sergeant Major," Hathcock answered. "Which Marine was he?"

"About a dozen men in your platoon!" Puckett said, trying not to raise his voice at the staff sergeant.

"I only have twenty-one men," Hathcock said. "That's more than half my platoon. That's a heavy quota. Do all the other units give up sixty percent of their Marines to burn shitters?"

"Don't get smart with me, Staff Sergeant," the sergeant major snapped. "We have priorities, and your men have not been committed to any action, therefore they will pull police duty or whatever else is necessary around this hill. They aren't paid for doing nothing."

"I beg your pardon, Sergeant Major," Carlos said. "My men have been working all morning. They will be working long after everyone else has kicked back for the night, too. We have a lot of lost ground and training to get caught up on so that we can get back into action. We will pull our fair share of duty. Every man, including myself.

"With all due respect . . ."

"Can it, Hathcock!" Puckett growled. "I'll hit the other units for quotas. You will pull your fair share, too. If I find one of your men lazing around the hill, I'll have your hide for it. Clear?"

"Yes, sir," Hathcock answered.

Then, standing at attention and looking as sincere as he could manage, he said, "Sergeant Major, I'm on your side. In fact, I would be honored if you would consider joining us. I'll set you aside one of the best rifles.

"I just need your help. I need supplies. My men need working uniforms. You help me get this and I will give you a sniper platoon that 7th Marines can brag about."

Puckett expected an argument, not an invitation to join what he considered a band of outlaws. Now, suddenly confronted with a red carpet and a welcome mat, he could only do what all his years as a Marine, always loyal to his troops, dictated.

"I don't want your best rifle," the sergeant major answered, "any one of them will do. You give the best rifles to the men who will need them most. I'll do what I can for you, if you're serious. Don't you embarrass me."

Carlos reached inside the large cargo pocket on the leg of his camouflage trousers and pulled out a list that he had typed in the low light of a small lamp early that morning. "Here's a copy of my shopping list. I sure appreciate the help."

As the sergeant major folded the paper, Carlos walked back to the jeep where David Sommers waited, and then left with him.

All the way down the hill, the two men laughed.

"Hell, Hathcock," Sommers said, "he'll probably deliver the stuff himself. You sure stuck your chin out, inviting him to become a sniper. The sergeant major's just gunji enough to do that."

"Good!" Carlos exclaimed. "If he's one of us, then he can't be against us."

"Yeah," Sommers agreed. "But he will still be a pain in the ass. You know, he's got to take care of everybody else, too. Your platoon isn't the only one hurting for new uniforms and boots."

"I hope he does take care of everybody else, too," Hathcock said sincerely. "I just want to be left alone long enough to get my platoon back into action. I have to start all over again and sell the sniper program from the ground up, here. I can't do that with my men on police duty. We've gotta produce kills, and show these company commanders how adding two snipers to their ranks can make the enemy turn tail."

"He's not going to leave you alone. He'll grab every

loose body you have around your hooch," Sommers said.

"I plan to keep them in the field," Carlos said. "I'm gonna start farming them out as soon as I'm satisfied they can go on an operation and kill the enemy without getting killed themselves. Meanwhile, they're gonna be in the field every day, under my personal control."

"Sergeant major's gonna get pissed when you're not at the hooch when he calls," Sommers said.

"He gave me a radio, remember?" Carlos said, grinning.

Sommers laughed as the jeep halted again where the sniper platoon continued to train.

Carlos smiled. "I've also got some radios in mind that will give me a long-distance punch, too. He didn't say anything about staying close, just in touch."

"You did all right with this first round," Sommers said. "But what about round two? That's when the other command sections start bitching about their people getting pulled for shit detail. There are a lot of gunnies and tops who have a lot more pull with the sergeant major than you do. I've got a hunch that he's going to want to get out of the middle of the mess real fast, too. Once the word gets around, there will be a bunch of folks wanting to pin your ears back."

"That's too bad," Hathcock said. "But I never got in this to become popular. I'm obliged to my men. I've got a job to do."

Sommers waved good-bye as he wheeled the jeep away and Carlos Hathcock went back to work.

That evening when the snipers returned to their area, Hathcock found the former platoon sergeant again lying in the rack. Carlos just looked at him.

"You think you can generate enough energy to answer this telephone if it rings?" he asked the sergeant.

"Yeah, no problem," the surly man answered.

"Good," Carlos said with a smile. "For the next two weeks, you'll be phone watch."

＊   ＊   ＊

IN THOSE WEEKS, HATHCOCK MANAGED TO GET HIS MEN shooting on the paper, acting again like snipers. In that time, too, he found an enthusiastic combat unit that welcomed his snipers, 1st Battalion, 7th Marines, commanded by Lieutenant Colonel John Aloysious Dowd, an officer who led with devotion and held Carlos's greatest respect.

During April, Dowd's battalion led the regiment in combat action. The Marines of One-Seven killed 160 North Vietnamese Army troops, 51 Viet Cong, and took one prisoner. The 2nd and 3rd Battalions, combined, killed 58 NVA and 85 VC in the same period. Additionally, during May, Dowd's Marines tallied 44 NVA killed in action, 41 Viet Cong, and took two prisoners, while the 2nd Battalion killed none and the 3rd killed 30 NVA.

While six snipers operated with One-Seven, Carlos sent eight others to the division's sniper school at Da Nang. Next month he planned to send four more, and two others after that. Based on their progress now, Hathcock expected that by August his platoon would be ninety-nine percent operational.

"Platoon's looking sharp now," David Sommers told Carlos one late June evening.

"Thanks," Hathcock said, and smiled while gazing at the stars in the clear night sky.

Then he looked across his shoulders at Sommers, wrinkling his brow.

"Still," he said, "those sticks of ours need work bad, and now. No matter what I do, they still shoot groups that look like a shotgun made them."

"Any word on that new assistant?" Sommers asked.

"Naw," Carlos said, looking back at the sky. "Boy, it'd be nice if this guy knew how to work on guns. You know?"

Both Marines laughed and their conversation quickly fell away to the subject of blind dates and embarrassing moments, allowing their minds to drift away to better times. More pleasurable times. Peaceful times when war and Vietnam did not exist in the language of teenagers in penny loafers, crew socks, and greased-back duck-tail hairstyles.

They told stories of their youth and watched the darkness—accented by the red streaks of tracers and orange bursts of artillery shells exploding in the distance—deepen from gray to black, blending the shapes of the hills where the battle now broiled into the shapelessness of the night sky. And as the roar of that war drifted across the wide valley that separated them from the fighting, it cued their thoughts back to that of war and reality and doom.

With those thoughts now filling each man's consciousness, they adjourned from their quarters to the low sniper bunker on Finger 4 where they could watch the fight in relative safety. The thought of lob-bombs and rockets and mortars coming their way prompted that unconscious survival response.

It was not long before Hill 55 came under attack along its long Finger 3 where sappers hurled explosive-filled satchels into the wire, blowing wide holes in it. Then, the enemy invaded through the caps, attacking the sentries positioned there. No Marines died. The Americans repelled the sapper assault and killed four VC.

That same night of June 22, 1969, while Carlos and David watched the light show from the top of the sniper bunker, while attacks continued at Charlie Ridge and Hill 55, a four-man reconnaissance team from the C23 Recon Company of the 31st NVA Regiment fell short of fully scouting out avenues of attack on Hill 327 when Marines on security patrol there caught them in-filtrating the wire. Three soldiers escaped, but the Marines captured the fourth, who told interrogators that his regiment planned to attack the communications facility there, as well as the Hoa Cam training center.

Several days later, Carlos poured over notes and reports of the various incidents. The documents provided him with the information that the Viet Cong no longer presented the primary threat—but that the 2nd NVA division, reinforced with the 90th, 141st, 1st, 3rd, 36th, and 31st NVA regiments and two artillery battalions who were now poised for attack from strongholds located all along the 7th Marines' western flank, were trouble. He talked aloud to himself, turning the heads of two snipers who sat on boxes, cleaning their weapons.

"Gonna get a lot hotter this summer," he said. "They're stocking up for the monsoons. Gonna get all the rice this year. That many troops—gonna be a big harvest of not enough to go around."

It did not take a tactical scholar to conclude that with less rice available for more people, the food-gathering program initiated by the enemy would be vigorous, to say the least Carlos had watched rice drops to hungry villagers, and based his assumption on that.

He laughed at the story a friend told him of a hundred people intermingled with hungry pigs and other farm animals, all waiting in a large circle where an orange *T* lay spread on the ground. They stood, staring at the sky, listening for the sound of airplane engines belonging to a C-117 that would drop sacks of rice into the large circle of people. Then, all of a sudden, the roar of the engines and propellers cut through the air just above the broken and mangled treetops. The pigs, too, turned their snouts skyward—their ears perked—and watched for the rice.

It was as though someone fired the starter's pistol when the bags fell to earth, several sacks bursting open. The people and the pigs ran for the rice—hungry and fighting for every grain, because the Viet Cong and North Vietnamese had taken their harvest from the season before and these regular airdrop deliveries, which occurred on a daily basis throughout the country, provided their principal means of survival now. No longer did rice come from the field, but from the sky, and the Marines who watched the event laughed.

Today, however, that memory haunted Carlos as he pondered the prospects of the enemy's rice-harvesting plan this year. That preposterous spectacle, which repeated itself throughout the country again and again, lost its humor and took on a menacing prospect.

"Gonna be a hot, hot summer." He sighed.

As HE SCRATCHED OUT MORE NOTES WITH HIS BLACK ballpoint pen on a yellow legal-sized tablet, sweat ran down his shirtless back and soaked into the top of his trousers.

The door suddenly burst open and two loud feet stomped across the sniper hooch's plywood floor. Carlos raised his head as he heard the thud of a hundred pounds of personal gear, bound inside a long green sea bag, hit the floor behind him. Before he could turn his head, a familiar voice boomed, "The name's McAbee—Staff Sergeant McAbee. Just call me Mack!"

Staff Sergeant Ronald H. McAbee was one of Carlos's best friends in the Marine Corps.

McAbee first met Carlos at Camp Lejeune at the end of the Marine Corps' rifle and pistol matches in the spring of 1967. McAbee had just finished shooting his .45-caliber "hard ball" pistol in the final day of individual competition when he met Carlos in the redbrick barracks at the rifle range near coastal North Carolina's Sneed's Ferry and Topsail Island. That night they crossed the tall bridge that led to the beach community and drank Jim Beam at a tavern there. McAbee was allergic to beer.

A month later, they were neighbors in the Chamberlain Village family housing area of the Marine Base at Quantico. Only a matter of days after the Hathcock family cleared their quarters, so did Staff Sergeant R. H. McAbee and kin.

McAbee knew that Carlos was in 1 Corps, but he did

not know where. He guessed his friend would probably be at the 1st Marine Division's Scout/Sniper Instructor School, now at Da Nang. He had no idea that Carlos led the sniper platoon on Hill 55.

After the exclamations, hugs, slaps, and cheers, Carlos got down to business with his friend, one of the best armorers in the Marine Corps.

"The first project on the agenda is to overhaul all these old sticks we've been shootin'," Carlos said. "You're gonna have your work cut out with them. They're in pretty humble shape.

"What this platoon needs is a set of rifles to choose from like a pro golfer picks clubs—the right one for the right job. Custom-fitted for each man. If you can get our weapons tuned up like that, we'll be the hardest thing to hit this country yet."

"Carlos, you get the parts and machinery and I'll do the rest," McAbee said.

"Soon as you get settled," Hathcock added, "you're gonna get a truck from 11th Motor T and head down to 1st FSR[2] at Da Nang and use their shop. I'll get the sergeant major to grease the skids.

"Let's go see Gunny Sommers and get you settled in our hooch."

IT TOOK THREE TRIPS TO DA NANG BEFORE MCABEE completed the major work on the rifles. From then on, he passed time fine-tuning each weapon at a bench he built in the sniper hooch. It was a job with no end, and he knew it. But with the new glass jobs and refitted and matched receivers and barrels, suddenly the sniper platoon's kills rose to a level that rivaled battalions.

July ended with the 7th Marines sniper platoon confirming seventy-two kills. Carlos felt certain it was a record.

For Carlos and his snipers, McAbee's arrival had

------

[2] Force Service Regiment.

sweetened their lives. His fine gun-smithing coupled with the keen training and leadership that Carlos provided resulted in a platoon that became one of the best in Vietnam. For their outstanding achievement the platoon received a Presidential Unit Citation, one of the few platoons to ever receive such recognition.

The accomplishments of the 7th Marines snipers, however, did not win the hearts of all who broke bread with them at the mess hall on Hill 55. There were those who admired and respected the snipers, and those who detested them.

Carlos often wondered in which camp the sergeant major really stood—sometimes it seemed as though the leathery Marine counted the days when the trio of McAbee, Hathcock, and Sommers would be gone, and other times they were certain the man was their friend. But there was never a doubt about the master sergeant who headed the Interrogator Translator Team. He hated them.

That hate grew the first week that McAbee arrived. He and Carlos had enjoyed a bottle of Jim Beam much of the afternoon and felt the euphoria that the 86-proof bourbon packed.

As the two Marines relaxed on the staff NCO hooch's small plywood porch, Carlos noticed a group of peasants walking through the checkpoint where the highway crossed the top of Hill 55. Several men and women, yoked with large buckets hung on the ends of long poles balanced across their shoulders, hurried through the gate, followed by several empty-handed children, all unchecked by the sentries who stood guard there.

Carlos jumped to his feet.

"They just let those hamburgers through the wire without so much as a how-do-you-do!" Hathcock snapped. "Mack, come on. Let's see what that bunch is carrying in those buckets."

Both Marines slung their rifles across their shoulders and headed off the band of peasants.

"Hold on there!" Carlos shouted to the woman who led the group. "What you got in the buckets?"

The woman smiled, showing a mouth filled with black teeth. "Got fish. Go sell fish."

"Everybody got fish?" Carlos asked.

The woman smiled again and bobbed her head up and down quickly, stooping her shoulders up and down with her hearty nod.

All the buckets brimmed with large fish. Many fish. Too many fish.

"You catch them down in the river?" Carlos asked, pointing his finger at the silver ribbon of water that flowed to the sea in the distance.

The woman smiled and bobbed her exaggerated nod again.

"You have the best luck I've ever seen anybody have out of that river," Carlos said. He looked toward McAbee and grinned. "I smell a fish!"

Both Marines chuckled at the irony of the comment. And as Carlos reached for a fish, the woman suddenly tensed.

"That's about the hardest fish I ever felt," Hathcock said. "Feel that, Mack. That old sucker must have arthritis! What's that, a rock fish?"

McAbee grinned. "Wonder if it might be something he ate?"

Both men laughed again, and Carlos pushed his middle finger down the fish's throat.

"Mack, you're right. This old sucker swallowed something." And as he withdrew the contents of the contraband hidden inside the fish, Carlos said, smiling at the woman, "He swallowed himself a bunch of bottles of penicillin. I'll bet that just surprises the hell out of you."

Carlos frowned and lowered his rifle at the group. McAbee followed the lead, tilting his weapon down at the men and women and several children that followed along. "I've got guard of the rear. Carlos, you lead on."

Dutifully, the two snipers marched the group of peasants to the camp stockade, and there turned them over to the commander of the guard. The Interrogator Translation Team chief spent much of the evening listening to the interrogations. And once word of the mass capture reached the colonel's ears, the angry commanding officer responded with a policy that each group of peasants wishing to pass through the gate must first pass a careful examination by one of the ITT Marines.

THE FINAL WEDGE, HOWEVER, CAME ONLY A FEW DAYS later, when Carlos and McAbee returned from a hunt with a prisoner. They met the master sergeant from ITT at a checkpoint, and there he very promptly began to question the soldier dressed in a white shirt and black shorts.

Each time the top asked a question, the man responded and the Marine said, "What?" and looked at Carlos and McAbee who simply smiled and shrugged.

Finally the frustrated master sergeant looked at them and said, "This man is Laotian. I need to send for a Lao language interrogator from Da Nang. You'll have to watch him for a while longer."

Carlos and McAbee sat quietly with their prisoner for several hours, waiting for the interrogator to arrive from Da Nang. Finally, after the ITT chief went through the trouble of dispatching a jeep and driver to Da Nang to bring the interrogator back to the checkpoint, the Marine arrived, and met the same confusion that had confronted the master sergeant.

"I can't understand him," the ITT chief said. "It's a dialect that I've never heard."

Carlos stood and looked at the master sergeant. "Reckon one of these hotdogs out here might understand him? At least they might be able to tell you which flavor of translator to get next trip."

The top looked coldly at Carlos, put his hands on his hips, and yelled to a farmer squatting near a hut no more than fifty yards away, who had watched the entire episode with great interest. The old man walked as quickly as his ancient, stiff legs could carry him. He bowed his head and removed the straw hat from his head before speaking to the Marine.

After a brief exchange in Vietnamese, the old man looked at the prisoner and spoke. The prisoner responded in a pleading tone. The old man laughed, looked at the master sergeant, spoke several words, and pointed to the prisoner, who in response opened his mouth and pointed to his tongue.

The interpreter from Da Nang smiled and looked at Carlos and McAbee, who grinned, too, anticipating a humorous explanation.

"The man's tongue-tied," the Marine said, laughing. "He was talking Vietnamese all along. He just has a speech impediment."

Carlos and McAbee howled and guffawed. The humiliated master sergeant remained silent. He took the prisoner, set him in the back of the jeep between the Marine from Da Nang and a guard, jumped in the front seat, and told his driver, "Home!"

The two snipers continued to laugh as the jeep spun its tires on the rutted roadway and left them standing in a cloud of dust.

CARLOS AND HIS SNIPERS AVOIDED ANY UNNECESSARY contact with the ITT Marines, and others who shared their opinion of snipers. As Carlos saw it, a sniper's place was in the bush, not drinking coffee in somebody's hooch. Out of sight, out of mind proved to be an effective philosophy for the snipers to adopt when dealing with the support troops on the Hill. But Sergeant Major Puckett was another story.

Hathcock's and McAbee's disappearing acts had become a constant irritation to him. Every time he asked for one of the two Marines, both were out patrolling somewhere. Meanwhile, he could only speak to the lance corporal or private who answered the telephone, only able to say, "I'll give him the message, Sergeant Major."

Puckett gave up on the radios when he realized the men generally hunted well out of direct range. As weeks disappeared, so did Hathcock and McAbee with more and more frequency.

Whenever Carlos and his men finally returned to their headquarters, Sergeant Major Puckett roared at them. Carlos and McAbee remained close for several days. After things cooled a bit, they would take off on another adventure. Puckett would storm, they would batten down their hatches, and repeat the drill.

When Captain Rick Hoffman called for Hathcock and Company to go on a "Rice Denial" patrol with his 1st Battalion, 7th Marines company, Carlos and McAbee disappeared again.

"HOW'S YOUR BACK?" CAPTAIN HOFFMAN ASKED AS the two snipers stepped inside Bravo Company's command tent. "You got some room to carry explosives?"

"Sure. How much?" Carlos said.

"Forty pounds each," Hoffman said. "We have satchels filled with C-4, and each man will carry one on this patrol. Go on out to that six-by and the gunny will get yours and Mack's.

"How you feelin', Mack?"

"Fine, sir," McAbee said.

"You're a whole lot slimmer now than when you got here. You been eatin' okay?" Hoffman asked.

McAbee laughed. "I've lost a good twenty pounds, maybe more."

"Dieting?"

"No, sir. Hathcocking," McAbee said with a grin. "First words that Carlos says to me is, 'Mack, you sure put it on around your middle. Come on and we'll go walk some of that stuff off of you.'

"Sir. That's when you and I first met. Remember?"

"Sure do," the captain said, leaning back against his

footlocker. "That's when I noticed you were a regular butterball. And that's one of the few times I've seen Carlos wear a helmet and flak jacket."

"Yes, sir, I think he did that on purpose, too," Mack continued. "He made me wear my Army hat and all that other garbage to conform to regulations—he said."

The captain laughed.

"He wanted to wear me out!" Mack said, laughing, too.

"I had four canteens of water and when we got to the place where he and I dropped off from your company, I had run completely out."

"It was hot that day, too," the captain said.

"Carlos only carried two canteens and both his were still nearly full," Mack continued. "I think he's half-camel, on top of everything else.

"But, we sat there and I finally asked him for a drink because I was sick from the heat."

Carlos looked at the two Marines and said, laughing, "You were just about the same color as the skipper's writing paper there. I crushed up a couple of salt tablets in my canteen cup, and after you drank that you were all right. Right?"

"I don't think we ever walked that much since then!" McAbee said. "We covered a good twenty miles that day—all at a dead run."

"Well, Mack," Carlos said, "I told you that I was going to walk that fat off of you."

"Yeah, Carlos, you sure did," McAbee said, shaking his head and chuckling. "But you didn't have to do it all in one day!"

"You look real good, Mack," the captain said. "You up to another heavy hike like that one?"

"Sir, it can't be worse than that one," McAbee said. "I don't have all that spare weight and I ain't loaded down with that Army hat and flak jacket. Forty pounds of C-4 won't mean a thing."

Carlos looked at his friend and said, "I want to hear that again, about this time tomorrow."

The captain smiled. "Let's get going. You get your satchels and I'll meet you outside."

A group of lieutenants and staff sergeants, notebooks in hand, huddled around the captain to hear the operations order. The mission was to search for caches of rice or other stored food in the Arizona Territory and destroy it all with the explosives that each man carried.

After a round of questions, the lieutenants and many of the staff sergeants hustled away to formulate their operation orders, issue them to their respective squad leaders, and assign them the detailed tasks of the overall mission.

As the captain folded his map, he looked at Carlos. "I saw a curious sight the other day. Something that really got my attention."

Carlos arched his eyebrows with anticipation. "What was that, sir?"

"I had to rub my eyes. I couldn't believe it. Now, am I crazy, or is Gunny Sommers's career planner hooch really bright red and yellow?"

Carlos fell back on his heels laughing. "Last time the sergeant major grounded me and Mack, we had to have something to do. We figured that Gunny Sommers would get a lot of business if folks knew where to find his hooch. We got a couple of gallons of red and yellow paint and made his hooch visible."

"Real visible!" the captain chuckled. "Charlie shoot at it?"

"No!" Carlos said. "Not at all. You know how it sits right between the Operations hooch and the mess tent? The mess tent still gets the rear end blown out of it every day, and Operations still gets thunder shot out of it, too, but they haven't so much as sent even one small-arms round through ole Gunny Dave's hooch. That's the safest place on Hill 55."

"How does Gunny Sommers like it?" Hoffman asked.

"He thinks it's great," Carlos answered. "He even

helped paint, once he saw Mack and me out there working."

"How about Sergeant Major Puckett?" the captain said smiling.

"He hit a grand slam!" Carlos said with a twinkle in his eyes. "I have never seen the sergeant major blow more fuses at once. His neck bulged and all his veins poked out on his face. He turned red as that hooch.

"The sergeant major had all three of our butts at once," Carlos said, slapping his hands on his thighs.

McAbee said, "That was yesterday morning. He told us to have that thing green before the sun went down."

"Is it?" the captain asked.

"Partially," Carlos said. "The front still looks like a used car lot, though."

McAbee beamed. "You want to hear something better than that? Carlos, tell him about the shower."

"I don't think that's so funny," Hathcock said. "We needed the convenience, Mack."

"Just tell the skipper, Carlos," McAbee said smiling.

"Well, sir," Hathcock began, "you know how we are always having to go heat that water in the barrel over at the area head? Have to light off that jet engine they call a submersion heater?"

"Oh yeah. If you're lucky the damn thing won't blow up in your face," Hoffman said. "Hell, I'd rather go dirty sometimes."

"Well, I got tired of lighting that thing off," Carlos continued, "and either getting the water too hot or not hot enough, or having that thing burn off all my hair.

"I found a wing tank that somebody lost. It holds about fifty gallons and is long and thin, and when the sun heats up that water all day and you open the little pit-cock valve, it pours nice warm water out.

"Now, we take real good care of our friends over at the supply tent, and they take care of us. It just so happened they had some scrap angle iron and a bunch of nuts and bolts, so me and Mack and Dave Sommers built us our own private shower.

"Nothing wrong with that."

"No," the captain said. "Sounds fine to me."

"Tell him the rest," McAbee said, elbowing Carlos.

"We needed canvas to cover it so that we wouldn't be standing outside naked. And we figured that it would be kind of nice to be able to walk from our racks to the shower without having to go outside, so we cut this *greeeeeat* big hole in the side of our hooch, pushed the whole thing halfway through the hole and used the spare canvas to cover the outside. It looks beautiful."

McAbee started laughing hard. "Sergeant Major Puckett lost it all when he came in to inspect our hooch. He turned green, and then he turned bright red. He yelled and fumed, but we got to keep the shower. Damage was already done.

"He told every staff NCO in that hooch that each man would have his pay docked for the price of that hooch."

"Don't worry about that. It's so full of bullet holes nobody will ever care anyway," Carlos said.

As the three Marines sat in the shade of the six-by truck, telling stories, passing time, waiting, several more Marines joined the group. Orders had finally reached the last fire team and now the company was ready.

In an hour's time, helicopters had lifted Bravo Company into the combat area called Arizona Territory. First Battalion, 7th Marines had assumed responsibility for the entire Arizona Territory, relieving units from the 5th Marine Regiment to participate in an operation called Durham Peak.

As the platoons disbursed across their areas of operation, the enemy watched. The enemy that the Marines encountered these days was more often North Vietnamese than Viet Cong. It seemed to Carlos that these days the NVA represented the real enemy, as opposed to the VC in 1966 and '67. He saw few NVA then. Now NVA were the commonly sighted threat.

This enemy that now watched, restrained himself. Elements of the 2nd NVA Division, reinforced by the 90th and 36th NVA Regiments, along with the 577th NVA Artillery Battalion spent their major efforts gathering and storing rice for the monsoon season that would begin in October. They preferred to harass and outmaneuver their enemy rather than confront him with their full force. But, the tenacity of the 7th Marine Regiment, and Lieutenant Colonel Dowd's 1st Battalion in particular, would prove too much of a liability for the NVA to face. Eventually, they would meet head-on.

"HOT, HOT, HOOOOOOT!" MCABEE SAID AS HE WALKED twenty paces to the right of Carlos.

"Keep your eyes peeled for trip wires," Hathcock responded. "That's a bad way to go home, your bottom half-blown apart."

McAbee looked cautiously ahead of his steps after the prompting, recalling the men he'd seen lose their lives by the explosives hidden beneath their feet, triggered by a piece of fishing line or a grass-covered pedal. He did not know which was worse. Getting blown apart by a booby trap or getting torn to shreds by shrapnel from the rockets, shells, and lob-bombs that the enemy dumped on the Marines who sat in compounds.

He thought again of the Marine he had watched die on his first day at the Hill. A lob-bomb sailed into a truck and blew hundreds of heavy metal pieces in every direction. One long shred of shrapnel, a chunk of iron that looked like an oversized lawn mower blade, sailed straight out from the explosion and struck a Marine who ran toward a nearby bunker. The ragged-edged, heavy piece of iron severed the man's upper body from his lower, spilling him across the ground. He died in one long, sad cry.

"Mack!"

"Yeah, Carlos?"

"You look a little green. You okay?"

"Yeah. Just hot."

"Maybe once we check out that bunch of huts up

yonder, we can take a break," Hathcock said.

The sun blazed in the cloudless sky as they walked from the tree line's cover into the nakedness of a clearing 1,200 yards long and nearly 1,000 yards wide. The huts stood at one end of the clearing, next to a low stone fence that encircled the entire clearing, divided by low dikes that crisscrossed it like a checkerboard. Only weeds grew in the fields now, and the huts appeared long deserted.

Carlos and Mack squatted next to the lieutenant who led the platoon they accompanied. They watched as a fire team ran toward the huts, scouting for signs of a possible ambush. The four Marines took cover along the knee-high stone fence. One by one they vaulted over the wall and ran to the huts.

Five minutes passed and the fire team leader waved his arm above his head—all clear. One fire team at a time, the two squads crossed the open land while the third moved into the area of the huts. Carlos and McAbee followed them.

When the two snipers joined the squad leader, who squatted next to a hut, Carlos told him, "Mack and I are gonna sit here awhile and set up next to one of these huts. With all this thrashing around we've been doing, no telling who might be coming to visit us."

The squad leader radioed the lieutenant who now waited at the far end of the clearing, 1,200 yards away. He agreed that it would serve the platoon well, and they could use the break. But the lieutenant ordered the third squad to move on to a hill where they could observe the area and warn the platoon of any approaching patrols.

Just as the third squad prepared to depart, a rifleman shouted, "Found something!"

Carlos and McAbee walked with the squad leader to a bare spot where a Marine squatted, scratching through the dirt with his knife.

"Careful of any booby traps," the squad leader called to him.

"Got one right here," the Marine answered.

"Blow it in place," the sergeant ordered.

The Marine broke a chunk of C-4 from a long stick, pressed a blasting cap in it, and folded the claylike explosive over the small, metal primer, and formed a doughy ball. While he did that, the other Marines took cover behind the low stone wall.

"Fire in the hole! Fire in the hole! Fire in the hole!" the Marine shouted as he jumped behind the wall and squeezed the handle of the small electrical detonator three times, sending electricity down the wires and setting off the charge.

A dusty bang opened the top of a gigantic crock buried in the earth and filled with hundreds of pounds of rice.

"Charlie's gonna go hungry around here," Carlos said, looking down at the gigantic round jar that was nearly five feet tall and four feet in diameter, and sat in a square hole that had been shored with thick wooden slats along the sides.

The Marines peeked down the black gaps between the outside of the jar and the boards that covered the dirt on the sides of the hole.

"We'll get rid of this rice. You better get on that hill before Charlie comes running. No telling whose attention that explosion may have drawn," Carlos said.

The squad quickly moved away from the clearing where the huts stood and where Carlos and McAbee hid. They planned to drop a few of the one-pound sticks of C-4 down the sides of the jar and blow it when they departed. But for now, the two snipers took cover to wait and see who might come in search of them.

Carlos's radio squawked five minutes after he and McAbee had settled into their hide.

"Get out of there, now!" the message came from the excited squad leader. "Charlie's coming up the hill just below you two! Get going!"

Carlos looked at McAbee. Their closest fire support

lay hidden in the ragged jungle on the edge of the clearing more than 1,000 yards away.

"Blow the rice! Blow the rice!" the lieutenant's voice commanded on the radio.

"One thing for sure, we don't have time to make up any fuses," Carlos said. "We'll have to go with the timed fuse in the satchel."

McAbee pulled the forty-pounds of plastic explosive off his back and dropped it at his feet. "I'm not going to try to run from those clowns with that on my back! No way. It's too damn heavy!"

"I'm not taking mine either!" Hathcock said. "Eighty pounds of C-4 is about seventy-five pounds too much, though."

"I don't care!" McAbee said. "They want this rice blown, they're gonna get it blown good!"

Carlos chuckled as he stuffed his forty-pound satchel down the side of the rice and then stuffed McAbee's on top of his. "Gonna make some kind of mess out of this rice."

"Yeah," Mack said. "Puffed rice. Shot from guns!"

Carlos pulled the round green lighter on the end of the time fuse and both Marines ran to the little stone fence, 100 feet away. They lay against the wall and felt the ground shake as though an earthquake had struck when the explosive charge detonated.

"Shit!" McAbee said, raising up and looking at Carlos. Hundreds of pounds of rice rained down on them, mixed with dirt and splinters. "It's like it's snowing!"

Carlos started picking rice out of his eyebrows and hair. Rice stuck to both Marines as though they had been tarred and feathered with it. The grain filled their ears and every opening in their clothes.

As they stood to run, rice kept falling, snowing, covering every inch of ground. Both Marines' ears rang from the tremendously loud explosion and they laughed. They laughed so hard they couldn't run. They could only stumble down the 1,000 yards of open ground to the jungle's edge where the lieutenant waited with his platoon, on line, ready to engage the NVA patrol that now fanned into the village behind the two snipers who staggered, out of breath, howling hysterically like two drunks on liberty rather than two Marines running for their lives.

Automatic weapons fire cracked across the open ground while Carlos and McAbee could only stagger breathlessly, sprinkling rice with every step and finding that hilarious, too. Miraculously, none of the enemy bullets came near the two Marines.

14

Dance with the Devil

A THUNDEROUS BOOM SHOOK THE STAFF NCO TENT on Hill 55. The peacefulness of midnight suddenly came alive with the sound of Yankee barking his alarm and the clatter of Marines, roused from their sleep, searching for boots and helmets, and scurrying to shelter.

Carlos opened his eyes, blinking in the bright moonlight, listening for the sound of more artillery rushing through the air on their deadly arc into the lower fingers where Marines waited in bunkers, their rifles aimed outward, ready for an assault.

"They're firing short," Carlos called out in the darkness, but no one listened. The scurrying took priority over rational thought.

"Carlos! Come on to the bunker!" McAbee shouted. "Incoming! Incoming!

"Where's my Army hat!"

"It's short rounds, Mack. They're going for the wire," Carlos moaned, but his friend did not hear him.

McAbee found his helmet—a steel pot with a fiber

liner that he called his Army hat. But the excited staff sergeant, who still wore his white Stateside skivvies, could not find both his boots.

As a salvo of Ketusha rockets devastated the side of Hill 55, as though some mammoth shotgun had blasted the lower slopes, McAbee forgot his boot and ran for the bunker, just outside the front door.

A singular *clomp, thud, clomp*, sounded down the plywood floor, pounding toward the door, and roused Carlos enough to look and see his friend hurrying to safety, one foot bare and the other booted, "Army hat" on his head, and baggy white long-legged skivvy shorts flapping in the breeze.

Carlos began to rumble with laughter. But when Mack fell into the bunker, Carlos lost all control and howled.

Lately, Carlos had been reluctant to go into that bunker because it had partially filled with water—some groundwater, but mostly water from the indoor shower. It was not the splash that made Carlos fall off his rack laughing—it was Mack's scream and sudden stream of blue-tinted words after the crash and splash that sent Carlos reeling onto the floor.

After the shelling stopped, and Mack emerged, covered with mud and limping, Carlos apologized. Mack had not yelled from the near drowning that he took, but from the nail on which he had stepped, which caused him to leap forward and fall headfirst into the water-filled bunker.

WHEN THE CORPSMAN FINISHED DRESSING MCABEE'S injured foot the following morning at the regimental aid station, the lanky, blond-haired Marine hurried back to the hooch. He had news.

"Carlos, we're moving. Gonna go over to LZ Baldy. I just got the word that we're giving up part of Arizona for the Que Son Hills. Word is that we'll be gone in a week to ten days."

Carlos sat at his field desk and smiled. "I hear that area's full of hamburgers. Word is that the Americal Division and the 196th Infantry Brigade has the 1st, 3rd, and 36th NVA Regiments giving them fits.

"Plus I heard Division is realigning tactical boundaries of the entire TAOR. So a move over to Baldy makes sense."

"I got this from one of the guys in Operations," McAbee said. "We're gonna be spread all over creation down there. We're gonna have Fire Support Base Ross and Fire Support Base Ryder, and we're gonna build a new one called Bushwhack."

"Bushwhack," Carlos said with a look of inspiration, "I like that. Bushwhack. It sounds like a good place for snipers to live."

"You're talking September for that," McAbee said, sitting on a straight-back chair and unlacing the jungle boot off his sore foot. "Meanwhile we're going to live in sea huts that the Seabees will hammer together once we get there. It's gonna be a mess."

That night, Carlos and McAbee joined David Sommers in a long, green canvas-walled, hardback hut that served as a staff NCO club. A thundershower rumbled outside as a crowd of sweating men sat jammed together on low wooden benches watching and cheering John Wayne in the *Green Berets*. Water poured in on them from a thousand punctures in the tin roof—holes made from night after night of the enemy's harassing fire.

As the 16-mm projector flickered through the pall of cigarette smoke and body steam, rain splashed on the small, flat sheet-metal cover that one of the Marines from 11th Motor Transport Battalion had erected above the movie machine to shield it from the overhead leaks.

Just after the first reel change, a bullet ripped through the tent—a prelude to this night's bout. Outside, heavy gunfire erupted, yet the movie played on while bullets ripped through the tent and sent several of the newer arrivals diving to the floor and scurrying on their knees out the door.

"Crap!" Carlos said, flopping down on the wet, muddy floor, and carefully setting his drink in front of him. "I'm stayin' put. They're not gonna keep me from watchin' John Wayne bust hamburgers in this movie!"

Mack rested on his elbows next to Carlos and nudged his partner. "There's one more reel to this movie. When this one runs out, who's gonna stick that last reel on the projector?"

Carlos looked at David Sommers, who also lay on the floor with several other John Wayne diehards, and chuckled. "He will."

They watched the rest of the *Green Berets* that night, rain running through the sievelike roof and hundreds of bullets ripping through the tent at shoulder-high level. The projector, which sat on a three-foot-high stand in the midst of the fire, suffered only one shot through its sheet-metal roof.

Carlos changed the final reel.

It was the last movie Carlos watched on Hill 55.

ON THE MORNING OF AUGUST 12, FIRST BATTALION, 7th Marines moved through Arizona Territory on a major sweep, searching out and destroying enemy strongholds and food stores. Lieutenant Colonel John Dowd led his Marines on this operation, searching in particular for the 90th NVA Regiment, reinforced.

The morning climaxed several days of random attacks when two of Colonel Dowd's combat outposts came under heavy fire. As the day ended, Dowd's battalion rushed in hot pursuit of two battalions of the 90th NVA, who would run, try to hold, but ultimately have to run again.

Carlos wanted in on this action and Captain Hoffman had extended him an invitation to go along several days earlier. In response to the captain, Carlos sent three sniper teams, but with the move coming up, he could not go and lead these men himself. Instead, the staff sergeant spent much of his time packing sniper platoon gear. On top of that, on this day August 13, he had the commander of the guard watch.

Already, word circulated of the heavy fighting from the day before and Carlos found it difficult to concentrate on his duties. He knew that out there, where tall plumes of black and gray smoke rose from the hillsides, he would not be so restless.

"I'm getting cabin fever, Mack. I wasn't meant to hang around here and wait for the troops to report home. I'll tell you, if I had the chance to pick up and go to the field—any excuse—I would. Duty or not."

"Sergeant major would have your butt. You know how he gets when you jump off without telling him, and he'd take it especially hard with you having the duty," Mack said, honing a rifle part that he had clamped in a vise. Carlos moaned and continued stuffing folders and stacking gear.

Hathcock checked his watch and looked at McAbee. "Lunchtime. Gotta go to the mess tent and check the chow. Duty calls."

McAbee nodded and kept filing on the steel piece.

For Carlos, the afternoon of August 13 was one of the most boring days he would ever recall of his war experience. But as he finished checking posts at five P.M., the day suddenly filled with excitement.

"Turn that off!" Carlos shouted as he stepped into the sniper hooch.

The strained Cajun voice singing the song called "Joli Blond" sent chills through Carlos. "Every time I hear that song, I have bad luck. Something bad always happens!"

"You're serious," McAbee said, walking to the transistor radio that sat on the other end of his workbench. He turned the tiny black wheel on the top of the small plastic radio until it clicked off.

"Sorry," he said and went back to work on the rifle that he had nearly finished rebuilding.

"I just got One-Seven's situation reports from yesterday's operations," Carlos said. "They're taking some heavy losses, but kicking hell out of the NVA. Listen."

McAbee sat on the cot near his workbench and listened as Carlos read the brief reports.

"At 6:50 yesterday morning Delta Company got sucked into an ambush. Two hamburgers drew them into where twenty of their buddies waited. Ended up killing one Marine and wounding three. They didn't get any of them.

"At 8:50, Alpha Company lost a Marine when he set off a booby trap—a 105-millimeter artillery round with a pressure fuse. Apparently one of the platoons saw six of the hamburgers who set the thing; they killed one and wounded the other. Everybody they engage so far is NVA. One of the men they killed had a Chinese pistol."

"An officer," Mack said, resting his chin on the heels of his hands.

"Most likely."

Carlos thumbed through the printed pages and said, "Here. Here's where things start happening.

"At 11:45 in the morning, Echo Company took incoming into their position and had six Marines wounded. They swept their forward area and killed one NVA hamburger on his getaway.

"Then all hell broke loose when they began their battalion sweep. The NVA hit Bravo and Delta companies. They had units out on the sweeps, and when they started taking fire back in their camps, they hotfooted it home. They got back just in time to catch the full attack. Bravo and Delta, and Charlie Company, too, started taking RPGs and 82-millimeter mortar hits, and all kinds of small-arms fire.

"This lasted all night. NVA killed eight Marines and wounded thirty-three. At first light, they went out and picked up fifty-eight dead NVA and two wounded ones. They also picked up 100 AK-47s, three light machine guns, three RPG launchers, fifty-two Chicom rifles, and a world of ammo.

"While all that went on, the NVA was hitting One-Seven's command post, and elements from Charlie Company along with Alpha Company went into where the NVA had dug in along the tree line. When the dust settled, they lost five Marines, had twenty-two wounded, but killed eighty-two NVA.

"This morning, they went out from the battalion command post and picked up four wounded hamburgers and 147 dead ones. Also, the battalion got all kinds of 82-millimeter mortar tubes, some 120-millimeter mortars, and a world of small arms and ammo.

"I guess Colonel Dowd is finally getting at that raft of gooners that have dogged him for the past two months."

McAbee took off his glasses and rubbed his eyes.

"I'll bet our little rice denial program has gotten the NVA and Charlie in a pinch trying to get stocked up for the monsoons," Mack said. "Sounds to me like we've got their backs to the wall and they're trying to make a stand."

Carlos stood and looked outside. He could see the distant smoke of a battle.

"They're still at it," he said. "There must be thousands of those Communists going at our folks."

A worried expression spread over Carlos's face.

THAT AFTERNOON, IN THOSE SAME HILLS WHERE THE smoke of battle rose, heavy artillery shells and air-delivered bombs and napalm pounded and burned the 90th NVA Regiment, and what was left of its supporting units. Now they fought for their very existence against the battalion commanded by Lieutenant Colonel John A. Dowd.

India Company, 3rd Battalion, 7th Marines, joined Colonel Dowd's force when the fighting began to get heavy.

At five P.M. on August 13, 1969, John Dowd commenced a battalion sweep across a wide valley near the place they called Dodge City in the Arizona badlands. They were advancing on the enemy, who had dug in again along a tree line, determined to hold their ground.

Dowd stood in the midst of that front established by India Company, and led the advance on the tree line. The enemy had committed everything to this battle, and now waited, watching as the Marines came closer.

It felt like the quiet one encounters as a huge storm cloud rolls across the hills, just before the first gust of wind sends torrents of rain and hail, lightning and thunder.

Lieutenant Colonel John Aloysious Dowd, a Marine loved by his men, deeply respected by his peers, and one of the greatest warriors that Carlos Hathcock had ever had the pleasure and extreme honor of serving and calling friend, never heard that thunder.

In the time that an eye can blink, or bare skin can feel the prickle of the afternoon sun, the time that it takes to call out to warn a friend when a sudden rifle crack shatters the quietness of a warm summer afternoon while jungle birds sing in the trees, a man can die.

In the instant that a volley of rifle and machine-gun fire burst forth from the line of trees that edged the valley where John Dowd led his men, his life ended.

At just past five P.M. the commanding officer of 1st Battalion, 7th Marines, along with four of his men, died.

At just past five P.M., the smoke of battle that Carlos watched from his hilltop command post marked the spot where those five souls departed, and thirty-two other Marines lay bleeding from wounds while Spooky[1] flew overhead, churning and chopping and riddling the tree line to shredded and burned rubble.

---

[1] A twin-engine, fixed-wing aircraft, typically a C-117 (formerly a C-47, like the civilian Douglas DC-3), commonly used for cargo and troop transport, but in this case heavily loaded with 20-millimeter chain guns, rockets, and other significant firepower.

"Hey! Staff Sergeant Hathcock!" Corporal Perry shouted as he ran toward the sniper command post. "They're calling for volunteers to fly out to help One-Seven! They're taking hell!"

As Carlos watched that faraway smoke, the 90th NVA Regiment, reinforced by elements of the 2nd NVA Division and the 577th NVA Artillery, made their last stand against a reinforced battalion of Marines who fought with great vengeance for their many fallen brothers who now lay zipped in black bags at the rear area. Now, those avenging Marines fought against a superior-sized enemy force who was attempting to over-run them.

"Mack! Take my duty!" Hathcock shouted as he sprinted from the hooch, slinging his rifle and looping the straps of his pack over his shoulders while he ran. Carlos felt compelled to help. Compelled by that part of him that would never stand and watch while others needed aid.

"What about the sergeant major?" Mack yelled to his friend.

"He'll understand," Carlos called back, feeling that no Marine could resist the sounding of the alarm—his call to duty.

Hathcock ran up the rear ramp of a CH-46 Sea Knight helicopter that squatted with its twin rotor blades turning, waiting as forty Marines bounded aboard, filling its long and narrow belly.

The crew chief wore a heavy white aviator's helmet, decorated with zigzagging green and orange tape, and had its dark-tinted visor dropped down, hiding his eyes and much of his nose. He stood facing out at the foot of the ramp, pointing to his left, and yelled above the roar of the turning blades, "Bravo Company!"

He shouted again, "Charlie Company," and pointed to his right.

Carlos thought of Captain Hoffman and ran to the left where other volunteers, heading to help Bravo Company, sat, buckling themselves to the long, grease-stained, red nylon fabric seat fastened to a tubular-aluminum frame that stretched the entire length of each side of the aircraft's cargo bay.

These Marines who sat, apprehensive of what they may encounter—scared that they might die—were mostly Marines who spent much of their time cooking in field kitchens, typing in command tents, driving trucks, or a dozen other jobs that do not normally involve direct combat.

Carlos admired them for their bravery. To him they were heros.

Shuddering under the strain of its heavy cargo of men and arms, the helicopter rose from the landing zone, following three other similarly loaded aircraft, and disappeared in the blackness of the night sky.

Carlos edged his way to the front, near the window where another Marine wearing a white, tape-decorated aviator's helmet stood behind a .50-caliber machine gun. Hathcock stood near the Marine, and watched the black hills and jungle and hidden rubble of war pass just below the belly of this green giant filled with Marines.

Below, in the blackness of the jungle, he saw red streaks of fire reaching toward him, passing below and above the helicopter as it pressed onward toward the hills of Arizona Territory.

A ridge line rose from the blackness of the ground and touched the gray sky with its jagged edge. Down the side of this ridge, thousands of red streaks streamed into each other. The nighttime exchange of gunfire, accented by tracers, reminded him of one night in bootcamp when he joined in and first saw the Final Protective Fire that Marines termed "The Mad Moment."

A sudden tug on his pack startled Carlos. He was tense and frightened, too, by what he saw.

"Charlie Company!" a Marine with the face of a child yelled at him. "Which side is going to Charlie Company?"

"This side is Bravo Company. Charlie Company is over there!" Carlos yelled to this young man, still in his teens, whose face offered little wear for a razor, and whose mother probably worried for him each day.

The Marine turned to cross the helicopter, and before he could step, that mad moment below them turned skyward and filled the inside of the lumbering green giant with hundreds of red glowing bullets. Seven Marines, including this young man who wanted to help Charlie Company—who wanted to save the lives of his brother Marines pinned on the hillside below—fell dead.

Carlos had taken a step toward the Marine who fired the machine gun out the helicopter's window. As smoke and red glowing bullets and spraying hot hydraulic fluid filled the helicopter, Carlos fell to the floor with a sudden burning pain in his right upper thigh.

He scrambled back to his feet and saw the floor, covered with wounded and dead Marines. He looked between the two pilots' seats and saw a firework- and tracer-filled sky through the bullet-riddled windscreen. He imagined headlines that he feared Jo would read: "More than 40 Marines Die As Helicopter Is Shot Down."

He closed his eyes for a moment and waited.

Then the helicopter banked sharply left and Hathcock opened his eyes. Again, he looked out the front window and this time he saw blackness and stars. Smoke still fumed and oil still sprayed, but the bullets had stopped. Carlos knew that the attempt to get this helicopter down and reinforce the Marines on the ground had failed. They were going home.

When the leaking, limping aircraft touched down, the pilot did not make a textbook landing. The wheels hit the ground hard, jolting every Marine aboard. But Carlos knew that the pilots did not care about the smoothness of their landing this night. They were just glad to be alive.

"What happened?" Mack said as Carlos limped inside the command hooch.

"We took too much fire to get in there."

Mack looked sadly at Carlos. "Colonel Dowd got killed when that ruckus began this afternoon."

Carlos said nothing at first. He thought of the other good Marines he had known and lost.

"Good man. Outstanding Marine."

A hot lump tightened in his throat, choking him, and he turned his face toward the screen so that his friend would not see the sudden well of tears that he fought hard to conceal.

"I'm *suuuure* gonna miss him," Carlos said with the audible gurgle that often accompanies fought-back sorrow—the sound of one's soul fighting to find its voice and cry out.

After a moment, Carlos breathed heavily and pulled his emotions together. The sight of seven Marines dying at his feet and the news of the colonel's death had left him drained. He stared out at the darkness that engulfed the world where the distant flashes of the battle that he had departed continued to glow, yet he saw nothing but the faces of those men in his mind's eye.

"What's that on your leg?" Mack asked, seeing the blood that turned Carlos's trousers dark.

"Aww, that's nothing," Carlos said, taking a deep breath of the stale and steamy night. "A little scratch. I'll put something on it later."

He walked out of the hooch without looking back at his best friend, who felt the grief, too, and who worried as well about this man he considered his brother.

The rounds from checkpoint to checkpoint seemed much more distant to Carlos as he limped with a bullet lodged in his thigh. He thought of Sergeant Major Puckett and what he would say if he got wind of his volunteer effort.

It was certain that the sergeant major would find out from any doctors who attended Carlos's wound. He also knew that the sergeant major might never know if he let his leg heal without going to sick bay. But by first light, the pain signaled that he could not just let it mend on its own.

After passing the watch duty to his relief the following morning, Carlos went to the regimental aid station.

When the corpsman said, "You just got a Purple Heart," Carlos swore at him.

"Don't you write that down! Put it down as a cut or something. I don't want no Purple Heart," Hathcock said.

The corpsman laughed. "Don't be so humble. We give out a hundred a day around here."

"I get a Purple Heart," Carlos argued, "and the sergeant major will have my butt. That's why I don't want it. I don't need him mad at me!"

Three days later, Carlos stood before Sergeant Major Clinton Puckett and received his Purple Heart, as well as a sound lecture on what it meant to be Commander of the Guard. But because of Hathcock's noble purpose, the sergeant major did not place him on report for reassigning his duty without permission.

AT THE END OF THE THREE-DAY SWEEP IN ARIZONA TERritory, near the valley they called Dodge City, the 1st Battalion left those badlands with the 90th NVA Regiment virtually destroyed and 226 of the enemy killed.

Two days after that, the regimental headquarters, along with 3rd Battalion and the sniper platoon, moved to Landing Zone Baldy, a hilltop twenty-three miles south of Da Nang, while 2nd Battalion moved to Fire Support Base Ross, a hill seven miles southwest of Baldy.

During the move, Carlos, McAbee, and a driver assigned to them from 11th Motor Transport Battalion drove a six-by truck with a high canvas cover over its cargo bed to Da Nang. They had completed their portion of the move and now headed to I Corps' main supply point where they were to pick up thirty-five R-and-R kits—small green and yellow plastic "ditty" bags with shaving gear, prophylactics, and toiletries inside. It was a good excuse to take a vacation to the city and eat a sit-down lunch in the modern dining hall there.

All of June and July, and thus far in August, many items were in short supply on Hill 55. Utility uniforms and boots loomed at the top of that list. All three Marines who sat in the cab of that truck had holes worn in the knees and seats of their uniforms. When they walked up to the large dining hall, a Marine dressed in white and wearing gunnery sergeant stripes sent them away.

"You boys go change into decent uniforms and take a shower," he told them.

All the Marines that Carlos saw there in that rear area wore fairly new utilities, and it increased his humiliation and anger.

"Let's go on to the warehouse and get those kits. To hell with eating there, you don't have to dress up to eat C rations," Hathcock growled.

When the truck stopped in front of the Quonset hut that sat at the head of several long warehouses, a very young, frightened-looking private stepped through the doorway.

"Your boss around?" Carlos asked, jumping from the cab.

"No, sir," the private responded. "They're all gone to chow."

Carlos looked at his watch; it was 11:25 in the morning, and he knew that despite the fact that a person could get fed at the dining hall as early as 10:30 A.M., normal chow time did not start until 11:30.

"You boys stay pretty busy here, don't you?" Hathcock said with the sound of innocence in his voice.

"No, sir," the private said. "We'll move pallets and load orders during the day, but we don't push it too hard around here."

Carlos thought about the men back at the fire bases and outposts squatting in the dirt with no supplies. The

treatment at the dining hall and now the revelation that
the people at the supply point were in no special hurry
to get the much-needed supplies out to the line companies made him boil.

"You boys get plenty of utilities?" the staff sergeant
asked.

"Sure. Many as we need," the private said proudly.
"That's the advantage of working here."

"We come to pick up thirty-five R-and-R kits. I got
the paperwork right here," Carlos said.

"You all go on down and get them. They're in that
first warehouse," the private said. He walked inside the
hut, took out a set of keys hung on a large brass clip,
and tossed them across the counter to McAbee, who
followed him inside.

"We just go out and get them ourselves?" McAbee
asked.

"Sure," the private answered. "Just drop off the keys
when you're done. I gotta stay here. I'm just the phone
watch.

"You can drop the paperwork off when the gunny
gets back."

Carlos smiled at the young Marine. "Come on,
Mack. We got some shopping to do."

McAbee grinned and climbed inside the truck.

Carlos trotted back to the Quonset hut and returned
the keys, rather than drive the truck by. He did not
want the private to see the back of the truck stuffed
with boxes of utilities and boots, along with thirty-five
R-and-R kits.

When they backed the truck up to the 7th Marines
supply point, McAbee looked at the Marines who ran
out to meet the truck—the canvas top bulged like
Santa's overfilled sack of Christmas gifts.

"Don't ask. Just be thankful," he called to them.

Carlos and his sniper platoon, David Sommers and
many of the Marines in the regiment got new uniforms
that mid-August week as they moved to Baldy.

After their success of wiping out the 90th NVA Regiment, the 1st Battalion stacked arms and stood down for R-and-R at China Beach. Because of that, they moved to LZ Baldy last.

While the 1st Battalion took advantage of the Stack Arms program, a period of rest and recovery, the remaining two battalions of 7th Marines set about clearing the Hiep Duc Valley in the Que Son Hills with the 196th Infantry Brigade.

On August 28, this major push of combined U.S. Marine and Army forces finally dislodged the stubborn enemy.

Ron McAbee and David Sommers sat on the porch of their new sea hut. They sipped ice-cold Coca-Cola and listened to Armed Forces Vietnam Radio. And, consistent with its "play-it-all" format, the selection that followed Led Zeppelin's "Whole Lotta Love" was a country song. A song that many country music fans who especially enjoyed the songs of the bayou country of Louisiana had requested. "Joli Blond."

"Shut that off!" Carlos shouted from inside the hooch.

"Damn! I'm sorry, Carlos. I forgot all about that," McAbee said, turning off the small transistor radio.

David Sommers shouted to Carlos, who rested on his cot, "That song doesn't mean anything, Carlos. It's a real popular piece now. You just connect every time you have a bad experience with it. It's not the song!"

Carlos got off his rack and walked through the door. "It's a durn good country song. I like the way it sounds. But every time I hear it, something bad always happens.

"I don't need to hear that when me and Mack are going out to meet up with Three-Seven."

"Okay! Okay!" Sommers said, drinking more cold soda.

"You two going out with Three-Seven, huh? You've made a lot of progress in three months' time. I can remember when all you were good for was shit detail."

Carlos playfully slapped Sommers on the back of his

head. "Watch it. I don't need to hear that from a no-account career planner.

"My troops have done real good for themselves. And, those schools I held for all the platoon and company commanders in the regiment didn't do any harm either. Now my men are on a heavy demand. Everybody wants snipers."

"Everybody except the folks on the top of the hill," Sommers said with a smile.

"Well they don't need snipers," Carlos responded with a grin. "They call in air strikes!"

McAbee laughed loud and hard. "Right! That was the funniest thing I've seen in years."

David Sommers looked puzzled. "What's the big joke?"

"You didn't hear about the big air strike on Hill 55 the day before we left?" Carlos said proudly. "I thought everybody heard about that!"

"You know I don't run with that inner circle up there," Sommers said, sipping more cold Coke. "You'll have to fill me in."

McAbee leaned forward, on the straight-back chair. "They were unloading fifty-five gallon barrels of gasoline on Finger 3 and one of them got away. It rolled way down into the wire. Too far for us to get to, and just right for Charlie.

"They sent a patrol down toward the barrel to put a charge on it and blow it in place. Charlie must have seen it coming because they had a sniper out there picking at those Marines every time they got within fifty yards of the barrel.

"Carlos wanted to help. He told that top that he would put a couple of rounds through the barrel and get the gas to leaking good, and then put a tracer in it to light it off. Hell, anybody in the sniper platoon could have done it. It wasn't anything spectacular.

"But *nooo*. They wanted to do it their way.

"Carlos and I sat down and watched while they

popped willy-peter[2] rounds down there with mortars and 105s. Hell, we sat and started laughing because they were blowing hell out of their wire and not coming near the barrel.

"I went to the top and offered again. I figured that he just didn't like Carlos, and would be a little more receptive to me. But *nooo*. He wanted to do it his way.

"Then somebody—and nobody is claiming credit—decided to call in an air strike on that stupid barrel of gasoline! I mean, really! An air strike?

"We spend a million dollars and risk a pilot's life to blow up a barrel of gasoline when Carlos was right there and could have burned it in a minute."

Mack took a big gulp from his Coke, waiting for Sommers to ask the inevitable question.

"Did the air strike get it?"

Mack and Carlos both howled, "*Noooooo!* He blew a whole section out of the wire!"

"What happened to the barrel?" Sommers asked. "Did they ever get it?"

Carlos smiled and said, "Don't tell nobody, but one of my snipers shot it, and set it off with a tracer."

"Really?" Sommers said.

"Yeah!" Hathcock answered. "You know ole Jones with the bad feet—can't walk so we put him on that .50 up in the tower?"

"Sure."

"That top looks up at the tower and forgets that it's a sniper up there. He yells for Jones to open up on that barrel.

"It took about four shots to set that gas off, and then the top looked at me like, I showed you. And walked off feeling smug.

"I didn't have the heart to tell him that the .50 in the tower was mine!"

Sommers shook his head. "I don't know. I'm really

---

[2]White phosphorus artillery rounds.

not surprised, I suppose, considering some of the hard-
heads we have around here."

"Their loss," Mack said, sipping more cold Coke.

"That walk-in refrigerator that the Americal Division
left behind has sure added to the comfort level around
here," David Sommers said, drinking down the last of
his Coke. "All this cold stuff is gonna spoil me."

Mack looked at Sommers. "You want to get spoiled?
Come with Carlos and me next time we go to cool off
and eat a little cheese and wieners."

Sommers smiled. "It's you two. I should have
known."

Mack laughed. "It's so damn hot! That walk-in
makes a fine little place to beat the heat. And its always
full of cheese and hotdogs. We can go in there and cool
off and eat, too."

"They just keep putting a new lock on the door,"
Carlos said with a grin.

"And we just keep cutting it off," Mack said, cack-
ling. "All they have to do to keep us out is put a guard
on it."

Sommers smiled. "Of course, Sergeant Major Puckett
will have our skins when he catches us."

Carlos winked at Sommers. "That will never happen."

It never did.

The humor on the porch lasted until Carlos saw the
helicopters.

"Mack. Time to go," Carlos remarked, picking up
his pack and rifle, which he had set next to the hooch
door. In a minute both snipers were gone.

THE TWIN-ROTOR HELICOPTER SHUDDERED ABOVE THE
Hiep Duc Valley where 2nd Battalion pushed an esti-
mated two NVA regiments from the east while the
Army's 196th Light Infantry attacked from the west.
The sky full of churning helicopters carried 3rd Battal-
ion and the two snipers.

Four other sniper teams already advanced with 2nd Battalion, and in 3rd Battalion Carlos was there to reinforce the Marines on the ground and help overpower the enemy regiments who remained entrenched there.

In one of the helicopters that carried Kilo Company, Lance Corporal Jose F. Jimenez—a fire team leader—rode with his platoon. The chopper set down in a hot landing zone, and Jimenez and his patrol quickly found cover at the edge of this valley, crisscrossed with rice paddy dikes.

Here they faced an enemy who held the terrain—entrenched in holes and tunnels. Success weighed on a balance, tipped by the courage of Marines—youngsters just out of their teens—whose valor would take them well beyond those measures that determine the call of duty.

As the helicopter that carried Kilo Company into the area of hostile fire set down, another chopper churned in low, clipping the treetops, dropping into an adjacent landing zone.

Carlos stood near the front window, next to the door gunner whose machine gun chewed the ground below them. Small holes popped in the helicopter's skin, and Carlos looked at Mack. Each Marine could see the anxiety written on the other's face—a look of concern that creeps across most men who embark on a tightrope where death laps at their heels.

Ron McAbee turned his head to look out the large open side window where the machine gunner sent pounds of lead drilling into the bush and snags below. And when he looked back, Carlos lay on his back, a look of total surprise and wide-eyed horror on his face.

"Carlos!" Mack shouted, and reached down to pick up his friend. As he wrapped his large hand beneath the base of Hathcock's many-pocketed NVA pack, he felt sticky, warm wetness.

"Oh, no!" Mack cried out, sending greater fear into Carlos because he felt nothing—no pain. He had only felt the impact of the bullet as it picked him off his feet and hurled him to the helicopter's floor.

Then McAbee took his hand away to look at the blood, and Carlos stood.

It was yellow and sticky.

"Turn around!" Mack yelled above the roar of the turbine-driven engines. And McAbee began to laugh as he sniffed his hand.

"Skeeter spray!" he yelled. "The bullet got your skeeter spray!"

THE BATTLE LASTED THROUGH THE NIGHT AND THE TWO snipers spent much of it moving quietly across the paddies, from hide to hide, sniping and blocking the NVA as they attempted to hold and bolster their positions. When they crossed into the open, Carlos shot them— killing their leaders and leaving the surviving soldiers in the shambles of confusion and fear of this random death merchant who once again wore the white feather.

Throughout the night, he and Ron McAbee killed several NVA but confirmed none. Too often, there was no company or platoon commander, or third-party staff NCO or officer to confirm the dead. They were too busy fighting to keep count or give credit. And for Carlos and Ron McAbee, that was fine.

For Lance Corporal Jose Jimenez, the body count also made no difference. He was dead.

But Jose Jimenez—a youthful leatherneck from Mexico, who joined the Marines for the same reason Carlos and thousands of other such honorable men had—dealt a deciding blow to the enemy before he died.

As his fire team moved away from that hot LZ where the helicopters had left them, entrenched NVA soldiers turned their wrath on his platoon. Jimenez faced a choice of holding and allowing the enemy to enjoy the advantage or to charge—to seize the initiative—and turn the attack on the enemy.

The dark-skinned, square-jawed Marine took up his

rifle and charged forward, leading the assault and personally destroying an antiaircraft gun that the NVA soldiers hoped to protect.

Jimenez turned to see his fellow Marines follow him, and the lance corporal yelled as he charged forward to within ten feet of the enemy. As he approached the trench, firing and shouting—leading his men and defeating the enemy—he fell to machine-gun fire.

Kilo Company took their objective. Third Battalion, 2nd Battalion, and the Army's 196th dislodged the enemy from the Hiep Duc Valley. And Lance Corporal Jimenez earned the Medal of Honor.

15

Holding On and
Letting Go

WHEN RON MCABEE RETURNED TO 7TH MARINES'
new home on LZ Baldy from Da Nang with his new
glasses, Carlos had already gone. Had taken Perry with
him.

The two staff sergeants had planned to rendezvous
with 1st Battalion, 7th Marines, when the unit returned
to their base of operations on the east side of the Que
Son Hills from the Hiep Duc and the Nghi Ha valleys.
The entire 7th Marines Regiment had just finished
clearing out two NVA regiments there. The two snipers
had learned from battalion operations that the 3rd and
36th NVA regiments, the GK-33, and the 1st Viet Cong
regiment had concentrated their forces in the Que Son
area. Carlos saw it as a fruitful opportunity for his entire sniper platoon, most of whom had participated in
the Hiep Duc and Nghi Ha operations and remained
with the battalions, now heading for the eastern Que
Son Hills.

The night of September 15, 1969, cooked the men
who slept indoors, so Ron McAbee had decided to sleep

outside, on top of the bunker with Yankee. Hardly a breeze stirred that night, but outside, lying on his poncho liner, Mack could at least breathe.

The tall blond staff sergeant had stretched out on the bunker roof, and had laid his last pair of unbroken glasses on the sandbags that ringed the bunker, just below the roof. He had unlaced his boots but kept them on his feet, should he need to flee for cover during the night. Yankee slept with his head on McAbee's chest. The dog had adopted Mack much as he had Carlos.

In the early morning, well before dawn and while the moon shone brightly, Yankee raised his head from the Marine's chest and perked his ears. A small rumble began to grow in the dog's throat. His lips curled above his teeth, and the rumble deepened to a growl.

Just as Yankee made his first bark, Mack's eyes snapped open. Before he had time for any rational thought, his feet swung to the side and he stood, about to run. The sound of crunching plastic and glass stopped him cold.

The next morning, he had pled for Carlos to wait for him until he had returned from Da Nang with a new pair of glasses. Hathcock told Mack he would wait, but not much past noon.

Carlos hated waiting. Boredom ate at his soul as he checked his watch again and again. He sat impatiently, dreading the two more hours he knew it would take before Mack could possibly return, when Staff Sergeant Boone from 1st Battalion's intelligence section told Hathcock that a convoy was about to leave and that they had room for him and one other Marine. After a half-hour more of waiting, Carlos gave up and told Corporal Perry to grab his pack and come with him. They were heading south.

Seeing the sniper hooch deserted, McAbee told his driver to wait. The lanky staff sergeant ran inside and in a few seconds returned to the jeep with his pack and rifle. He planned on catching an afternoon helicopter south to Fire Support Base Ross and then hitchhike from there to 1st Battalion, 7th Marines' bivouac.

"Skipper," Ron McAbee shouted to an assistant operations officer as he jumped from the jeep in front of 7th Marines Operations. "How long ago did they leave?"

"A little after ten o'clock I think," the Marine captain said as he stepped through the hooch door.

Mack looked at the officer and saw his down-turned mouth and sad eyes. He saw the tension in the captain's jaws. There was something else. Something troubling.

At the same time a Marine, who did not see the captain standing to the left of the open door, jogged outside the operations hooch. Seeing McAbee he said in an excited voice, "They finally got Staff Sergeant Hathcock! I think he's dead."

Mack frowned at the captain. The captain gave the Marine a cross glance, and then looked at McAbee.

"Staff Sergeant Hathcock, Corporal Perry, and about a dozen other Marines took a hit on an amtrac," he said, keeping his eyes fixed squarely on McAbee. "Sergeant Major Puckett is doing his best to get their status right now. He was really glad you two were not together. He said that is exactly why he had been so adamant about you not going on patrol together in the past. We would be without a sniper platoon leader now, you realize that?"

"Yes, sir, I do," McAbee said. "What happened though?"

"All we know right now is their amtrac took a hit from a big mine, command detonated. Killed everyone inside, and burned all the Marines on top. Some have said Hathcock is dead, but honestly we do not know.

"I was on the radio with Gunny Boone. He said Hathcock stood in that fire and threw everybody off before he jumped off.[1] By then he was burned to a crisp. So it doesn't look very good."

---

[1] When the explosive detonated under the amtrac, the blast ruptured the vehicle's fuel tanks, immediately engulfing the amphibious personnel car-

McAbee's normally reddish complexion turned fish-belly white. His heart beat so hard that it hurt. He could hardly catch his breath. For a full minute he stood staring at the captain, saying nothing.

"Mind if I use one of the Ops phones?" the staff sergeant finally managed.

The captain motioned with his head toward the hooch door. "Use the one on the gunny's desk," he said.

Mack looked back at his driver. "Don't shut the motor off. Don't go anywhere."

Then in two long steps, Ron McAbee was inside the hooch and in front of the gunny's desk, where the Marine sat scrawling notes.

"Hathcock and Perry were on an amtrac that got ambushed," the gunny began.

Mack looked at him. "Yeah, the skipper just told me out front."

"The VC set off a 500-pound box mine[2] under it," the gunny continued. "Blew that sucker sky high. All the Marines were burned bad—real bad. I don't know whether he is dead or alive. He looked bad when they put him on the Med-Evac chopper and sent him out to the *Repose*.[3] I didn't get any word on Perry, but he's on the *Repose*, too."

McAbee took off his glasses and wiped sweat out of his eyes. "Thanks, Gunny," he said, and turned the

---

rier in flames. Carlos Hathcock was the only Marine riding on top that remained conscious after the explosion. Rather than leaping to safety, Hathcock stood in the fire and rescued the seven other Marines riding on top with him. They included Privates First Class Roberto Barrera, Lawrence Head, Keith Spencer, Thurman Trussell, Lance Corporal Earl Thibodeaux, Corporal Perry, and 1st Lieutenant Edward Hyland. Hathcock suffered third-degree burns over forty-three percent of his body.

[2]High velocity explosives packed in a nonferrous container, such as a large wooden box or clay jar, that does not produce an electromagnetic signature on typical mine detection equipment. Viet Cong would commonly bury the container in a roadway or trail and fill it with explosives. When a target entered its kill radius, guerrillas watching from a hidden vantage point would detonate the device.

[3]U.S. Navy hospital ship, USS *Repose*.

crank on the side of the canvas-covered box that held the field telephone. He held the receiver against his ear and then pressed the button on the side of the handle and spoke, "Master Sergeant Gunderson," Mack began. "Eugene G. Gunderson. Yes, Moose. That's him. Can I talk to him?

"Okay. Well, then would you mind giving him a message to please get ahold of me? Yes, Staff Sergeant Ron McAbee, at LZ Baldy, 7th Marines snipers. I just heard about Staff Sergeant Hathcock and was hoping Moose could fill me in.

"He's gone out to the ship? The *Repose*? Reckon I can get a ride out there with him?

"Okay, I am on my way. Marble Mountain, right. I know where it is. Out by China Beach. Right. Thanks."

Staff Sergeant McAbee clipped the receiver back into its case and offered the gunny a half-smile.

"I'm headed out to the ship to see Carlos," McAbee told the gunnery sergeant, and in two giant steps the six foot, two inch Marine jumped in the jeep and roared away, slinging gravel and dirt.

Mack held the jeep driver's M-16 in his right hand by its pistol grip as the two Marines raced northward on Highway 1. The lance corporal behind the wheel beat the horn button with the heel of his right hand each time they passed groups of Vietnamese walking or riding bicycles, motor scooters, or carts along the roadside. He never released his foot from the accelerator pedal that he kept planted against the floorboard. When he passed the people, he left them choking in a swirl of dirt and gravel.

A few kilometers north of the bridge that crosses the Song Ky Lam, the driver skidded the jeep in a right turn off of Highway 1 and onto Route 4, which headed east through Hoi An. At the beach that Marines had nicknamed the Riviera the roadway bent northward and then ran parallel to the beach, leading past the Marble Mountain air facility and terminating at the tip of a peninsula called China Beach.

The jeep slid to a stop in front of the Marble Mountain tower and operations terminal. Ron McAbee was already out of the vehicle and running to the door when the driver switched off the ignition.

"Top Gunderson," Mack said as he hurried to a counter where a sergeant stood on one side helping two pilots opposite him with paperwork. The three Marines looked blank-faced at the staff sergeant.

"Big guy," McAbee continued, "Master sergeant from 1st Division Ops on Hill 327. He would have come here to catch a ride to the *Repose*."

"Can't help you, Staff," the sergeant behind the counter said. The two pilots shook their heads. "I just came on duty, and the sergeant I relieved has gone to chow."

"You have anything headed out to the *Repose*?" Mack then asked.

"Not unless you can frag a chop out there," the sergeant offered. "Try hitting some of the squadron operations sections. They might have a crew needing to fly a sortie."

One of the pilots, a captain, looked at McAbee. "That's probably a wasted shot, Staff Sergeant," he said. "Just about anything flyable is supporting operations down by the Que Son Hills. Charlie burned up a bunch of Marines down there. Then units started taking hits from all over. You can try, but you might be better off spending your time heading on up to China Beach or into Da Nang and catching a boat out to the ship."

McAbee could already see the writing on the wall. He walked back to the jeep and collapsed in the passenger seat.

"Well, Cadillac," he told the driver, "want to take a spin up to China Beach? Maybe into Da Nang?"

The lance corporal behind the wheel looked at McAbee.

"Lot of shit between here and there," he said. "I will if you want me to, but lot of shit goes down on this road. Charlie will clip a few rounds at us, at least."

McAbee looked at the Marine, and then at the afternoon sun dropping lower in the western sky. If Gunderson had been here, he was already gone now. He had no guarantees that anything going outbound would be at China Beach or in Da Nang.

"I guess it's not worth the risk," he muttered. "Let's get back to Baldy, and I'll buy you a Coke."

Ron McAbee slept again on the bunker with Yankee. The evening was cool, but he could not lay on the cot next to Carlos's bed. The sight of his best friend's clothes and footlocker, and not knowing if he was dead or alive, was something he could do without.

As he lay on his poncho liner, he thought about his chore tomorrow, having to pack his buddy's gear. He had watched other Marines in other units do it. No one in the sniper hooch had had to do it until now. Now they had two men to pack out.

THE NEXT MORNING, DAVID SOMMERS STUCK HIS HEAD through the door. He saw Mack folding Carlos's clothes and separating out gear that he had to turn back to regimental supply.

"Want some help?" Sommers asked.

Mack shook his head no, and said nothing.

When he snapped the combination padlock shut on the hasp that fed through the three grommets in the top flaps of Carlos's sea bag, closing the satchel shut, he simply let it fall by Hathcock's cot, and he walked out the door. He needed to take a breather before packing out Perry.

Mack had not eaten breakfast. He did not feel like it this morning. He walked to the Operations tent instead.

"Can I call division on your phone, Gunny?" McAbee said to the gunnery sergeant sitting behind the desk. It did not look as if the man had moved since yesterday. He wore the same utility uniform. His coffee mug showed the same stains on the outside lip.

The Marine said nothing and nudged the field phone toward Mack.

"Thanks," Mack said as he turned the crank on the canvas-covered box.

"Top Gunderson? He there?" McAbee said.

"Shit, Moose," Mack began, "you heard about Carlos, I'm sure. Any word on his condition?

"Thank God!"

"I'm not sure if that is good or bad, Mack," Moose Gunderson said. "Carlos is burned over ninety-percent of his body. Half of that is third-degree burns.

"Carlos had them call me yesterday. I talked to the doctor and he said that most people die after a few weeks with the severity of Carlos's burns. They're loading him on a plane to San Antonio right now. His only real chance is getting to the burn center there at Brooke Hospital."

"How is Carlos doing?" Mack asked. "I mean, is he conscious? In a lot of pain?"

"Oh, he's been talking a blue streak since yesterday," Gunderson said. "You know him. He's gonna be all right whether or not he is. He's acting like it's just a scratch. He don't want anybody worrying.

"Doctors gave me an address, if you want to write him in Texas."

That night, Ron McAbee wrote Carlos a long letter. He told him how it was just good luck that they both did not go on that amtrac together. He told him how he drove all over the area trying to catch a ride to the ship, and that he was awfully sorry he could not get out there. He told him that Moose Gunderson had filled him in, and had given him the address for the burn center. He told him that he had heard "Joli Blond" play on the radio and because Carlos said nothing about it, he had ignored it. He told him he was sorry.

CARLOS REMEMBERED READING MACK'S LETTER several weeks after he had arrived at Brooke Army Medical

Center at Fort Sam Houston, Texas. But now, as he lay in his bed in Virginia Beach, nearly thirty years later, he also thought of the pain. He had endured the horror of daily debridement, having the scabbing flesh of his terrible burns scraped away. They put him in whirlpool baths, and then tried as gently as possible to remove the dead tissue. But there was no gentle that was gentle enough.

Later they began to surgically transplant skin to those full-thickness burned areas of his body. Since he had so little skin left that was not damaged, doctors had to use donor skin and skin from specially grown pigs.

However, as Carlos lay in his bed, living the last hours of his life, he considered the physical pain as nothing compared to the mental anguish he suffered, not only from the disabling effects that the burns had on him, but from the multiple sclerosis that he believed the injury had set off in him.

Throughout the early 1970s life had become a daily fight for him. Stress from pushing himself to remain active in the Marine Corps left him often disagreeable. Despite his efforts to rebuild himself. Despite his efforts to make his badly scarred body flex and stretch into shooting positions. Despite pushing himself so hard he often passed out on the firing line. He would never shoot a rifle again as he once had. He could not even hold a decent group.

Moose Gunderson had rejoined the Marine Corps Shooting Team after finishing his tour in Vietnam, and spent hours each day practicing positions and shooting groups with Carlos on the 1,000-inch range.[4]

Hathcock could only manage shooting from the prone position with any accuracy. He had spent several hours lying on his belly with the rifle sling cinched

---

[4] A miniature shooting range 1,000 inches in length using small targets to simulate long distances, enabling marksmen to work on rifle operation, holds, and techniques with minimal influence from elements such as wind.

tightly around his upper arm, working to stabilize his technique.

"Carlos, you look a little peaked," Moose said, seeing Hathcock's face, wet and pasty-white.

"I do feel a little light-headed," Carlos responded.

He had the heavy leather shooting jacket strapped tightly around him, so his movements resembled those of the Tin Woodsman in *The Wizard of Oz*. The tail of the black coat struck Hathcock at the thighs and clinched snugly at his neck, allowing nearly no ventilation on this hot Virginia afternoon.

Carlos pulled the tail of the shooting sling that he had cinched above the biceps of his left arm. As he released the pressure and let the loop fall past his elbow so that he could lay down his rifle, blood suddenly gushed from his sleeve.

"Oops," Hathcock said, trying to chuckle. He smiled at Gunderson, who immediately noticed the blood. "Guess I sprung a leak someplace."

"Here, let me give you a hand with that," Moose said, unhooking the several straps down the front that held the shooting jacket closed around Carlos.

As Gunderson released the last strap, Hathcock peeled it back and let it slip off his shoulders.

What used to be a yellow cotton shooting-team sweatshirt was soaked red, and now dripped blood down Carlos's trousers without the pressure of the shooting jacket straps to constrain it. His skin, losing its elasticity from the burn scars, now broke open and bled with very little pressure or strain.

Moose Gunderson was a tough Marine. Tough as they come. Shooting team Marines used to joke, "He's so hard that he's got muscles in his do-do." However, the sight of his friend Carlos sent the battle-hardened Marine back-stepping.

"Shit!" Gunderson said, gasping a breath. Then a prankish smile crept across his face as he looked at his friend's wide eyes. "Carlos, I'd throw up if I didn't have such a hard stomach."

Hathcock laughed out loud, while Moose filled a canteen cup with water he drained from a yellow and red plastic insulated jug, and then handed it to Carlos.

TIME AFTER TIME, HATHCOCK ENDURED THE SAME SORT of experience, trying to get himself back in shape. Carlos never quit trying. He joined the other Marksmanship Training Unit Marines in their daily physical training, struggling through calisthenics, running, and performing pull-ups. It took him months before he could raise his chin above the bar even once. He finally accomplished two pull-ups, once, and that stood as his record for the rest of his life.

Carlos's stubborn nature would not allow him to accept assistance. He carried his own gear when he fired the rifle, and he pulled his own targets when it was his turn in the butts. He wore white cotton gloves to protect his fragile skin from the steel and wooden framework of the target carriage. By the time he finished the relay, bloodstains spread from his palms to the tops of the gloves, and from the fingertips to the blue knit cuffs.

At the end of his target duty, he went to a hydrant and rinsed the gloves, so that he could use them later that day or the following morning. Any of the Marines serving with Carlos would have gladly pulled his targets for him. Yet the proud Marine sniper could not allow it. If it was at all humanly possible for him to do, he did it himself.

Carlos smiled as he lay on the bed, his eyes still closed, yet he saw the bright sun and black pavement in his mind as he relived walking across the parking lot at Weapons Training Battalion after another day of shooting. He began to stagger as he made his way between a second row of cars, trying to reach the armory window that opened behind the Weapons Training Battalion headquarters building, located at the east end of the parking lot.

A team member saw Carlos weaving across the asphalt, and shouted, "Hey! You all right?"

The Marine ran to Hathcock in time to see the sniper's eyes roll upward and his knees buckle. But rather than grabbing Carlos, the team member snatched the rapidly collapsing staff sergeant's rifle instead.

It amused Carlos to remember that incident. So typical of a shooting team Marine. Scrapes heal, lumps and bruises fade away. But damage to a rifle will forever change its shooting characteristics.

In February 1972, Carlos transferred to Camp Lejeune where he discovered one thing he could do well on a shooting team. Coach it. That year he gave 2nd Marine Division a championship, and in 1973 Hathcock moved back to Quantico, Virginia, as a shooting coach on his beloved Marine Corps Shooting Team.

Paradise disappeared for him as he pinned on gunnery sergeant stripes. The USS *Simon Lake*, a Navy ship based at Rota, Spain, needed a new NCO in charge of the Marine detachment aboard it. Carlos's name fell out of the hat for the duty. In October 1973, he reported aboard to Captain Howard Lovingood, a former enlisted Marine.

The captain took Gunny Hathcock's wounds into account when he required his Marines to drill and physically train. Lovingood knew the price Carlos had paid and respected the capabilities that he still had intact. Hathcock performed outstandingly in his leadership of the detachment Marines.

However, when Lovingood transferred in July 1974 and a by-the-book captain named Walter A. Peeples assumed command of the *Simon Lake* Marine Detachment, any allowances made out of respect for Hathcock's wounds left with Howard Lovingood.

Peeples pushed Hathcock. Tested him physically. And when Carlos failed the Marine Corps Physical Fitness Test and could not climb a steel ladder to an elevated gun position, he sent the Marine sniper packing. Carlos was crushed.

However, the stern Captain Peeples may well have saved Hathcock's life by sending him to the doctors at Marine Barracks Rota, Spain. By May 1975, Hathcock was at the U.S. Naval Hospital in Portsmouth, Virginia, where doctors discovered that multiple sclerosis was rapidly destroying the sniper's nervous system and muscles.

Carlos always looked back at that time with mixed feelings. He believed that Peeples could have shown more compassion and respect for him. However, he was thankful that he received help. It also put him in the position to return to Quantico. This time as the first-ever Senior Sniper of the Marine Corps, and NCO in charge of the newly established United States Marine Corps Scout/Sniper Instructor School.

Jim Land, now a major serving as Marksmanship Coordinator at Headquarters Marine Corps, had worked with others involved in Marine Corps marksmanship and had developed the concept of a permanent Marine Corps Scout/Sniper specialty field with its own Table of Organization and Table of Organization and Table of Equipment. In 1977, Commandant of the Marine Corps, General Louis H. Wilson, established scout/snipers as part of the Marine Corps' infantry battalion support elements. He authorized the three active duty and one reserve divisions to establish scout/sniper schools. Each infantry company would have a Surveillance and Target Acquisition Platoon, made up of scouts and snipers.

As part of the Marine Corps' Marksmanship Training Unit, General Wilson had authorized the creation of the Marine Corps Scout/Sniper Instructor School. Captain Jack Cuddy headed the school as its first officer-in-charge, with Hathcock as his senior enlisted scout/sniper instructor.

For the next two years, Carlos lived what he considered nearly a dream come true. An entire training and tactics philosophy and curriculum grew for the most part from Hathcock's experiences and insight. The Marine Corps valued what he had in his head, respecting his advice.

During the two years, Carlos worked from before daylight until after dark, and often on weekends. He had the coffee made in the morning before anyone else arrived, and he turned out the lights at night. He trained not only sniper instructors for the division schools, but Navy Seals and other operations specialists, Army and Air Force specialists, too, and government civilians working in the FBI, the intelligence community, and hostage rescue specialists.

The long hours pushed him over the line, and the multiple sclerosis advanced rapidly. Doctors prescribed heavy dosages of Valium for the pain. Carlos took thirty milligrams a day. He also began drinking every day, and quickly became addicted to the Valium.

In January 1979, the Marine sniper finally collapsed.

Carlos Hathcock awoke in a hospital bed, numb from the neck down. Several days later, he recovered feeling in the right side of his body, but never again in the left side. Making matters worse, he could not eat, he could not sleep, and began shaking violently. It was withdrawal from the Valium.

Several weeks later, Carlos returned to Bethesda for a follow-up examination by the head of the National Naval Medical Center's neurology department.

"How are we doing today, Gunny Hathcock?" the doctor asked Carlos, meeting him and Jo in the lobby area of Bethesda's neurology department.

Hathcock smiled and stood straight in his Marine Corps green alpha uniform, to show the doctor he was still fit. "Good as ever," Carlos responded, tucking his chin and puffing his chest. His gold shooting badges sparkled under several rows of ribbons pinned exactly one-eighth inch above the left breast pocket of the green surge blouse that he wore.

"Well then, let me watch you walk down the hallway to the examination room," the doctor said.

After seeing every other step a stagger, the doctor followed the sniper into the room. He watched as Carlos struggled simply to seat himself on the edge of the padded examination table with a wide strip of white paper stretched down its middle.

"Take off your blouse and hang it on the rack in the corner," the doctor continued. Carlos struggled with the buttons. The fingers of his left hand slipped and shook as he pulled the cloth over each button. Sweat beaded on Carlos's forehead and above his lip.

"Now," the doctor said, "extend your right arm straight out from your shoulder, hold it there, and bending only your elbow, touch your nose with your index finger."

It reminded Carlos of a sobriety test he had seen policemen perform on drunk driving suspects. He smiled as he brought his right index finger directly to the tip of his nose.

"Let's see the same thing with your left arm," the doctor asked.

Carlos could barely get his left arm to extend straight from his shoulder. Then, as he tried to touch his nose with his left index finger, his arm would fall. He sweated more.

"Okay, Gunny," the doctor said. "Stand up and tap your right toe on the floor."

Carlos did.

"Now tap your left," the doctor said, fully expecting the result.

Carlos's left foot only dragged. When he tried to tap his toe, the entire foot struck the tile floor. The gunny bowed his head and sat back on the exam table. The doctor sat on the stool at the side of the table and looked Hathcock squarely in his eyes.

"No more talking, Gunny Hathcock," the doctor said. "This is it. You're going out of the Marine Corps. Otherwise it will kill you."

Carlos wanted to argue, but he could see the doctor stood his ground. No getting past this one.

All the way back to Quantico Carlos thought about what he would do. Clearly the doctor was right. It had been a long fight, but it was time to accept life and quit fighting it. He thought of Jo, and of Sonny, and how much he really wanted to live and enjoy their company.

On April 20, 1979, Gunnery Sergeant Carlos N. Hathcock II brought his active duty Marine Corps career to a close. Weapons Training Battalion's commanding officer, Lieutenant Colonel David J. Willis, himself choking back tears, presented Carlos with an M-40A1 Marine Corps sniper rifle, complete with a 10-power Unertl scope, and a walnut and brass plaque that simply said:

"There have been many Marines, and there have been many marksmen, but there has been only one sniper—Gunnery Sergeant Carlos N. Hathcock. One Shot—One Kill."

16

Marine Sniper

CARLOS HATHCOCK HAD JUST RETURNED FROM THE Bait Barn and a morning-long shark-fishing excursion when the telephone rang. Jo was not home, and Sonny was at Parris Island going through Marine Corps Recruit Training, so Carlos answered.

"Gunny!" Colonel David J. Willis said. He was still the commanding officer of Weapons Training Battalion at Quantico. The majority of the Marine Corps' marksmanship, competition-in-arms, and scout/sniper programs operated under his direction.

"I have a friend here I want you to meet," he said.

Carlos smiled. He was always happy to see anyone from the Marine Corps, especially someone Colonel Willis had introduced.

During the four years since his retirement, Hathcock had seen the extremes of depression. Like so many other men and women whose life was the Marine Corps and suddenly it was not, severe depression spread its black cloak over his life. He hid himself in a back room of his home—"The Bunker"—and there, surrounded by mementos of his entire adult lifetime as a Marine, he grieved for more than two of those four years.

He spoke to hardly anyone. Not even Jo or Sonny.

In those low depths, men consider the value of their lives. They think of what life has left for them. Quite often, the depth of their melancholy is so far below anyone's understanding that they put guns in their mouths and pull the triggers.

Jo saw it coming. She tried every means of coaxing him into a new life that she could imagine. Cutting grass, taking walks. The strain often left Carlos collapsed in the yard. Yet, he still fell back to the dark room with its walls covered with Marine Corps pictures, plaques, and gun racks, and its depressing solitary confinement.

Finally, pushed to her limits, Jo Hathcock started packing.

Carlos asked her where she was going, and she told him she would not remain married to a dead man. She was serious.

The emotional charge raised Carlos's better side and he began to fight the depression. He began to make himself live.

Then one day he discovered the Bait Barn, shark fishing, Steve McCarver, and Steve's boat, the *Shark Buster*, a small open craft with a layer of stainless steel sandwiched in its fiberglass hull.

For the past year, Carlos had begun to live and smile, and drive himself, in his old pickup truck, to the Bait Barn. There he teamed up with his friend Steve, and hunted a new kind of quarry. Not nearly as hazardous as hunting men, but plenty dangerous in its own right.

Sharks often attacked the small fishing boats, biting holes in their nonarmored hulls, tearing pieces from their gunwales. Some of the deadly fishes would even thrust themselves out of the water and inside the boats, snapping and trying to maul the fisherman who had attacked them.

On one occasion, a lemon shark had lunged over the

top of the *Shark Buster*'s outboard motor, just behind Hathcock.

Carlos loved every second of it.

In his first tournament, the Marine sniper hauled in a 277-pound lemon shark, winning second place. Steve's daughter took third with a 236-pound lemon shark. But these great fish were like minnows compared to Old Scar-Face.

A legend of the Virginia Beach bait shops, several fishermen told of hooking into the great white shark that had to weigh 1,200 to 1,500 pounds. Each time anyone challenged the big fish with rod and reel, he easily turned and swam away, stripping off all the line from their reels, and then breaking the heavy monofilament as if it were cotton floss.

"Hell, you could pull a truck with that fishing line," Carlos would say, "but it's nothing for Old Scar-Face." Then he would break into his typical throaty "he-he-he" laugh.

When Carlos answered the telephone, his hands and clothes smelled of fish chum. Chicken blood stained his jeans and white sneakers. His face and neck were dark tan, and his cheeks filled with color.

"Yes, sir, Colonel Willis," Carlos said. "Who is he?"

"He's a trigger puller like you," Willis continued. "Only he can write, too."

Carlos hesitated. Many times since Vietnam, and especially since he retired from the Marine Corps, writers had approached him. They wanted to interview the man who wore the white feather, quite often for mercenary-oriented magazines.

Hathcock wanted nothing to do, ever, with anyone who wrote for publication. He reminded Colonel Willis that it had been a Marine who wrote the story in Vietnam that appeared in the *Sea Tiger*, and that provided his and Jim Land's names and likenesses to the Viet Cong. That had turned Carlos Hathcock against the press and anyone who reported for any sort of media, even in the Marine Corps.

"Carlos," Colonel Willis said, "I can tell him you would rather not. But listen to me for a minute. This man is one of us. He knows the program. I know him, and he's a good man. You know, if he writes a good story about you, it could be worth a few points for us. It could help the sniper program."

THREE DAYS LATER, THE WRITER, HIMSELF A CAREER Marine, knocked at Carlos Hathcock's front door. He spent the next two days in the Hathcock home, and the two Marines became friends.

The writer spent the next several months driving from Quantico to Virginia Beach, staying weekends with Hathcock, taking notes and tape-recording the Marine sniper's story.

What began as a speculative feature that the writer might sell to a Sunday magazine quickly became a book. Stein and Day published the first hardcover edition of *Marine Sniper* in 1986, and Berkley followed with a paperback edition the next year.

The *Chicago Tribune* called it a sleeper, a silent bestseller. It came from nowhere and in a matter of days sold out its first hardcover printing.

However, Stein and Day owed unpaid bills to its printers and binders. They refused to manufacture or release to distributors any further copies of *Marine Sniper* until they were paid.

Stein and Day kept all earnings, royalties, and license advances, refusing to pay the writer. He filed suit, and Stein and Day filed bankruptcy.

The writer had to pay the bankruptcy court $5,000 to return the rights for *Marine Sniper* back to him. Stein and Day kept all the money that *Marine Sniper* initially earned, and failed to fulfill the tremendous market demand for the book.

With the limited number of Stein and Day hardcover books in circulation, collectors began selling single, unsigned, first-edition copies of *Marine Sniper* for as much as $350 at gun shows and trade fairs. An autographed copy drew even more money.

It was not until Berkley released the paperback edition in the spring of 1987 that *Marine Sniper* became a book read around the world.

The costly lawsuit and the gross injustice shown the writer angered Carlos.

The two Marines sat at a coffee shop one morning in 1987, eating breakfast before meeting with 2nd Division snipers and marksmen at Camp Lejeune, North Carolina. Carlos expressed his dismay.

The writer looked at his friend and said, responding to Carlos's anger, "It's really not about money. I actually had never considered it until after the book came out.

"I wrote your story because it needed to be told. Young Marines needed it because the legendary Marine Chesty Puller died years ago. Our competition-in-arms and sniper programs needed it, too.

"I wrote *Marine Sniper* for the lance corporals sitting in the barracks. They needed a living Marine hero. I wrote it for the green lieutenant sitting in his room at The Basic School. They, too, needed a living hero. Plus it just might help them to more greatly appreciate and respect enlisted Marines.

"We succeeded in reaching those goals, my friend. Look where we are this morning. They know about Carlos Hathcock. They know that marksmanship, competition-in-arms and scout/snipers are important for our Corps' future.

"I even heard that a Marine Corps major cited parts of the book in his thesis at the Command and Staff College. That's a serious mark, and quite a tribute for snipers."

From 1987 forward, Carlos Hathcock was the Marine everyone wanted to meet. He became the living legend—White Feather.

Each year following *Marine Sniper*'s publication, Carlos traveled as a guest of Marines and former Marines, security forces, police departments, and state and federal law enforcement agencies throughout the United States. The FBI/Marine Corps Association paid tribute to him at their annual Marine Corps Birthday weekend celebration in October 1988 at Peekskill, New York. There, Carlos received honors as the reviewing officer for the annual parade of Marines and former Marines, along with U.S. Marine Color Guard, Silent Drill Platoon, and Drum and Bugle Corps. He stood next to the Commandant of the Marine Corps, General Alfred M. Gray, and FBI Director William Sessions.

The National Rifle Association paid tribute to Carlos Hathcock, issuing a resolution recognizing him at their national convention. Organizations named scholarships for him. He was the guest of honor at Marine Corps birthday balls at every major Marine Corps installation in the United States.

President Ronald Reagan even wrote Carlos a personal letter praising his patriotism and the example he set, and sent him an autographed picture.

In the midst of the swelling numbers of Hathcock fans, an increasing number of ardent supporters emerged. They recognized the great sacrifice that Carlos had made, standing in the fire in 1969, suffering severe disabilities while saving the lives of seven other Marines with total disregard for his own life. They were disgruntled that a grateful nation had not paid appropriate tribute to their hero. Carlos had not even received a Meritorious Mast for his heroism.

Captain Edward Hyland, who lost an arm in the fire and retired to Arizona, came forward and wrote a formal summary of action and medal recommendation. He cited what Carlos had done September 16, 1969, saving his and six other Marines' lives.

Hathcock had told Hyland in the hospital in San Antonio that he did not want recognition. When Hyland said he wanted to recommend him for a medal, Carlos said that if he did he would refuse it. Now, twenty years later, because of the desires of so many people, he reluctantly agreed to accept one if it came.

Petitions went to the United States House of Representatives and the Senate, pleading that Congress pass an exception to a statute of limitations imposed on awarding the Medal of Honor. No recommendations for the nation's highest tribute for heroism could be issued by any branch of the armed forces so long after the fact, unless Congress approved the action.

It took two years, but the approval finally came. An awards panel at Headquarters Marine Corps reviewed the recommendation, and downgraded the recommendation to the Silver Star. Since Carlos's action had not directly affected the tide of a battle, his heroism on the amtrac that day did not warrant the Medal of Honor or Navy Cross. However, they agreed that he had earned the nation's third highest medal for heroism that day.

Many people believed that the Medal of Freedom would have been an appropriate additional tribute for the United States to pay Carlos for his career of dedication. He had made significant contributions to America's defense through his pioneering of modern sniper warfare and its applications for police and security agents as well as for the modern soldier.

The mementos and plaques meant a great deal to Carlos, but what meant most to him was the tribute that young Marines paid him each time he stood before a group of them. For him, these new faces in both the enlisted and officer ranks, these Marines who revered him, gave the Marine sniper his greatest award—their love and respect.

For the writer, his greatest tribute came from Carlos Hathcock himself.

"It's like you were there with me," Carlos told him.

However, the writer's most significant and humbling moment came one afternoon in late October 1995 when he retrieved a handful of letters from his mailbox at his home in Lawton, Oklahoma. A brown envelope lay among the stack. From his publisher. Forwarding mail to him from readers.

Inside the envelope was a letter from Palm Harbor, Florida. Clearly, the handwriting on the front was from a woman. Unusual fan letter for *Marine Sniper*, he thought.

The woman wrote:

Dear Mr. Henderson,

I would like to introduce myself—I'm Jerry Ann Burke Bouchard, sister of John Roland Burke, Lance Corporal, USMC.

Your book, Marine Sniper, *was picked up by my cousin in Miami (ever since John was killed he—my cousin—has been an avid reader about Viet Nam). Before he even read it he called to tell me he had found a book about John. I went that very night to get a copy for my brother Bill and me (there were only two copies at "Book Stop" and since I wanted a copy for all seven of our children I ordered more).*

John was an "Oops-I-thought-I-couldn't-have-any-more" child for my mother. I'm 13 years older, my brother 15 years older. John was a delight, if ever there was a "perfect" child, he qualified. When I married he was only five. My husband, Roger, and I lived across the street from my parents, and John was like our first child. You can imagine the devastation we felt when we were notified of his death!

I really never knew (or didn't want to know) what a sniper did until I read your book. It was very hard reading about John, and I could only read a little at a time. But you did a wonderful job telling the story. I have never heard of Carlos Hathcock, but feel as if I know him, and would love to meet him and talk to him about John. He knew a boy that we never knew.

I would be very grateful if you could call or write to me, we would like Mr. Hathcock's and Mr. Land's address also.

Thank you for your time and effort that went into this book. Your literary skill made it a success and finally made me understand why John did what he did.

I hope to hear from you soon.

Jerry Burke Bouchard

The writer called her that night.

17

Shark Bait and the Mustard King

"**B**ILL," CARLOS SAID ON THE TELEPHONE TO THE writer who sat at his home in Staten Island, New York. Although his name was Charles, his close friends called him Bill—from his middle name of William—a throwback to his childhood. "I'm not sure what is going on, but I can't get into either airport in New York City, or into Newark, but I can get to Islip, Long Island."

"Take it, Carlos," the writer said. "Ray Doner lives close to the Islip airport and can very easily pick you up there. Oh, and we have a thirty-five-foot Hatteras called the *Sundowner* chartered for day after tomorrow. Twin-turbo diesel. Gonna be some deepwater fishing. We're gonna hunt *Jaws*. Also, I have our rooms locked on at Montauk Point, too. So you just get your butt here."

"Okay," Hathcock said cheerfully and then told the agent at the American Airlines counter in Norfolk to go ahead and switch his ticket to their next available flight to Islip's MacArthur Airport.

At two o'clock that afternoon, Ray Doner, a retired

police detective from the Nassau County force, a man who looked like he had just stepped out of central casting—slightly wind-tossed silver hair, a nose scarred and broken from bare-knuckle conflicts with New York gangsters, and Robert Mitchum eyes—wheeled his two-tone blue Buick into a parking slot next to the chain-link fence at the Islip airport. A half-smoked cigarette dangled from his lips as he slammed the car door shut and stepped onto the sidewalk where he could watch the tarmac and runways, and see Carlos's plane arrive.

Doner, a former Marine and member of the FBI/Marine Corps Association, had met Carlos in October at Peekskill. His close friend, Charles Henderson, the writer, had introduced the two men. They had immediately formed a friendship.

Ray and Jim Kallstrom, a supervising special agent at the FBI's New York Bureau, fascinated Carlos. Both men had spent careers going after organized crime figures. They, too, knew what Ernest Hemingway meant when he said, "There is no hunting like the hunting of man . . ."

Rumor had it that Kallstrom had crawled through Gambino family boss John Gotti's window to bug his office at the godfather's infamous Queens, New York, social club.

Doner, like Kallstrom, had crawled through his share of windows, too. *La Cosa Nostra* had his respect, but constant attention. Like Kallstrom, too, Ray down-played the seriousness and great risk involved in his work. Carlos liked that kind of humility. He appreciated what it meant. Their work gave the three Marines a kinship that only they and men like them truly understood.

Carlos enjoyed his membership in the FBI/Marine Corps Association because he met and became friends with many others like Ray Doner and Jim Kallstrom. Colonel John Riply had blown the bridges at Dong Ha, South Vietnam, in the Easter Offensive in 1972. Colonel Barney Barnum earned the Medal of Honor in Vietnam. Hector Cafferita earned the Medal of Honor while losing the use of his right arm in Korea. They were company with whom Hathcock fit in, felt comfortable. All of them just regular guys, just doing their jobs, just like Carlos. All with the same brand of humility. None of them considered themselves heroic. No better than any other Marine.

Unanimously though, they did consider their brothers and sisters who died in battle, who lost their lives on the front lines—whether in some far-off war or some slum neighborhood in America—the real heroes. Each of them knew firsthand the prices that these people paid. They saw it happen. It defined true heroism for them. It had written itself in the lines of their faces, and in the tears they shed when they stood on the parade field in Peekskill and honored the memory of those heroes.

So when Carlos stagger-stepped off the airliner and down the ramp, and saw Ray Doner standing there smiling, he hugged the man instead. Real friends do that. Especially tough-hided Marines.

"Bill is on his way out from Manhattan," Ray told Carlos. "He'll meet us at my apartment. Then we will go out to dinner and stop by the Marine Corps League in Masapequa, where I'm a member. I told them I would bring you by. All the guys want to meet you. Do you mind?"

"No, not at all. I like meeting Marines anytime," Carlos said as he stretched out in the Buick's wide front seat and lit a Salem cigarette when he saw Doner light one, too. He had not smoked since he left Norfolk. It felt good to relax.

THE WRITER PICKED UP BOTH MEN AT SEVEN O'CLOCK the next morning and sped westward to New York City. They would stop by the Marine Corps recruiting station in lower Manhattan first, then park the car at Henderson's office, and catch a taxi to the "21" Club, where owners Pete Kriendler and Jerry Berns would show them around. Then they would have lunch on the second floor of the former speakeasy with building giant Zachary Fisher, Jim Kallstrom, Lasard Fréres investment banking firm senior vice president Dick Torykian, Henderson, and Doner. All of them called Torykian the Field Marshal.

Any time the former Marine and banking executive attended any formal event, while others wore black-tie and tuxedo, Dick wore camouflage green tie, white shirt with black studs, camouflage tuxedo jacket, and camouflage cummerbund. He did wear black trousers. And he always had a pocketful of Cuban cigars that he generously shared with friends.

After lunch, the Field Marshal supplied everyone at the table with a Monte-Cristo Habana, 49 ring, Especiales No. 2. Carlos lit the $20 cigar, smoked about a third of it, dashed it out, and lit a Salem. He had no pretense about cigars, even Cuban Especiales rolled on the glistening thighs of nubile Havana virgins.

"How far to Montauk Point?" Carlos asked, taking a sip of the Sprite that he ordered. Everyone at the table laughed. Clearly he had shark fishing in the forefront of his thoughts.

At two P.M., Carlos stood before the senior class at Chaminade High School, a private school on Long Island. Dick Torykian had graduated from there, and his two sons as well. The boys stood in a long line, waiting to have the Marine sniper autograph their books. Patiently Hathcock signed each book and spoke to each student, and shook each hand. It made him feel good that at this high school they taught patriotism, too.

WHEN THEY FINALLY REACHED THE SMALL FISHING VILlage that sits at the farthest tip of Long Island, it was well after dark. John Britt, a member of the Navy League and Marine Corps Combat Correspondents Association, and a "Combat Poet," had joined the men after lunch and accompanied them to Chaminade and on to Montauk Point.

Filmmaker Erich Kollmar and documentary producer Woody Dougan rendezvoused with Henderson, Britt, Doner, and Hathcock in Montauk at the motel. Kollmar was an older gentleman yet very fit. As a young man he had served as a lieutenant in the German Navy. Like so many other young men in Germany during World War II who were patriotic to their country, but anti-Nazi and anti-Hitler, Erich Kollmar spent the war serving as second officer aboard a submarine. He had been trained and destined to operate the two-man U-boat, always a suicide mission. He was thankful that the war ended before he ever faced that fatal task. However, it was bad enough on the regular submarine. According to Lothar-Günther Bucheim's novelized memoirs of his tenure in the World War II German submarine service, *Das Boot*, of the 40,000 men who served aboard U-boats during the war, more than 30,000 did not make it home.

Carlos sat mesmerized hearing Kollmar tell him about life on those submarines.

"It was always cold in the North Atlantic," the white-bearded veteran said. "They put electric heaters on the boats, so we could not use them. We had to save the juice in our batteries. So, everything stayed cold and frozen in the sub.

"We slept two men to a bunk. One slept while the other stood watch. Every time, when I woke up, I had to break the ice off my leather suit. Thank God that we at least had those fleece-lined leather suits to keep us warm. But our toes and noses still froze."

Carlos laughed when Erich described the smell after several weeks at sea: vomit, urine, excrement, and body odor mixed with diesel and battery acid fumes.

"Quite a lovely bouquet," Erich said laughing, too.

Because they had arrived so late in the evening, all eating establishments had already closed. Only an ice-cream stand that sold only ice cream and soda, and a

7-Eleven late-night market remained open. Carlos, Erich, and Woody remained at the motel while the others went for the food.

An hour later the three returned with paper cups and plates, plastic forks, spoons, and knives, several large bottles of Coca-Cola and Sprite, two large bags of potato chips, two loaves of bread, three pounds of bologna, and a large squeeze bottle of French's Mustard.

John Britt spread the food out across a dresser and the television set in assembly line fashion. "It's easier if one man does the work," he announced, and looked at Carlos. "You've got a choice: bologna sandwich with mustard, chips, and a Coke, or bologna sandwich with mustard, chips, and a Sprite."

"I can't handle caffeine," Carlos said, "so give me a Sprite, and two of those Arkansas round-steak sandwiches. I'm hungry."

Britt spread a smile across his chubby face and stroked his salt-and-pepper Ernest Hemingway–style beard, the way a French chef in New Orleans might. "And will that be on white bread or white bread?" he said with an aristocratic air.

"White bread, if you don't mind, sir," Carlos said.

John wheeled on his toes and laid four slices of bread on a paper plate. Then he snapped up the squeeze bottle of French's Mustard with his left hand, tossed it in a high arch, and caught it nozzle down with his right.

Everyone clapped.

Britt began to squeeze, and nothing came out. Everyone watched but said nothing.

He rolled his eyes and smiled. "Oh, I need to twist open the little spout."

Grasping the nozzle between his right thumb and index finger, he very authoritatively twisted the yellow plastic applicator top. John had a master's degree in literature from the University of Southern California, but he had aspired to be an actor. Despite his difficulty with the mustard lid, he remained in his haughty French chef character.

Again he held the squeeze bottle in his right hand and began circling the nozzle above the bread, applying more and more pressure. Nothing happened.

"What the hell is wrong with this?" John said, finally losing character. He squeezed harder and harder, and still no mustard. The five others smiled, but still said nothing.

Britt pounded on the bottom of the bottle, and squeezed all the harder. His face began to glow red with frustration.

He looked at the hole in the nozzle. He unscrewed it completely off the lid. Held the yellow plastic cone up to the light. All clear.

After screwing it back in place and again giving it a half-twist to open the valve, John Britt squeezed again. This time with both hands. He wrapped himself around that bottle of mustard like the proverbial monkey on a football.

Suddenly, *splosh*! The entire lid, nozzle, and the white paper and plastic foam tamper-proof seal that he had neglected to remove blew off the plastic bottle, followed by most of its contents. A huge glob of mustard slopped across the television set, splashed across the dresser, and splattered on the mirror and white wall.

"Oh, shit!" John Britt cried out as the mess also gushed yellow globs across his gray Polo shirt and navy blue trousers. Several other spots of mustard dressed the green carpet and the tops of the now embarrassed poet's cordovan loafers.

The five nonsplattered men shouted and laughed. Carlos howled especially hard, and looking at John Britt he announced, "I've been wanting to figure out a good name for you, and now I have it. From now on, you are the Mustard King."

Enough mustard remained to barely dress ten sandwiches. John Britt, the Mustard King, did what he could to clean up the mess with a handful of napkins and bathroom towels. But it probably took a paint job to finally cover the mess.

*   *   *

"WAKE UP, JOHN," CARLOS CALLED FROM THE BATH-room. "It's five o'clock and the day's half gone. I'm already dressed and shaved."

John Britt moaned and pulled the bedcovers over his head.

"That skipper aims to leave at seven, and I aim to get me some vittles before we launch out," Hathcock said more seriously.

Ray Doner pounded on the door. John Britt fell out of bed and threw on his clothes. He took a look in the mirror at his rumpled hair, flashed his teeth at his reflection, and said, "Fuck it," and rumbled out the door behind Hathcock and Doner.

The others had dressed, and waited at the end of the upper walkway at the head of the stairs. They sipped coffee from paper cups as a drizzling rain fell on them.

"Could get to blowin' pretty good out on the water," Carlos said, taking note of the decaying weather.

"Fuck it," John Britt said and rumbled down the stairs.

At seven sharp the six now hearty and well-fed souls tromped down the wooden pier at Captain's Cove Marina. They splashed through puddles on the rain-soaked planks as they walked to the slot where Captain Tom McKinley had tied his thirty-five-foot, twin-turbo diesel sport fishing boat, the *Sundowner*.

"I don't like the looks of those waves," Woody Dougan said, seeing the increasing chop on the sea.

Doner and Henderson carried an ice chest filled with beer and ham sandwiches. Both men glanced back at Dougan, who walked next to Erich Kollmar, just behind Hathcock and Britt.

"You don't have to go with us," Henderson called back. "But we're going fishing. If that boat can handle it, we can handle it."

"Semper Fi," Ray Doner said.

"Me, too," Carlos said.

"Fuck it," John Britt said.

The six men stood on the pier next to the boat as Ray Doner called up to McKinley, who sat perched in a big swivel seat in the pilot's station above the main cabin, "Permission to come aboard, sir."

McKinley smiled and waved his hand, motioning the men to step aboard the *Sundowner*.

Doner stopped short of stepping aboard, clapped his heels together, and saluted toward the fantail, where the National Ensign fluttered on a small staff fastened to a grommet on the left rear corner of the boat. Each man followed suit and stepped aboard.

"You look a little green, Woody," Carlos said, noticing the documentary film producer clamping onto the ladder that led to the upper deck.

The small boat pitched in the chop that now splashed across the top of the pier, rocking the small boat. Dougan looked sallow.

"We'll cast off as soon as my mate gets here with the chum," McKinley called down to the men. Noticing Woody hanging on to the ladder, he looked at Kollmar, who stood nearest to Dougan, and asked, "He okay?"

Woody Dougan nodded. He would not be a wet blanket, despite already being soaked by the rain, his nose running, a chill making him shiver slightly, and his stomach rolling so hard he felt as if it might leak out his ears at any moment.

Seasickness can strike even the best and toughest sailors. It's something to do with the inner ear and one's vision relative to the motion beneath one's feet. However, Dougan did not want to appear a weak sister and quit before starting.

Seemingly from nowhere, Tom Quigley appeared carrying a two-foot square cardboard box covered with frost and a white five-gallon bucket with a lid snapped on the top. The man stood at least six foot, three inches and pushed the scales toward the 300-pound mark. His hands were as big as chuck roasts, and the girth of his arms would rival most men's legs. He wore a baseball cap over his short red hair. His eyes sparkled and he carried a grin that etched long wrinkles in his ruddy cheeks.

"By damn, they told me Marines were coming aboard," the hulking first mate cheerfully bellowed to the men. "Ain't it a beautiful day?"

Woody Dougan could only hang on to the ladder and try to hold down his sausage, eggs, biscuits, and gravy breakfast and two large cups of coffee.

Erich Kollmar had eaten lightly. He knew the sea well and how a man's stomach can get to tossing with the waves when it is full of sausage, eggs, biscuits, and gravy. He had mostly eaten fruit. As did Carlos and the two other Marines. John Britt had only drank coffee and a glass of orange juice.

"I wasn't in the Marines," Tom Quigley boomed in his deep Long Island voice as he cast off the bow line and hurried to release the stern line. "Rangers. U.S. Army Rangers, I'm not ashamed to tell you."

Captain McKinley pushed the throttles forward and turned the boat toward the right side of the channel. As the craft with a long walkway dressed with a waist-high, stainless steel rail increased its speed, its keel sank downward as the twin screws turned with greater force. White foam billowed from the rear corners of the craft as Tom Quigley carried the small American flag up the ladder to the top deck and fastened it on a small tower above the pilot's station.

"He may have been in the Army," Ray Doner said to Henderson, watching Quigley, "but he knows flag protocol on a seagoing vessel."

"I'm really proud to be with you fellows today," Tom said as he worked on the deck, unwrapping gear, getting it ready for today's shark hunt. "I've heard about that sniper. Is that him?"

"Carlos come here and shake the man's hand," Ray called to his friend. Hathcock had sat on one of the padded benches inside the cabin. He wore his green nylon Marine Corps Shooting Team windbreaker and

fumbled with the snaps, shutting it against the strengthening wind that drove the sea spray and rain across the
boat.

"Let me go inside, don't get up," Quigley said, seeing
how Carlos struggled to even button his coat.

Carlos stood anyway, and walked out to the deck
before the first mate could take two steps. He offered
his burn-scarred right hand, and Quigley took hold of
it and shook hard.

"It's an honor, sir," he said.

"Don't call me sir," Carlos said with a laugh, and
together with Quigley and several of the other men finished the sentence, "I work for a living."

Woody Dougan heaved his first spillage of breakfast
over the side as the boat entered the open sea. Swells
raised the craft several feet and then dropped it. The
boat's bow cut through the top of the next wave, riding
up as it rolled beneath the hull. The nose dropped down
the back side of the wave, and then rose up again,
crashing through the crest of the next swell.

"He okay?" Quigley said, pointing his thumb at
Woody Dougan, clinging to the ladder, now in great
agony.

Henderson had passed out a handful of Cuban cigars
that Dick Torykian had given him for the fishing expedition. Doner and Britt joined the writer, lighting up.
They each also had a beer, swigging and smoking. The
smell mixed with the boat's exhaust sent Dougan leaning over the side once more, heaving and spewing.

"Woody!" Ray Doner called to him. "How about a
ham sandwich and a beer?"

The men laughed as Dougan waved back at Doner
to go away and leave him to his misery.

Three hours passed before Captain McKinley throt-
tled back the thirty-five-foot, twin-turbo Hatteras.
Quigley immediately stripped away the cardboard from
around a frozen block of ground fish, entrails, and
blood. He tied a long nylon cord around the block of
chum and let it hang over the side, tying off the other

end of the cord to a cleat on the right rear corner of the boat.

"Already making an oil slick," Carlos said, knowing exactly Quigley's shark-hunting tactic. "That fish oil and blood slick will draw sharks for miles."

Quigley then popped the lid off the white five-gallon bucket and dumped several splashes of fresh blood and more entrails over the side.

He then took out four fishing rods, thick as his thumb at their necks, and with large reels mounted at the head of their two-foot-long, rubber-tipped wooden handles. One by one he tied hooks, long as his hand, on steel leader, and fastened them to the heavy fishing lines. As he tied on each rig, he ran the hook through a foot-long bait fish and cast it off the fantail. Quigley took hold of each fishing line near the reel and pulled it to an outrigger where he clipped it onto a clothespin.

"Shark hits, he'll pop the line off the outrigger, and darn near hook himself from the snap of the slack," Carlos said, observing the first mate.

Quigley smiled back at him. "You still better give her a yank when she pops."

While the boat drifted, the waves grew. By late morning they had reached twelve to fifteen feet in height. A person could not see the horizon from the deck, only water towering around the vessel, and the rainy, gray sky directly above.

"Bit more chop on the water," Carlos mused.

Quigley looked at him and grinned. "We don't have to worry about running into any other boats today. That's a guarantee. Only you Marines are crazy enough to fish for sharks in this kind of sea."

Ray Doner, Erich Kollmar, John Britt, and Henderson drank beer and ate ham sandwiches. Carlos sipped a Sprite and finished a bag of potato chips. Woody Dougan held fast to the ladder.

Britt first noticed the large fins cutting in and out of the waves that rose high above the boat. Then Carlos took note and laughed. "Looks like we got us a bunch!"

John Britt answered him, "Sure as hell don't want to go over the side."

Woody Dougan threw up again, leaning his head over the side.

"Stick it out too far, and a shark just might jump out and take your head," Quigley joked to Dougan.

One at a time the clothespins popped off the outriggers. Tom Quigley grabbed the first rod and gave it a hard jerk.

"It's a big one," he said, and looked at the men. "Who wants first crack?"

"Carlos," several of them said together.

"If we only snag one, Carlos ought to have the honors, since the rest of us live around here," Ray Doner said.

Hathcock flashed a wide smile at his friends and took the heavy rod. He locked his knees against the gunwales and pulled up on the wooden handle and then let it drop. As it dropped, he cranked the big reel.

"You need some help?" Quigley said, reaching to hold Carlos by the shoulders.

"Don't need no help," Hathcock growled as he fought the shark. "Just stay out of my way!"

Quigley laughed and stepped back, but not so far that he could not reach Carlos before he went over the side, should the big shark pull him off balance or he slip on the wet deck. Then he looked back at the other men, all of them laughing and cheering their hero on in his battle with the shark.

"You sure he's okay?" he said to them softly, hoping Carlos did not hear him. No one answered him.

"I'd feel better if he would sit in that fighting chair," McKinley called from his seat where he operated the engines in coordination with Carlos and the big fish.

Quigley put a harness over Hathcock's back and one at a time fed Carlos's arms through the loops and then fastened the harness to eyelets on each side of the fishing reel. But the Marine sniper stood his ground when the first mate tried to guide him back to the fighting chair.

Carlos wanted to feel the fish against his knees and back as he leaned over the fantail and pulled back, drawing the fish closer with each cycle.

After a half-hour of watching Carlos fight, the captain called from his station, "I'm going to have to insist he sit in that fighting chair. He looks tired."

Carlos glared over his shoulder at the man seated above and behind him. Then he looked at Tom Quigley and let the big man guide him back to the chair, where Hathcock finished the fish in another fifteen minutes.

It was a blue shark, well over 300 pounds. The largest fish Carlos had ever caught.

They took pictures of Hathcock and his fish as it lay alongside the boat in clear water as the growing waves tossed the boat ever higher. Once they finished with the camera, Tom Quigley reached over the side and cut the leader, allowing the shark to swim free.

"No point in killing a creature we can't eat," he said.

"Yes, sir," Carlos agreed. "That steel leader and hook will dissolve after a while. He'll be good as new, but I bet he don't bite no more hooks."

Ray Doner pulled in a shark and released it. So did Erich Kollmar and John Britt. Henderson waited to be last, and fought his shark for an hour. Well over ten-feet in length, Quigley estimated the fish weighed several hundred pounds.

Each time the writer managed to pull the shark close enough to the boat for a picture, the great fish swam out, stripping off-line, spinning the reel against its drag. He had set it at the maximum tension that would prevent the line from snapping under the shark's pull. Nonetheless, the fish stripped off-line easily.

After pulling the shark to the boat three successive times, the writer called to his friends, "Who else wants a turn at this? I think three times counts as a catch."

Ray Doner took the rod and fought the shark to the boat once more. Then Tom Quigley cut the line.

Woody Dougan still held fast to the ladder.

"You mind if we go in a little early?" Tom McKinley

called down from his station. "You Marines proved your point to me. Drinking beer, smoking cigars, eating ham sandwiches while catching five sharks in these conditions has me convinced."

Tom Quigley laughed. "The skipper is tough as they come. It's got to be bad for him to want to head home early."

Hathcock and his friends agreed. They had done what they set out to do. Ray Doner waved to McKinley to head for home.

That night at one of Montauk Point's more colorful pool hall bars, five of the six men reveled in their day's accomplishment. They stood and drank beer beneath the mounted front half of a great white shark, enjoying this moment in life, and their day with Carlos Hathcock.

For several months after their fishing event, people at Montauk Point, Long Island, still talked about the "crazy Marines" who went shark fishing in fifteen-foot seas, rain, and a gale. They also spoke with pride that Carlos Hathcock had gone out from there and caught shark.

18

Honors

Conscious thought returned to Carlos Hath-cock, yet his world remained dark. He willed his eyes open for a few seconds, seeing only pale-green light cast from a source somewhere above his bed. Then he let his eyes fall shut. His body still felt the motion from the sea. It was good to remember such a time.

These were the good memories. Yet so were many of those from Vietnam, the Marine Corps, and his life of teaching Marines that the deadliest thing on the battle-field is one well-aimed shot.

How many times had he said that?

At least several hundred. He had long ago lost count of the receptions, graduations, balls, shows, and trib-utes with him in the spotlight. At each of them, he had always concluded his remarks with the phrase ". . . one well-aimed shot."

Within his heart, he felt satisfaction. His life had sig-nificant meaning for hundreds of thousands of people. Not just soldiers or Marines, but students, teachers, mothers, sisters, just plain people who identified with the standards of honor and decency that he had exemplified throughout his life.

AS CARLOS LAY IN HIS BED, FEELING PROUD, HIS MIND'S eye carried him back to a warm summer day at Marine Barracks, 8th and I streets, Washington, D.C. It was August 25, 1989, one of the greatest days of his lifetime.

"Carlos, you old horse thief," David Sommers said with a laugh, extending his hand to his friend. When the president had named General Alfred M. Gray Commandant of the Marine Corps, the Marines, in turn, selected Sommers as their top enlisted man to serve at the Commandant's side.

Hathcock took Sommers's tan uniform shirt's short sleeve in his fingers and traced the three up and four down stripes indicating the rank of sergeant major. However, in the open space between the three upward-pointing chevrons and the four downward-curving rockers was the symbol that only one man on active duty could wear: a tiny Marine Corps emblem flanked by a star at each side. Sergeant major of the United States Marine Corps.

Hathcock took Sommers's hand, and in a moment the clasp turned to slaps on the shoulders, and then the two Marines hugged. Tears streamed from the corners of Carlos's eyes. He felt extremely proud of his friend.

Sergeant Major Sommers chuckled because he, too, felt a lump gather in his throat and his eyes moistened.

"Oh, I puddle up a lot these days," Carlos said, laughing, too, and looking at Jo who had accompanied her husband with Sonny on this important day.

Sommers had also invited writer Charles Henderson and his wife for this special occasion. He and the sergeant major had known each other at Quantico in 1983, before the idea of writing *Marine Sniper* had ever taken shape. Henderson had graduated earlier that same year from The Basic School, making the transition from enlisted Marine to officer, and had just returned from combat duty in Beirut when he first met Sommers, then sergeant major of The Basic School. The writer stood with his wife several paces behind Carlos, and next to Jo and Sonny Hathcock, watching the two old friends greet each other.

The sergeant major had sent a driver to Virginia Beach to bring Hathcock and his family to Washington, D.C., for this special day. Henderson had driven there the previous evening from his present duty assignment in New York City.

"Colonel Pete Pace, commanding officer here at 8th and I, is anxious to meet you, Carlos," the sergeant major said, leading the small group along the sidewalk, around the parade field, and into the headquarters building.

Respecting protocol, Sommers handed escort of the visitors to the Marine Barracks' sergeant major. He then led the people to the colonel's office.

Pete Pace did not wait for Hathcock to enter the room before he was at the door shaking hands and introducing his teenaged son, who had come to the barracks to meet the legendary Marine sniper. Both father and son were sincere Carlos Hathcock fans, and true believers of the value of one well-aimed shot.

Tall and dark-haired, Pace looked too young to be a colonel, yet the ribbons on his uniform shirt and the eagles on his collar quickly convinced anyone that this Marine had seen most sides of the Corps, and his share of combat. He had a gentle nature and kindness in him, tempered with discipline and respect for the chain of command, and appropriate behavior among differing ranks. Put simply, to Marines, Colonel Pete Pace had class.

"We have a special ceremony that the staff NCO's want to perform for you this afternoon," the colonel said cheerfully, his tall, dark-haired son following in trace with the group as they crossed the street, south of the Marine Corps' oldest active post.

"They have a new library at the staff barracks," Pace continued, and said no more until the group entered a room filled with every staff noncommissioned officer stationed at Marine Barracks, 8th and I streets, Washington, D.C.

Tears streamed from Hathcock's eyes as he saw the hand-carved, burnished wood sign above the library's doorway. It read: GUNNERY SERGEANT CARLOS N. HATHCOCK LIBRARY.

"I think usually you're supposed to be dead to get something named after you," Pace said, jokingly. Then he added in a serious tone, "I am not aware of any other place or facility in the Marine Corps that does carry the name of a still-living person."

Carlos stood before his family, friends, and smiling brethren, struggling to speak. He could only beg their forgiveness for his tears and his inability to make a proper speech, and added, "Now you really made me puddle up."

The Corps can offer no greater honor to one of its own than to preserve his or her name on the face of a building, facility, or in this case, a library. Carlos knew this grand gesture usually went to famous generals or Medal of Honor heroes. To be alive and to see one's own name enshrined on a building humbled Carlos more than anything had ever before in his life.

At 6:30 that evening, the writer, his wife, Carlos, and his family walked up the back steps of the commandant of the Marine Corps' home, located at the far end of the 8th and I parade field. General Al Gray greeted the group at the door, and invited them inside to the reception held in Carlos Hathcock's honor. High government officials and senior officers of the Marine Corps filled the historic residence, each of them also excited to meet this night's honored guest.

"I want you boys to come upstairs with me," General Gray said to the writer and Carlos. "I have something to show you."

The three Marines wound their way through the

crowd to a small upstairs room that had a wooden desk built into the corner. Above it, and at its sides, on both walls, matching wooden shelves stood lined with books and mementos. The burly, silver-haired Marine general pointed to the blue spine of a hardcover first edition of *Marine Sniper*.

"This is where I keep the books I like best," he said.

Throughout the evening Carlos kept looking through the crowd. "I don't see E. J. and Elly," he said, referring to Jim Land and his wife, who had flown to Washington, D.C., that day from Denver, where Land headed a firearms company.

"Reckon something happened to them?" Carlos then asked, clearly worried about two of his dearest friends. "I know there is no way under the sun they would miss this unless something really bad happened."

Later that night, Carlos discovered that Jim and Elly Land had come to the reception, but were turned away. An administrative error had kept their names off the guest list. So Jim and Elly found bleacher seats at the parade field and waited. After all, they had not made this trip to see the inside of the commandant's home. They came to see Carlos honored. There was no way that either of the Lands would miss it.

At eight o'clock, as the summer sky grew dark, guests began walking from the back of General Gray's home, along the sidewalk that led to the center seats, reserved for special guests. Then at 8:30, the stadium lights dimmed and a spotlight turned to the end of the parade field where Carlos Hathcock stood with the commandant and the sergeant major of the Marine Corps. Together, they marched to the first row, center seats, where Jo and Sonny had gone earlier.

Several thousand people packed the stands that lined the south and the west sides of the parade field. Billed as the best show in Washington, D.C., visitors often waited many weeks to obtain tickets.

For the next two hours, the "President's Own," the United States Marine Band, marched and played with the United States Marine Drum and Bugle Corps. The musical units posted at opposite ends of the parade field. Directly across from the audience, several companies of Marines wearing dress-blue jackets and white trousers stood in formation with M-1 rifles at their sides.

Centered among the units stood the United States Marine Corps Color Guard. The Colors Sergeant of the Marine Corps held the official flag of the United States of America. Next to him, another sergeant held the official Marine Corps Battle Colors, the head of the staff from which it flew festooned with colorful silk streamers representing every conflict, war, and expedition fought by United States Marines. Silver bands with the names of the battles engraved on them covered the staff. Flanked by riflemen, they marched forward and posted the colors.

Since this evening's event was the annual parade for the sergeant major of the Marine Corps, David Sommers stepped to the center line and received the colors and formal honors. When he sat down, one of the greatest performances of music and precision drill that a person can see anywhere in the world began.

Tears streamed down Carlos's cheeks throughout the entire two hours of drills, music, and ceremony. The Silent Drill Platoon drew cheers from the audience as they performed their intricate rifle drills with chrome bayonets fixed on their M-1 rifles, all polished brightly. Every move, every step, every turn, every toss of a rifle, came without oral command or cadence. The platoon of Marines, all junior enlisted men, demonstrated what teamwork truly meant.

Carlos stood and applauded when the three ranks of privates first class, lance corporals, and corporals, led by a sergeant, concluded their drill and marched back to their place in the formation of Marine Barracks companies. Then came the highlight event of the evening. The Marine Band played the War of 1812 Overture accompanied by gun crews firing actual artillery pieces in concert with the music.

Carlos was overwhelmed.

Then the moment that everyone who knew and loved Carlos Hathcock had waited for all day finally came.

The commander of the guard called out, "Sir, the parade is formed!"

Sergeant Major Sommers stepped to the center line and in his forceful, former drill instructor voice, he responded, "Pass in review!"

A Marine then led Carlos Hathcock to the side of his old friend. A voice on the public-address system announced, "Ladies and gentlemen, tonight's reviewing officers are Sergeant Major David W. Sommers, Sergeant Major of the Marine Corps, and retired Marine Gunnery Sergeant Carlos N. Hathcock the Second!"

The entire mass of onlookers rose from the stands and applauded and cheered the simple, dedicated American hero who grew up with a single ambition in life—to be a Marine.

Carlos staggered. David Sommers took his hand, and discreetly held him steady. As the colors of his country passed him, Carlos placed his hand over his heart. At the same time, David Sommers snapped a drill-instructor perfect salute.

Every Marine that marched past saluted their sergeant major with a hand salute, sword salute, or eyes right. And standing beside their sergeant major, deeply touched and standing at the best position of attention that his wobbly legs could hold him, they also saluted a great Marine, a living legend, Carlos Hathcock.

CARLOS NEVER AWOKE AGAIN. HIS BREATHING AND HIS heart stopped at 5:30 Tuesday morning, February 23, 1999.

Lieutenant General Pete Pace grieved at his desk later that day when he received the news. Ten years ago, the colonel who admired Carlos Hathcock, like most Marines did, had watched from a seat near General Gray as the Marine Sniper received one of the greatest tributes given to any person. Now he wore three stars on each collar, and held command of the Fleet Marine Force, Atlantic.

He had found delight at his Norfolk, Virginia, duty station. For one reason, it had returned him to contact with one of his true heroes, who lived in nearby Virginia Beach. Carlos had been thrilled to see his friend now wearing so many stars on his collar. He believed the Marine Corps had made an excellent choice by promoting Pete Pace to a rank of such great authority.

Three days later, more than 600 people, each of them a friend of Carlos Hathcock, stood at his graveside and watched eight Norfolk police officers carry the man who had personally trained them in SWAT and sniper tactics to his final resting place. A botanical garden of flowers surrounded the grave site. Many of the people who stood in honor of their friend had traveled across the country for the privilege of personally paying respect. Dick Torykian had postponed important business that week and had traveled down from New York. Jim and Elly Land stood near him.

A squad of Marines fired their rifles in the air, and Marine Corps musicians sounded taps. Lieutenant General Pace saluted as Carlos's pallbearers lifted the flag from his casket, folded it, and presented the banner to Jo and Gunnery Sergeant Carlos Hathcock III.

Someone once said, "When you are born, you come into the world crying, while those surrounding you smile. Live your life so that when they lay you to rest, you will be smiling as all those around you cry."

More than 1,200 streams of tears flowed that Friday in the mid-Atlantic coastal community cemetery. One can be sure that Carlos Hathcock was smiling.

From the author of *Silent Warrior*

Charles Henderson

MARINE SNIPER
93 Confirmed Kills

The incredible story of the remarkable
Marine Carlos Hathcock, whose 93 confirmed
kills in Vietnam have never been matched by any
sniper before or since. Features harrowing stories
of a man who rose to greatness not for personal
gain or glory, but for duty and honor.
This is a rare inside look at the U.S. Marine's
most challenging missions—and the man who
made military history.

0-425-18165-0

AVAILABLE WHEREVER BOOKS ARE SOLD OR
TO ORDER CALL:
1-800-788-6262

B530